Fore ...

I T WAS the year we first hear
and what the Spice Girls i
many others, 1996 was the i
Yugoslavia. We, the British
years. A lot of us had been before a~ ~u.. ~. ~.~ ~.., ~..~.......... terrible things, while some were never to come home. This operational tour for me came after several Northern Ireland stints in which
we were up against a known but unseen enemy on familiar-looking
ground. Bosnia felt like a chapter that should have been consigned
to history after the Second World War, a distant conflict that people
watched in grainy black and white footage. Yet here we were, wit-
nessing a modern European country being torn apart by atrocities
fuelled by deep-seated hatred and nationalism, as neighbour turned
against neighbour. What scared me was that the entrenched animosities within Yugoslavia had been unsettlingly close to the surface and
not too dissimilar to what Northern Ireland experienced. Could it
ever happen in the UK on the same scale?

Tito once said, "I am the leader of one country which has two
alphabets, three languages, four religions, five nationalities, six republics, surrounded by seven neighbours, a country in which live
eight ethnic minorities."

He ruled Yugoslavia, or kept a lid on this melting pot, as some
say, from 1944, when he and his partisans liberated it from the Germans, until his death in 1980. He was in power in many different
positions of national governance during his tenure, but no matter
which one it was, he was always the big boss of the 'Land of the
South Slavs'.[1] His message of Brotherhood and Unity, held the
country together and he suppressed any notions of nationalist in-

1 The literal translation of the word "Yugoslavia."

surrections, such as the Croatian Spring in 1972. He himself was born to a Croat father and a Slovene mother in Kumorvec, a village in Croatia way back in 1892, thus you could say he was a good model of the Yugoslav dream.

After his death, there was nobody of a similar imposing, authoritative or commanding character to fill the void, and Yugoslavia began to falter from that point. One of the key figures to emerge after his death was a Serbian politician called Slobodan Milošević. Climbing through the ranks of the Communist Party, ousting opponents as he progressed, he eventually became the President of the Serbian Republic in 1989. He was an advocate for Serbian nationalism, which exacerbated ethnic tensions and, as Yugoslavia began to disintegrate, his policies contributed to the outbreak of conflicts in Bosnia, Croatia, and Kosovo. He was finally charged in 1999 with war crimes by the ICTY[2] during the NATO intervention in Kosovo. His downfall came soon after amid demonstrations over disputes in the recent presidential elections and he resigned from the Yugoslav presidency in 2000. He was arrested by the Yugoslav authorities in 2001 and then extradited to The Hague to stand trial for genocide, war crimes and crimes against humanity. The trial began in 2002 and was a protracted case, but before it was concluded, he was found dead in his cell in 2006. To this day he remains a controversial figure. He is viewed as a nationalist hero by some while others see him as the leading initiator of the widespread Balkan violence on the 1990s. His legacy had an effect on many in the world, not just the Balkans, including me and my military comrades, as his actions led to our deployment there.

This is my personal account of the first part of a six-month tour, which started early in April 1996. I was based in Croatia, but, because of my job as a Driver, I spent many days on the roads in Bos-

2 International Criminal Tribunal for the former Yugoslavia.

For Mum & Dad.
I hope I did you proud.

Also available in the Hurry Up & Wait Trilogy
Book 1: Licking The Taliban's Flip-Flop

Coming in December 2025
Book 3

Published by BA Press 2024

Copyright © James Lee 2024

The moral right of the author has been asserted

ISBN No. 9798300753009

Typeset in Garamond by Bus Stop Editorial Services

Cover by Gary Bainbridge

Sleeping In The Ditch

with ← Slobodan Milošević

JAMES LEE

BA Press

KENT

KEY:

BB - BLUEBIRD (ROUTE)   IEBL - INTER-ENTITY BOUNDARY LINE

BLMF - BANJA LUKA METAL FACTORY   SNP - SPLIT NORTH PORT

HB - HORNBLOWER (ROUTE)

VRBAS RIVER

PEGASUS · BLMF

IBEL

· BANJA LUKA

REPUBLIKA SRPSKA

BOCAC DAM

BOČAC LAKE

HB

MRKONJIĆ GRAD

BB

· JAICE

SIPOVO

DIAMOND

FEDERATION OF BOSNIA AND HERZEGOVINA

· VITEZ

EMERALD

SWAN

KISELJAK

· BUGOJNO

SNAKE

OPAL

· SARAJEVO

PARROT

KUPRES

· SARAJEVO

CROATIA

LIVNO

PELICAN

GORNJI VAKUF

GULL

BIG LAKE

TSG

MAPLE

KITE

SPLIT AIRPORT

SPLIT HILL

GULL

· LIPA CAMP

DJ BARRACKS

SNP

DALMA

KAMENSKO BXP

GANNET

ADDER

· SPLIT

OHIS

BRAC

MAKASKA

PACMAN

HAVR

· METKOVIC

VIS

· BOCE

KORČULA

PELJEŠAC

· DUBROVNIK

ADRIATIC SEA

nia. I have written it from my fragmented notes, faded memories, and from those of you I contacted to fill in the blanks. Twenty-eight years have passed since that tour and my getting it onto paper. The memories of locations and characters have become clouded because of the passage of time. A few places that I've described I visited just once. They might not be as how those of you who spent more time at these locations remember them. Those of you who served with me in 7 Regiment may recognise individuals, but with different names. I felt I had to change them, as I don't fancy a 'late-night' visit from you. I had to merge personalities too. It would be wonderful to include everyone, but it's just not practical to have more than a hundred great characters in a book, and I'm no Tolkien. It was a tragic period in modern European history, but we all played a role in promoting peace in the Balkans and bettering the lives of the Bosnian people. I'd like to think that I've captured the spirit of the tour for all those who served there with the one thing we always remember, talk about, and miss, now we're no longer serving. It's one of the best qualities that the British Forces have.

Humour.

1

Time to Check Out

I T WAS a scar, a long one and not straight. It followed a boundary on a map and didn't care for the people living in its way as it zigged and zagged across the countryside. And, like an old wound, it was a reminder of the past and the pain which came from that slash. I stood on this blemish, which was the former Inner German border looking out towards the Harz Mountains, panting from the run up to the top of the hill. I was doing last-minute panic fitness because of my impending return to the Regiment. The icy February air stung my lungs as I breathed it in deeply, and I knew I'd undoubtedly have snot hanging from my nose. A quick wipe on the back of my black fleeced glove produced a snail trail and confirmed my suspicion. I was on the track used by the border guards to patrol their given sector. It was two identical lines of perforated concrete blocks running alongside where the fence had been. It was so the guards could rush to where a suspected crossing was being attempted by some desperate soul fleeing to West Germany from the East German regime.

During October the previous year, the Regiment required an individual to run the Adventure Training Lodge at Walkenried, down in the Harz Mountains. It had been suggested to me it would be beneficial for the career development of a Lance Corporal and I was, indeed, of that rank. The actuality was they needed someone, anyone, just anyone to head down there now, so the box was ticked. I knew a good thing when I saw one, so I happily agreed to a deal of time away from the Regiment, with no uniform or bullshit. I wouldn't be running it either. I'd be looking after it as they solely needed somebody to change the light bulbs and hoover the carpet. My train had arrived at Slipper City.[3] It wasn't the cosy lodge in the mountains I was expecting, but a cheap-looking bungalow on a middle-class housing estate. It reminded me of my old primary school, with its 1970s architectural design. Before the fall of Communism in Europe, it had been an accommodation hut for the British Military patrolling this part of the border. It was possibly too good a thing to hand back to the Germans, so someone somewhere had the idea to use it for Adventure Training.

That term has brought a few memories flooding back, so I'm just going to go off on one and get it off my chest. "Adventure training" is a pretence of military training, minus the guns or the green uniform. My experience of this was walking and/or running up mountains at the pace of the fastest person who was normally in charge. In my rucksack would be the world's heaviest tent, and, before we set off, the one with the map would say:

"We'll take it easy today as we are here to enjoy ourselves."

Within a few hundred metres, we'd be going like the clappers,

3 Any cushy job which is far removed from the rigours of a normal military life.

10

as if the cafe on the top of the mountain would be closing soon. There's always a cafe on top of the German mountains. My head would be fixed, looking down at the ground as I strained to keep up with the pack. I'd then miss the wonderful scenery and not enjoy myself, despite the fact I'd been ordered to enjoy myself.

Even when we went skiing, it was a major workout. Everybody only wanted to do downhill as it was quite easy and you got to sit in the cafe on the mountain top for most of the day. In the eyes of the military, that type of skiing is too easy for the soldiers, so half of your time had to be spent doing the dreaded *'Langlaufen.'* Officially, that translates to 'cross-country skiing'. Soldiers, rightly so, translated it to 'cross-country running for lunatics.' The thinnest of skis were attached to your feet by a clip on the toe. When you fell over, the ski would twist so much you would feel as if you'd suddenly put a pair of shoes on five sizes too small. There was the expectation that you could somehow ski up a hill. You'd end up giving the impression that you were either skiing on the spot or walking up it after major back surgery. It was pure retribution for a few days indulging in a hot chocolate in the mountain-top cafés.

My time at the lodge changing light bulbs and hoovering up had been an easy one. Being on my own and distant from the Regiment, I had naturally gravitated towards the life of a civilian. I had a local pub to go to down in the village in the evenings and an Italian restaurant for a nice takeaway pizza on the way back. I met a British guy there one evening. He had been in the British Army many years ago, married a local girl, and settled down in Walkenried. I presumed he would be a little lonely, being the only Brit in an area far away from the big military garrison towns. I thought he would like the opportunity to converse in his native language. My assumption was incorrect. He only wanted me to bring him jars of piccalilli from the

NAAFI[4] as he couldn't get his hands on any locally.

My time in Walkenried was coming to an end. I had a date for my inheritor arriving, so I had to think about doing an extensive light bulb check and hoovering up at least twice. I checked the bathroom scales were working. At first, I thought they were broken, only to realise my extended stay at the lodge financially supporting the local pub and Italians had taken its toll. Life back in the Regiment would involve lots of running around doing soldiery type things. I had to get back at least to a level of fitness that wouldn't make me look like I'd been sitting on my arse for three months.

I returned to Bielefeld in late February, and one of the first things I did was to pop into the 'Big' NAAFI, to pick up a few things, piccalilli not being one of them. The 'Big' NAAFI was off-camp and was a proper supermarket selling big things. The 'Small' NAAFI was on-camp and was a small shop selling small things. I get to the till and as I was just about to hand over my Deutschmarks, the lady recognised me and passed on the big news.

"Are you looking forward to going to Bosnia?"

"I'm not aware I'm going," I replied, slowly, not quite understanding what I'd just heard from the checkout girl.

"Yeah, you are, the whole Regiment is going. That'll be 31.99, ta," she said, holding her hand out for my money. "You're all off in April, but at least you'll be home for Christmas."

This was how I found out how I was to spend the best part of 1996.

4 Navy Army Air Force Institute. They are proud to point out they have been fleecing – I mean serving – the British forces since 1920.

It's All Gone Pete Tongovic

The break-up of Yugoslavia was an extremely complex situation, especially if you don't know much about the history of the Balkans. I've found the best way to describe it is to depict the Yugoslav Civil War happening in the United Kingdom. It would involve significant changes in historical, cultural, and political contexts, but let's try to adapt the scenario. In this hypothetical situation, let's pretend the UK is a diverse country with regions representing different ethnic groups, similar to Yugoslavia.

England →→ Serbia
Norfolk →→ Slovenia
Wales →→ Croatia
Scotland →→ Bosnia
Isle of Wight →→ Montenegro
Yorkshire →→ Vojvodina
Cornwall →→ Kosovo[5]

We'll imagine England, Norfolk, Wales, Scotland, and the Isle of Wight as the main regions. There's also the two autonomous regions of Yorkshire and Cornwall. I'm inclined to leave out Northern Ireland, as I think they have had their own fair share with the troubles. We would also need to militarise the UK a tadge more. We have a sizable military. Just our ground forces consist of over half a million full-time soldiers and we could mobilise a million more trained reservists in wartime. This makes us one of the largest stand-

---

5 I haven't mentioned Macedonia. This was the only republic to secede from Yugoslavia peacefully and was always under the media radar. Even then, it got into a dispute with Greece over the name Macedonia, and had to go by the name The Former Yugoslav Republic of Macedonia for a while, before finally becoming the Republic of North Macedonia in 2019.

ing armies in modern Europe. The UK has been run by one person since the end of the Second World War, who was Welsh by birth, and we will call him Coffeefinger. He was head of the resistance during the German occupation from 1940 to 1945. His partisan forces liberated the UK with very little help from the Allies or the USSR Armies, unlike most other European countries who were occupied. After the war, he's hailed a hero and cements his place in power by purging the country of any prospective opposition. The Cold War begins and Europe falls into two spheres of influence, East and West. Coffeefinger is a strong leader and doesn't want to align himself with either. This annoys Stalin and they fall out with one another. After Stalin tries to have him assassinated, Coffeefinger has the balls to threaten Stalin in a letter.

> *"Stop sending people to kill me. We've already captured five of them, one of them with a bomb and another with a rifle. If you don't stop sending killers, I'll send one to Moscow, and I won't have to send another."*[6]

He rules well during his tenure, pleasing most of the citizens, but not all of them, while creating a robust economy. He holds the UK together and comes down hard on anyone showing any signs of nationalism or talk of independence from within the state. Coffeefinger creates a new collective Presidency to assume his role in the event of his death, as he lacks a direct successor to inherit the reins. Time catches up with him and he does indeed pass away. As planned, it falls to the Presidency to ensure the continued existence of the UK. How the Presidency works is that it comprises representatives of the Republics and the two autonomous regions. There are seven seats in this Presidency and there needs to be a majority vote to pass any

6 Stalin never sent another letter to Tito and kept this one in his desk until the end of his life.

policies. This is intended to stop any one country from becoming the dominant power and gaining the upper hand against the others. Tensions between these regions have simmered for years since the passing of Coffeefinger because of historical grievances, economic disparities, and cultural differences. This reignites the flames of nationalism, especially in England. The English, who over the years have settled across parts of Scotland and Wales, now have large populations there. They want to protect their own in the other Republics, and nationalistic ideas of turning the entire UK into a greater England start to sprout. The Presidency should stop these aspirations, but as Yorkshire and Cornwall are within England, they easily control their votes. They also install a Pro-English government on the Isle of Wight. England now have direct control of four out of the seven seats in the Presidency, so any policies not in their best interest won't get a majority vote. Norfolk, Welsh and Scottish leaders see this and worry they will be marginalised within the Kingdom. This accelerates their drive down the route of independence to get away from the now domineering English of the UK. Norfolk and Wales are the first to declare their independence. Initially, England is concerned about Norfolk leaving the UK and sends in the British Army. Any British Military personnel who are from Norfolk desert over to the newly formed Norfolk Defence Force. The British Army go in, expecting to be received as saviours, but they don't find this to be the case. They are genuinely shocked to find the Norfolkians aggressive towards them. They see them as invaders and make life hard for the British Army, such as blocking the major roads with trucks and tractors to inhibit their movements. The tiny Norfolk Defence Force gives the British Army a bit of a kicking. After ten days of this, England reassesses their situation and says, "sod this for a game of soldiers," and promptly pulls the entire British Army out of Norfolk. The English reasoning for this is that Norfolk is populated only by the Norfolkians, so they are not too bothered if they leave the Kingdom. England waves bye-bye, and the Norfolkian government in Norwich gives a huge tremendous sigh of relief.

Wales is a different matter. There is a significant population of English individuals living in Pembrokeshire and North Wales, who adamantly don't want to be ruled by Cardiff. The British Army is now sent into Wales, but this time there's a substantial English population who wants them there. As in Norfolk, quite a few British Military personnel from Wales switch sides and join the newly formed Welsh Armed Forces. They even take a few planes with them for the fledgling Welsh Air Force. Over the years, the English had put plans in place to ensure the majority of Officers, recruited and installed in the top jobs within the British Army, were loyal to England. The bulk of the other ranks in the British Military are English too. Which makes it a force for England and not the UK. Pembrokeshire and North Wales are occupied by the British Army. They are initially there to give the English protection from the Welsh Military and the recently established Welsh militias. To bolster this, the English population in these areas form their own militias for protection, and they are well-equipped with assistance from the British Army. Heavy fighting erupts, and, from the outset, Wales takes a beating. HMS Swansea of the Royal Navy shells Swansea. For the first time in British history, a ship shells a town of the same name.[7] Their shortage of military hardware is evident, and they soon concede large parts of Mid-Wales to the better equipped British Forces and their militias. There is heavy fighting in many places, but the Welsh ensure a stalemate. A ceasefire agreement is reached with the mediation of the EU. The fighting comes to a stop, but the English stay and keep the land they took. For now.

Scotland is a right old melting pot with Scottish, English, and

7 This actually happened in Croatia when the Yugoslav Navy frigate Split shelled the town of Split in November 1991.

even some areas with a Welsh population. They are all Scottish but the country is split into those who are Scottish Scots, who have a loyalty to Scotland, and English Scots and Welsh Scots, who have loyalties are to their original homelands. Scotland has a referendum for independence and most of the Scottish Scots vote, with 99.9% of them in favour of it. However, the English Scottish living there, who are entitled to vote, boycott it. They decide to create the Republic of EngScot with the capital city in Perth. Scot and EngScot soldiers, and even entire Regiments of the British Army, change sides. Now giving their allegiance to either the new Scots or EngScot Army. The British Army goes in, and, as in Wales, they arm the Republic of EngScot Army. Fighting soon breaks out almost everywhere across Scotland. Glasgow is surrounded by the British and EngScot Armies and remains under siege for 1,425 days with incessant shelling of the city. Thousands are killed and injured on all sides. The infrastructure and built-up areas are damaged or destroyed beyond repair. War crimes are committed by every side, with mass killings, rapes and torture against the civilian populations. The UN deploys the Peacekeepers, but with a mandate to deliver humanitarian aid and not to take sides. They try their best, but they find themselves between a rock and a hard place. Under international pressure to withdraw the British Army, the English simply transfer any remaining Scottish English soldiers or units to the Republic of EngScot's Army.

Efforts to broker peace and reconcile differences prove challenging, as deep-rooted animosities and grievances hinder progress. The conflict persists for years, exacting a heavy toll in terms of loss of life, displacement of populations, and destruction of infrastructure. The Welsh Scots strike up an alliance with the Scots against the Republic of EngScot. This lasts for a few years, until the Welsh see an opportunity to grab an extra bit of Scottish land and turn on their former Scots allies. When their fortune changes back again, they rekindle the alliance with the Scots. The Welsh, who had secretly been rearming their military, funded by donations from rich Welsh living abroad such as Tom Jones, Shirley Bassey and the Manic Street Preachers, launch Operation Red Dragon in Wales. They take back their land, expelling the English from their borders. The Scots and Welsh move the front lines back in their favour from a now weakened Republic of EngScot Army. Eventually, the world gets so pissed off that the leaders of England, Scotland and Wales are invited to Dayton, Ohio, in the USA, for a chat without tea and biscuits. The Yanks lay it on the table and say if they don't stop the fighting, they will stop it for them, with extreme violence. On the surface, this seems to make everyone see sense and come to an agreement which will be based around the current lines of conflict. The Welsh are more than happy with this after their recent successful Operation Red Dragon. The Scots are happy to have the ability to exist. And Scotland is to be divided into two entities. One of which is inhabited by the Scots and Welsh, as their alliance holds. The other is the Republic of EngScot. Overall, the English are the unhappiest at the recent loss of significant portions of land in Wales and Scotland. They have nothing left to bargain with and have no real choice but to go along with the agreement. In the background they are now setting their sights on cracking down on the Ethnic Cornish speaking population of Cornwall, who've been calling for more autonomy from England. The Kernow[8] Liberation Army (KLA) has evolved from civil resistance to the English Police forces in the early 1980s into a well-armed separatist militia. They want to create a Greater Cornwall that encompasses the entire SW peninsula, emphasising Cornish culture by removing all English influence, including the rich Londoners who have holiday homes in the region.

A massive NATO-led force is to be sent to Scotland. They're to oversee that the warring factions are returned to their barracks

8 Cornish for "Cornwall".

18

or disarmed so peace will return to the Glens. The scars from the conflict linger, and the process of reconciliation and rebuilding will take generations. The "UK Civil War" has far-reaching consequences, resulting in the formation of independent nations like Scotland, Wales, and Norfolk. Additionally, it brings about a restructuring of the relationship between England and the rest of the world.

The real episode is somewhat more complicated than the above. If you want to learn more, and you have a spare week, I would recommend you watch the BBC documentary *The Death of Yugoslavia.*

My part in this was to be in the period after the signing of the Dayton Peace Agreement by the warring parties on 14 December 1995. The agreement would bring an end to the conflict, which had been going on in the region since 1991. The responsibility of guaranteeing all signatories adhered to the agreed terms would fall upon a multinational NATO force named IFOR or Implementation Force. If not, then they would be liable for a good shoeing from them. The contribution of 7 Transport Regiment to this would be to supply the units comprising IFOR with paper plates, plastic cutlery, gas, and fuel, and to take away the sewage. This would allow team IFOR to carry out their task of ensuring that the parties were keeping to their end of the deal. If required, IFOR could administer military persuasion to those who were not keeping with the plan. I was to be witness to this historic event of finally bringing the peace to Bosnia under the name Operation Resolute.

While You Were Away

It's pandemonium on my return to the Squadron this morning, with people running around looking busy. I can't quite work out what they are busy with. We were to deploy in early April, but, from the morning's activity, you would have thought it was this afternoon we were going. The Squadron is in an old German Army barrack block dating back to the 1930s, and it was known as 'The Block.' It's one of many which made up the barracks that the Regiment inhabited. The Germans had called it Artillerie Kaserne[9] and Lauter Kaserne, but it was renamed Catterick Barracks when the British Army occupied it after the war. There were numerous camps of almost the same design all over Germany, and they had been used by the occupying powers in their respective zones. The building is oblong and constructed of solid stone with modern-looking double-glazed windows. The height of it reaches three stories, including a cellar and an attic. There was a rumour the structure descended as deep as it was high. The tale was always told by a senior Corporal, who was never so old, that he'd been there in 1945. Maybe the late 1970s at a push. He would then go on to tell you that under the Parade Square was where the Germans kept their tanks and that they were still there with their dead crew inside. I heard this story in every camp I ever went to, and the old Corporals always swore it was true.

The cellars are used for the stores and the armoury. The ground floor is occupied with the Headquarters and Troop Offices with a few more rooms used for briefings, or for us to sleep in. A couple are decked out with several hand-me-down sofas of various designs. They'd been unwittingly donated by soldiers who had left the Regiment and couldn't be arsed to take them with them. The two floors above are where the single soldiers lived. There are many buildings

---

9 German for "barracks".

on the barracks, some identical, some of a different shape — but in the same pre-war style — and some are of more modern construction. I'm a Driver by trade, and I had been posted to 17 Squadron, 7 Transport Regiment, RLC,[10] a few years earlier. My previous Regiment, in Münster, had been relocated to the UK. I had arrived in Germany in January 1990, missing the Cold War by a few months. With the threat from the East well and truly evaporated, the defence cuts started happening, as units were either disbanded or moved back to the UK. I was in no rush to go back to a home posting as Germany, and what was on its doorstep, was way more interesting. It wasn't anything to do with the extra pay, cheap booze, cheap fuel and tax-free cars.

It's said 7 Regiment has a tradition from history. It's not quite as ancient as those infantry types who could trace their origins to the Napoleonic Wars or further. Our quirky tale came from the Second World War.

So, after the big brawl ended, a Polish Colonel stuck in Germany decided, "You know what? I'm going to employ Polish refugees, forced labourers, POWs, and conscripts, and make a unit!" What did they do first? Guard German tanks! By 1947 they'd morphed into the Mixed Service Organisation, and they were moving Allied tanks across Germany. In 1965, 7 Regiment took on the Polish units, and by 1972 were replacing the retirement-aged Polish drivers with fresh-faced British Troops.

What did they get in return from their Polish counterparts? The Polish Orzel (Eagle) as a thank-you gift from the still-serving Polish personnel. This marked a significant milestone, as it was the first time British soldiers wore the Orzel, a symbol that became a cherished emblem of the Regiment's heritage. Further solidifying the Regimental bond with its Polish roots, shared traditions were culti-

10 Royal Logistic Corps.

vated. The Tank Transporter Troops were named after cities such as Krakow and Warsaw. The kerbstones in the barracks were painted in the white and red colours of the Polish flag and vodka flowed freely at Mess functions. Even the vehicles displayed the Polish Eagle in their windows, serving as a constant reminder of the enduring partnership between the two nations.

In 1998, during my second Balkan tour, I find myself stuck in a traffic jam on the Croatian coast road one afternoon. I am in a Land Rover that has the Polish Eagle in the back window and the bumpers painted in the Polish colours. I am approached by a small crowd of excited people speaking in a language which is like nothing I have heard before. Tourists were now returning to the Balkan popular destination, and this bunch turns out to be Polish holidaymakers. Their eyes sparkle with happiness upon seeing me, believing I belong to the Polish Army until I explain, in German, I was British. They walk back to their vehicle, utterly confused.

I feel like a spare part because, as I have been away for the last few months, I'm not sure where I should be or what I should be doing. I'm dossing around in the Troop restroom at the bottom of the corridor with a few other guys. We're trying to hide from the prospective shit jobs that are handed down during hectic times. Sergeant Jimmy Frazer enters the room with his big notepad in hand, which, we have no doubt, has a list of crappy jobs on it. Newly promoted, he is keen as mustard in his new role as Admin Sergeant. He's Scottish and likes a drink. He's also missing his bottom two front teeth, but I don't know if these facts are related. The gap in his teeth is occupied by a replacement denture which he constantly moves around in his mouth. He reminds me of a goat with a massive under bite.

"Ah, Scouse Lee," he says, pointing to me with his pen whilst looking at his notepad. I am not a Scouser. I am not from Liverpool, and I have never said I'm from Liverpool. I am from the Wirral, on the other side of the Mersey, but your Army mates never let geographical facts – or any facts – get in the way of a nickname when you have an accent. "You're on a fuel tanker course tomorrow over at 9 Squadron, now you're back from your holidays in the Harz Mountains."

"Who have I upset?" I ask. This sounds like a shit job.

"The Squadron will have two Troops for the tour. DROPS[11] Troop and Fuel & GT[12] Troop, and it's just the thing for the career progress of a Lance Corporal like yourself," he says, rattling off the familiar line.

What I want to say is: "You mean nobody else wanted to do it and as I was away, the easy option was to put my name down instead?"

But all that comes out is, "OK, I'll do it," as I didn't fancy getting a tooth knocked out.

→→→

The rest of the week is spent learning how to operate the 12,000 and 22,500-litre TTF[13] trucks with a few other unfortunate souls from my Squadron. The trucks are museum pieces, but with nothing modern to replace them in the immediate future, they are the best thing we have. They were made by a company called Foden and wouldn't look out of place in a 1960s film. The instructor is a Lance Corporal like me, but, because of his instructor status, he thinks he's

11 Demountable Rack Offload and Pick-up System. It was a modern truck which could pick up its own loads. A glorified skip wagon in reality.

12 General Transport.

13 Truck Tanker Fuel.

head of petroleum. He has a pool cue that never leaves his side. He uses it to point at everything from the information on the overhead projector screen to different parts of the truck and at us. I bet he goes home with it in the evening and points it at his wife, dinner, and his dog.

I saw him later in the year, after our return, in a downtown bar. He was lying on a sticky floor in a drunken state after falling off the stool. I picked up a pool cue, pointed it at the phone on the wall, and said, "Shall I call you a taxi?"

One day is spent in the classroom learning the dimensions, capacities and performances of the vehicles. There are too many unimportant things we're expected to memorise. There will be a test at the end and there is no way we are going to pass it.

"I'm popping out for five minutes. No fucking cheating," says the instructor during the test. He must be so proud of us, as everyone passes with 100%.

We pump thousands of litres from one truck to another and back for days on end on the Parade Square. The instructor always laughs at himself whenever he tells us to: "suck the fuel off another truck." Given we are humping the big reinforced pipes with their bronze handles whilst wearing uncomfortable rubber gloves and overalls, inevitably there are spillages. When we spill diesel, we have to put down absorbent granules to soak it up. One of us pours the granules on the fuel from a big bag and the other uses a brush to spread over the spill.

As I am putting the granules down with another guy, I say, "We wouldn't want any diesel getting onto the tanks stored under the Parade Square, would we?"

He stops brushing, looks at me, and says, "So you know the rumour?"

"It's horse shit," I reply.

"Nah, it's true. An old Corporal told me about it. Did you know the blocks go down as far as...?"

I stop listening as he drones on, repeating almost word for word what I heard years ago.

The interesting bit happens as we finally get to drive these lumbering beasts. As the fuel sloshes around in the tanks, the trucks wobble from side to side quite noticeably, and emergency stops are fascinating. Our task is to drive them on possibly the most inhospitable roads in Europe, so I envisage an intensive package of training. After doing two laps of camp, without crashing, the Instructor says, "well done," and signs my FMT600.[14] I am now a fully trained TTF Operator and I know it because I reek of diesel.

Sennelager: Probably the Worst Lager in the World

It's late in the afternoon and the entire Squadron is waiting outside the block for the German buses which would take us down to Sennelager Training Area. It's the week for our Pre-Deployment Training and, as if ordered by the hierarchy in charge, a blanket of snow has fallen on this part of Germany.

"If it ain't snowing, we ain't going," I hear someone say.

I'm leaning against the wall with two of my friends, Del and Scouse Platt. Del is originally from the Republic of Ireland and a natural comedian. He's continually telling jokes or stories and, with his accent, they always make me laugh. Scouse Platt is from Liverpool, but we call him Scouse Prat to make up for the geographical

14 The MOD driving licence which authorises you to drive whatever vehicles you have been trained on.

accuracy. He's got a dark black moustache, which makes him look like Ian Rush. "I'm going to sell T-shirts one day saying, Sennelager: Probably the Worst Lager in the World," I say as I shiver away in the cold.

"I'll buy one," says Del, "I'd buy several right now and put 'em all on. It must be minus 10 fecking degrees."

"Where's der fuckin' buses," adds Prat. "It's bastard freezing."

We aren't in the suitable kit for the temperature as the CO[15] had decreed that only issued kit is to be worn. Normally, when we go on exercise in this weather, we wear Matterhorn boots which we buy from the American PX.[16] They are insulated and waterproof. We also wear big heavy parkas issued from the stores and thick gloves from the German ski shop. Our state of dress is more suitable for a mild winter in the UK.

The buses arrive and the scene turns into one of bedlam. The luggage compartments on the side of the bus are opened. We throw our kit in without a care so we can get onto the warm bus. This is to the dismay of the German driver, who I know likes order. There is no orderly queue as 50 soldiers try to get through one door at the same time. The relief to get out of the cold is exquisite. We squeeze along the aisle. Some of us have our daysacks, but we all have our weapons, and we pick our seats. The cool soldiers don't get to sit at the back, it's just whoever got on first. The SNCOs,[17] or 'the adults' as I like to refer to them, always sit in the front few seats. It's not written down, but it's the natural order of the military world.

"Is anyone missing?" shouts Sergeant Frazer, standing at the front of the bus like a tour guide.

---

15 Commanding Officer. The one in overall charge of the Regiment.

16 American NAAFI. It always has good kit for sale and it's cheap.

17 Senior Non-Commissioned Officer, anyone above the rank of Corporal but not an Officer.

"Lord Lucan," shouts Del, with his hand over his mouth as if to fool him into thinking someone else said it.

"Shut the fuck up, Private Delaney," says Sergeant Frazer, looking directly at Del, his Irish accent betraying him.

The door hisses shut, and the bus pulls away. It wobbles as it navigates the speed bumps on its drive towards the Guardroom. By the time we exit camp, turning right onto Detmolder Strasse, the driver is already getting his revenge. He has set the heat to tropical and tuned the radio station to White Noise FM, so we are subjected to some mild psychological torture during the trip.

Doing training at Sennelager is as painful as always. Anything that involves a training area will always be uncomfortable. When soldiers get together and reminisce about the 'good old days', they talk about their comical experiences. They may mention the hours spent in the cold, trying to sleep in a wet ditch, or the time they were fucked about all night long. However, conversation will always steer towards the memorable incident, such as when Corporal Clutterbuck crashed his motorcycle into a German naturist's BBQ.

My mind has forgotten most of the uncomfortable bits, which is probably for the better. However, I still remember the incessant pain inducing cold during that particular week. The temperature continued to drop and I do recall it being minus 20 degrees at one point. The infantry unit running the training package for us were kitted out in warmer looking kit and stared at us with pity in our issued gear. There was lots of listening to briefs about the country, the threats to us, and how things might turn out if it went 'pear-shaped'. We watched demos of situations previous units had experienced. Then we were placed in scenarios with an angry, drunk local militia guy who was threatening to kick off. All of this was conducted outside in the crisp German winter.

This evening, we're doing a night shoot with tracer, which is something we Drivers rarely get to do. There are about 10 of us lined up in a long trench, looking down the range, waiting for something to happen. We've been given the order to 'watch and shoot', which basically means something is about to happen. There's a noise of metal-on-metal in the distance, and, even though we can't see them, we know the targets have come up into their standing position. As soon as one of us opened fire, the rest follow suit. Putting an abundant amount of lead down the range, we are witnesses to a violent firework display. We nearly always shot during the daytime and without tracer. The only thing you might have seen was a small puff of dirt as the bullet struck the ground. This was followed by the unmistakable sound of a ricochet as it spun off somewhere unseen. Tonight we can see where everything is going. Most bullets continue down the range, missing their target. They bow to gravity and seemingly slow down as they get further away from us until they appear to switch off as the tracer burns out. Some hit the ground and go straight up in the air. A few whizz wildly off into the woods on either side of the range. Now and again, one of them hits something hard and comes spinning back towards us. One lands a few metres in front of me and continues to burn brightly in the snow. I pause for a second, mesmerised by it, before I hear a livid, shouty voice over my shoulder.

"Get them fucking rounds down."

I continue to fire single shots in the target's direction, with some purposely above, so I can watch them light up and arc through the dark.

"Cease fire, cease fire," shouts another angry voice as we apply safety catches and stand upright away from the front of the trench. Everyone is buzzing with excitement. Once the procedure for unloading the weapons and checking they were unloaded is complete, we remove our ear defenders.

"I wish every day on the ranges were like dat," says Scouse Prat. "Dat was fuckin' ace, dat was."

He continues, giggling like a mad man, "I'd do dat again. It was fuckin' sound as a pound."

Del says with his Irish accent, "With all der snow and all dat I felt like I was on the eastern front keeping the Red Army at bay." His interest in history is obvious.

"Did you feel like the *Wehrmacht* or the SS?" I ask Del.

"Well, maybe the *Wehrmacht,* as I'm not really a bad lad you know. I mean, I'm fairly easy going and I'd have probably been kicked out of the SS for being too nice."

We clamber out of the trench and are herded off to an open-sided shelter with a corrugated iron roof. There are a number of large plastic insulated Norwegian containers, known as 'Norgies'[18]. They are green, oblong, with rounded corners and a thick flat lid. Their insides are cream coloured and are always stained from their contents over years of use. They are cleaned with bleach, normally by an overzealous soldier who has been given the task as a punishment. There's no distinction as to what would go in them, so having a tea with hints of spaghetti bolognese, orange squash and bleach is quite normal. They're propped up on their sides so we can dispense a hot drink from the nozzle. They are used for the transportation of food and liquids whilst keeping them warm. There's a type of spout on the lid with a rudimentary tap for pouring the brown water. A breather cap is also fitted in the lid, which can be unscrewed to allow the liquid to flow. Soldiers straight out of training are customarily told it's the switch for dispensing hot and cold drinks. We gather round the Norgies in anticipation of a warm drink. Simultaneously we all reach for our mugs, which are snugly fitted on top of our

18 I presume they are called so because they are from Norway.

water bottles in the pouch on our webbing.[19] The water bottle pouch is always fitted a bit too far around on the belt to reach easily. I see one guy twisting his body so much to get at his mug that he keeps turning around and around on the spot like a dog chasing its own tail. The light brown steaming liquid fills our mugs. A big spoon of white sugar is lifted from a brown paper bag and unceremoniously dumped in with a quick stir before we move on to make way for the next. In less than five minutes, the brown paper bag is ripped in half and the sugar solidified from the repeated use of the wet spoon.

We gather as we sip the brown liquid, and we comment on it.

"I'm getting hints of cheap NAAFI tea laced with cheaper coffee," says Del after taking a sip. He holds his mug up to the light of the Tilley lamp that is hanging off the corner of the shelter and pretends to inspect the fluid in his mug.

"It's almost as if they changed their mind when they were halfway through making this classic tipple," he says, while lowering his mug to look into it as he swills it around.

"I'm getting suggestions of range stew[20] with gentle under-tones of spaghetti bolognese," I add after my first sip.

"It's fuckin' awful," says Prat. "But at least it's warm and wet, and dat explains why our brothers in arms in der kitchens can get away with making dis shite."

Del pauses, then announces: "This cofftea. This cupperteano.

---

19 Webbing is the collection of various-sized pouches that are used to carry stuff you need to hand such as ammunition, rations and water. The pouches are attached to a belt with the important ammunition ones being just in front of your hips and the less important ones being further round the back. There is also a yoke to distribute the weight over the shoulders, and it's put on almost like one would put on a jacket.

20 An all-in stew that was served whilst on the ranges in the same containers which would be used later to serve drinks in.

This elixir of life. Long live der Cabbage Mechanics."[21] I spit mine out on the ground, splashing our boots.

Del looks at me, laughs, and says, "So we're a professional taster now, eh? Good on yer. We all need a career to fall back on when we get out der Army."

We get back to the accommodation in time to grab a few quick beers and a pizza at the NAAFI. Some are intent on downing as much as they could in one hour, like condemned men. One of them, Corporal 'Smeggy' Thompson, has a growing collection of German beer bottles lined up in front of him and is eating a grim-looking pizza covered in hot-looking chillies. I see him later in the night when I get up to go for a pee. He's sitting in the corridor, pissed as a fart, drinking from a big red plastic fire bucket which has a few dog ends floating about in it.

"All good, Smeggy?" I ask him.

"I'm fucking gaggin', man."

"Well, if we have a fire, we might need you to come and piss on it," I say as I wander off to the toilet.

Wait Training

On our return from Sennelager, we have to do some more Pre-Deployment training, but of a type that's more suited to our role as Drivers, which involves less shooting and more driving. We have to drive in convoy in our DROPS vehicles to a predetermined map reference in the middle of another training area. Our load is pretend palletised ammunition boxes containing gravel to simulate the weight. I'm teamed up with Prat and we ensure we have plenty of snacks to make life a bit more bearable. One of the positive things

21 Another name for an Army Chef.

about these driving exercises is that we don't have to carry everything on our backs but in our cabs, so we can make ourselves comfortable. The DROPS truck is fairly new and, compared with some of the antiquated vehicles that the Regiment still had on their books, it's like driving a Rolls Royce. It has a spacious cab with room in the back for a great deal of kit and a kip, should you feel tired, which we do frequently on training. It's an automatic so there is no playing about with the sort of broom handle-length gear sticks you have to fight with in manual vehicles to crunch it into the next gear. On doing so, it's followed by cries of "It's a gearbox, not a jukebox," or, "If you can't find 'em, grind 'em," from any onlookers or passengers.

We turn off the road and onto the training area and soon we come to a stop. I presume this is our pre-determined map reference as our convoy idly wait for something to happen. I don't want to get out of the cab, as the ground is a sea of slushy snow, ice, and mud. What typically happens is, as soon as you do get out, the convoy will pull away again. I poke my head out the window to try to see down the line of vehicles and I see Smeggy Thompson staggering through the filth like a drunk. He stops at each vehicle to speak to the driver. He arrives at ours and bangs on the door as if to wake me up, even though I have the window down. My head is already poking out in expectation for his big news. He gazes up at me and, even though we've only been out of barracks a few hours, he looks like he'd been out here for weeks, rolling about in the crap and in dire need of a bath.

"The local militia won't let us through their checkpoint, so we are going to have to wait," he says.

"OK", I say, as I'm more than happy to wait there.

"No questions," he asks me?

"I do have one."

"Fire away."

"How do you grow seedless grapes?"

He stumbles off through the quagmire, mumbling something about copulating with male chickens.

We stay there the entire night, practising our waiting. A guard roster has been made up by Smeggy. Each truck crew takes turns to carry out a roaming patrol up and down the convoy to ensure no builders are going to steal our boxes of gravel. I think Smeggy just wants us to look as dirty as him. I was hoping to keep out of the mud, as I don't want wet feet. When I have to take a pee, I clamber out of the cab, holding onto the bars on the roof which had been fitted with possibly this actual scenario in mind. I climb round to the back where there is just enough space to stand without holding on to something to relieve myself from a great height.

As the evening wears on, we make ourselves comfortable in the cab. Prat is laid down in the back, smoking a cigarette. I have put the passenger seat all the way back and have my feet on the dashboard.

"This is great for practising waiting," I say to Prat. "I doubt you could do it on paper or in a classroom."

"Or yer could do it in a classroom, I suppose," he replies.

"Yeah, but it'd be boring, not like this octane-fuelled roller-coaster waiting that we are doing now,"

"I'd rather be doin' it at home with der telly on."

I am awoken by a busting bladder which I try to ignore, but it's a foregone battle and I have to concede defeat after less than a minute. Unzipping my sleeping bag, I feel the chilly air envelop my body and I start to shiver. I slip on my cold boots and pop the door open so I am able to scramble out of the cab to the peeing spot. The joy of letting off the pressure is one of life's little pleasures. It arches down into the mud, creating a new steaming yellow puddle. I clamber back into the cab to grab my toothbrush. Behind the seats lies

Prat, looking like a green maggot in his dossbag.[22] I give him a gentle nudge with one of his boots as I send it flying in the direction of his head.

"Time for school, princess," I say.

"Fuck off," replies the green maggot.

The shivering becomes uncontrollable, but it's helping me to get the brush around my mouth with more efficiency. Smeggy hoves into view and is doing the rounds to see if everyone is up and ready to spring into waiting.

"You two good?" he shouts at me as he walks along our line of trucks.

I give him the thumbs-up as he passes by, splashing straight through my piss mud puddle. "Ready to move in 10 minutes," he yells over his shoulder.

I take a swig from my mug and gob out the mixture of water, toothpaste and saliva, just missing him. I bang on the back of the cab and shout, "WAKE UP YOU LAZY BASTARD, THE WAR IS OVER AND WE IS GOING HOME!"

The next 10 minutes are a flurry of activity as we have to finish our morning routine and check the truck. We check the straps holding the gravel boxes in place are still tight, make a brew, make breakfast, drink the brew, and eat the breakfast. Being highly trained, we manage this in under five minutes. Smeggy is doing his nut, shouting unintelligibly at everyone in his line of sight. He spots us sitting in the cab wearing our helmets. We are then ready to jump into action like a coiled spring and are waiting for his order to move. He points at us and continues screaming more incoherent words in our direction. Even though we can't make out what he's saying, we sense the tone and know they are obscenities. Some are aimed at us, but mainly it seems to be at everyone in his field of vision.

---

22 Sleeping bag.

"It's a job of a Corporal to shout incessantly at random soldiers," Prat tells me.

"There must be an Officer around somewhere he's trying to impress," I reply, looking at Smeggy and wondering if he needs a couple of sessions with a therapist. He disappears off to the head of the convoy to take his place in the front vehicle to prepare for our impending departure.

Two hours later, we set off.

Train Hard, Drink Easy

We continue this facade for a few more days. Because of a German law which bans HGVs on their roads at the weekends, we end up on an unusually small training area for the weekend. The morning is spent driving around and around it. After an hour, we have a London cabbie-style knowledge of the area with attacks of boredom and dizziness coming on. The Squadron Operations Officer and his team try to make things interesting for us with different scenarios. These include driving and waiting with a bit of First Aid or waiting and driving with a bit of rules of engagement. Some even combine more waiting with extra waiting. By lunchtime, their idea bank is exhausted. It is then announced that the rest of the day will be vehicle maintenance and the beers will be cracked open after this evening's dinner, which will be a barbecue. This news is received with loud cheers as this means checking the oil, cleaning the lights, then sitting around talking and smoking cigarettes. Even better is the barbecue, which means fresh food after days of living on compo rations.[23]

"Yer can only live on compo for so long, lad, before yer bowels explode," explains Prat. "I didn't shit for a week on exercise once.

---

23 Composite rations. I'm not entirely sure they were designed to block up your digestive system, but they did.

When I came back, I gave birth to a four-stone chocolate log. Nearly split me in two. I feel sorry for the missus now." The biscuits in the compo packs we've been eating are named AB Biscuits. I believe "AB" once stood for Alternative Bread. They were subsequently renamed by soldiers to Arse Bungers.

Instead of parking up the Squadron vehicles in a big line, it's decided that we should set up a sort of camp by arranging them in a defensive circle in the woods. If we had any women and children, they would have been placed in the middle. The next most precious thing we park in the centre is the strangely named G10 truck, which has now turned up. It's a Bedford 4-Tonner that carries the cooking equipment and other important stuff like toilet rolls, green string, and a Cabbage Mechanic. The man who owns the company that makes this string must have thought all his Christmases had come at once when he landed the contract to supply the military. We used it now and again when on exercise and I saw hundreds of full spools on shelves during my service, but I never ever noticed a near-empty spool. Every veteran across the world will definitely have unused ones in their sheds somewhere.

Drinking super-chilled beer in the freezing snowy German winter whilst standing about in the woods isn't much fun. Like drug addicts, we carry on regardless of our discomfort to get the alcoholic hit. The beer is so cold I have to wear one of my thick gloves to stop frostbite from setting in on the palm of my hand. The Cabbage Mechanic is cooking an assortment of meat on the almost standard oil barrel. The barrel is cut in half with metal fence posts welded to each end in an X-configuration, which will have been made by the unit metalsmith for a crate of beer or two. We anxiously wait in line with our collection of plates, some plastic, some made of metal, and the odd porcelain one that had been liberated from the cookhouse on a long-term loan. The traditional rectangular mess tins you see in most military films are still issued, but why rough it when you've got a great big truck to carry your crockery? I often take a pillow with me on these sorts of exercises. I always hear the words of one of my old Staff Sergeants, who had said he served in the SAS.

"Any idiot can be uncomfortable."

I don't think he had pillows in mind when he quoted this, though.

The call is made to inform us it's time to eat, so we slowly file past and get a moment's comforting warmth from the barbecue. The Cabbage Mechanic looks like a frantic music conductor as he ambidextrously loads up our plates with the steaming bratwurst, chicken and burgers at the same time as flipping the meat, which is still cooking. Next to the barbecue is Sergeant Frazer, behind a wooden table, offering a frozen bread roll and some chilled coleslaw.

"Just some bread please, Sarge," says everyone as they pass him.

"Wit's wrong wiv the coleslaw, yer big fannies?" says Sergeant Frazer, with a clean serving spoon in one hand.

"I'm on a diet," says Del.

"Yer fucking nee it, yer podgy basta."

As we huddled in our group, Del says, "I wanted to say at least I can lose weight, while you'll always be an ugly fucker. I think he would have cut my throat with his serving spoon if I'd said it to him though."

"Yer could ave fended im off wif yer berger," says Prat, proposing a culinary defensive plan.

"That would be against the Geneva Convention," I add.

"You'd end up in dat gaff in errr, what's dat country?" replies Prat. "Yer know, where day have shoes made out of cheese or wood or summit like dat."

"The Hague, in Holland?" says Del, bursting out in fits of laughter. "You excelled at geography, I see Prat?" he adds.

→» →» →»

Those of us lucky enough not to be on guard duty during the early hours awake to the sudden shock arrival of spring. The snow is melting fast. It's dripping off the trees at such a rate it's like being in a heavy shower. By the time we're packed up and ready to go, we look like we've been for a fully-clothed morning swim. It isn't only melt water that's soaked us, as our frantic exertion in the risen temperature soon has us sweating. We are now deemed to be highly trained in the art of waiting, so it is back to camp for a bit of Pre-Deployment leave before we fly out. It is the normal military-created chaos as the Squadron vehicles move about trying to line up in their order before departing. It isn't made any easier by the training area now resembling a massive mud bath.

Once the required shouting and screaming by the Sergeants and Corporals is complete, we move out. At the exit from the training area, I see Sergeant Frazer with a few other soldiers, and they are holding brooms. He's been tasked to sweep the mud off the road that our trucks would inevitably deposit as they depart the training area. This is so the locals won't crash their Mercedes on their morning commute. Del is in the DROPS in front of me and he stops briefly. He says something to Sergeant Frazer in that second, which is just enough time to make him throw his broom at him. Del floors it to get out of the way of his incoming broom. It strikes the back of his cab, clatters about for a moment and tumbles down to become wedged in-between the hydraulic pipes. I pass by Sergeant Frazer and I make out a string of Scottish obscenities directed at Del's rapidly disappearing truck.

I see the broom fall from his truck after half an hour and violently cartwheel off into a farmer's field.

"E'll get a fine fer fly tippin," says Prat.

"Is a broom fly tipping?" I reply.

"Well, did yer see ow it flew off into dat field? Looked like it was flyin to der tip to me."

"Let's dob him into the German council when we get back," I suggest.

Our arrival back at camp later that morning is celebrated with an uninterested courtesy wave from the gate guard. As soon as we switch the engine off, it becomes a race to get everything tidied and put away in the fastest possible time. This is so we can sit about for the rest of the afternoon waiting to be knocked off. Jimmy Frazer is looking for Del and approaches us several times, asking his whereabouts. Del has the gift of being about to complete his tasks without being seen, but we know he won't be able to evade him forever. The gravel boxes are offloaded, the trucks fuelled up, and their tool kits returned to the stores. Our unused weapons are cleaned, and the trucks are lined up on the Parade Square in such a neat style you'd assume we had OCD. Our trucks are not to be coming with us. We are to take on the ones already in the Balkans. There's a rear party left behind to look after the vehicles left behind, kicking the tyres every so often to make sure they are still drivable on our return.

The months prior to the Regiment being told of its impending deployment, it had been like a boat stuck in the doldrums. It was routine training, planning for an exercise, the odd job, sports and mainly ways for those in charge to keep us interested in being soldiers. After the news of our invitation to the Balkans, the tempo had gone up a few notches above manic. It was initially at least more exciting than normal. It made the time pass by quicker, but as the days to our departure became fewer, it was becoming a chaotic rush to ensure everything was sorted. There were personnel without passports, some lost intentionally, some missing inoculations, marital issues, child issues, grandparent issues and goldfish issues. There was so much to fit in. For us, it was a lot of waiting about for the next idea or problem.

Jimmy Frazer walks into the Troop restroom where we are waiting. Some are sleeping as tiredness has caught up with them from the last few days.

"Reet, listen in," he says.

He has his book, which no doubt has a list in it that he is going to go through.

"We're gonna try an git yers away on leave by tomorrow lunchtime? If the OC is happy wit things in the morning, there'll be a parade about 1200."

He looks around the room.

"Where's fucking Delaney?"

Del is in there. He's tried to hide himself between a couple of sofas and behind someone, hoping Jimmy won't realise he was there.

Careless[24], the Regimental grass, says, "He's there, Sarge," pointing at Del and giving away his hidey-hole.

"Eh," says Jimmy, looking for him.

Del pokes his head round from behind, smiling in pain, as he knows he has to face the music.

"Come and see me in my office straight after this," he says, pointing his pen at Del.

24 I'll explain this nickname later...

2

Let's Split

THE PLANE thumps onto the ground with the delicacy of an overweight whale doing a belly flop. We bounce in unison on our seats, leaning forward as the pilot abruptly hits the brakes, revealing a plot twist of limited runway ahead. The journey here had started in what our leaders would call 'the early hours of the morning' but we soldiers call 'the middle of the bloody night'.

→»→»→»

The entire Squadron was on parade in the April chill to make sure we were all present and correct with our bags. After some mildly aggressive shouting of names by various Sergeants — and the odd

41

Staff Sergeant when someone didn't answer — it became apparent we were indeed, with our bags, correct and present. Now and again, someone would shout an obscenity and run off into the block to grab whatever they might have forgotten. This would be followed by added vulgarities from Sergeants and Staff Sergeants. We were marched up to the gymnasium. But this wasn't the marching you might expect from Trooping the Colour. It was more like the rout of a beleaguered army. Some had one bag too many and, without having a free hand to carry it, they resorted to kicking it a few feet forward. Then they would have to walk up to it and repeat the process. It was less than a hundred metres to the gymnasium, and by the time the first of us arrived, some of the others were barely five metres from where they started. Some had given up with the kicking method and, once they'd dumped their bags outside, they would return for the ones which were left behind.

Inside the gymnasium, which had been set up as a temporary departure lounge, the Movement Controllers checked us in. I noticed the Movers didn't actually seem to do much checking-in and had somehow appeared to have coerced everyone else to do it for them. They had our clerks check ID cards and add the names to the manifest. A work party was weighing baggage on a set of scales which wouldn't have been out of place on *Antiques Roadshow*. They even got one of our own to read out the list of forbidden items we weren't allowed to carry with us on the plane. I considered becoming a Mover one day, as it seemed a lot more relaxed than driving trucks and getting shouted at.[25]

The RAF Police were looking in random bags just in case any of us didn't understand the list of forbidden items. As they always do, they eventually found someone who was not gifted in the depart-

---

25 It's all in my first book, *Licking the Taliban's Flip-Flop*. I eventually changed jobs for this easier way of life.

ment of following simple rules. Today, it was Staff Sergeant 'Gunny' Dawlish's turn.

His nickname came from Gunny, after the character played by Clint Eastwood in the film *Heartbreak Ridge,* which we knew he enjoyed being called. He was one of those individuals who gave me the distinct impression that he would have preferred life in an infantry unit. But, instead of taking that route, I suspect he chose to remain in the Transport Regiment, knowing he wouldn't stand out there the way he did among a pack of lazy drivers like us. He didn't look like the tough, no-nonsense Clint Eastwood character at that point, as the young Police Corporal emptied the entire contents of his bag. It was evident they'd discovered his hidden collection of mini-flares, which he was attempting to smuggle, and he appeared appropriately ashamed. He'd end up getting a discreet talking-to from the Squadron Sergeant Major, with maybe a hint that he might donate a few bottles of port to the Sergeant's Mess. If it had been one of us, it would have been an instant on-the-spot bollocking, followed by a charge. Captain Haywood, the Squadron 2IC,[26] got him at the end of the tour. Gunny had a box he was slowly filling in readiness for his return to Germany. Captain Haywood had cut around the bottom of the box with the precision and care of a gifted surgeon. Nothing looked untoward as Gunny filled it up to the top. He taped it shut and then as he picked it up to load it onto the truck. The contents stayed on the floor, spilling about, as Gunny lifted the box minus the bottom.

"Is Gunny thinking he's on a Rambo mission again?" asked Del.

"Those flares would have come in handy to scare the Operations Officer away when he came to him asking for vehicle availability."

"Maybe he needs them for reading in the dark." I replied.

"What in God's name is he thinking of? I mean, it's not like we

26 Second in Command.

have to buy our own pyrotechnics. What's wrong with the guy? Has his nickname really gone to his head or what?"

As time went by, a small pile of contraband had grown. There was nothing as bad as the flares, but I observed piles of gas cookers, bottles of spirits and quite a few German hardcore porn mags.

"Hope you enjoy your knees-up tonight in the cop shop," shouted Del, but not toward the RAF Police. I knew he did this to get a laugh from our guys, but didn't want to offend them in case his kit ended up in the Falkland Islands.

The baggage party, which was made up of Privates who had mostly been in trouble around then, was given this laborious task and carried our weighed bags out of the side door. The bags would be thrown onto a couple of waiting Bedford 4-Ton trucks. They'd have needed a three-hour head start to get to the airport due to them having a top speed that was impressive in the 1950s. I saw Geordie Munchester with a sweaty red face. He was chosen for this role after being caught smoking in a vehicle during the pre-deployment training.

"Sergeant Frazer 'volun-told' you for this job?" I asked him as he picked up another couple of bags.

"Aye man. It was this or babysitting for him," he replied.

Before I could question his logic of this being harder than babysitting, he said, "His kids are like him. They're fucking mental. They'd have kicked my head in for telling them it's time for bed."

"Fair one," I replied as I made my way out of the gym.

Soldiers babysitting SNCOs' kids so they could go and get smashed in the Sergeants' Mess was extremely common back then. We could be ordered to do it, as in the case of Geordie Munchester, offered a bit of cash or tempted by the 'help yourself to what is in the fridge'. In my previous posting in Münster, a friend of mine, Ned Horsfall, was given this offer by his Troop Staff Sergeant, Tommy Rave-on.

Not being one to disobey an order, he helped himself to what was in the fridge, which just happened to be a large quantity of beer. He helped himself to so much that Tommy had to consider breaking into his own quarter upon his return, as Ned was so helped out that he was horizontal on the sofa. Luckily, one of his kids opened the door before a forced entry destruction started. That was the end of his military babysitting career.

Next stop was the cookhouse for the last breakfast. We lined up for the greasy selection of sausages, eggs and bacon, and we took more than normal, as we didn't know when our next 'decent' meal would be. We knew we would get fed on the plane courtesy of the RAF, but experience told us to prepare.

The RAF passenger food budget was about the same as the yearly income of a Saudi Arabian life model. They would serve the in-flight meal in a white box which would contain a bland sandwich with something on it which nobody could identify. It'd include a Blue Riband, heavily salted crisps, a bruised apple or an overly ripe banana, and a bottle of cheap fizzy cherryade that wouldn't quench the thirst caused by the crisps. I knew Pratt would have had all the Blue Ribands from people who didn't want them, as he was a proper scrounger for sweet stuff.

With our full bellies, we headed back to the block to wait in the Troop restrooms for the buses to arrive. After a good deal of waiting, we heard engines, which must have meant our ride had arrived. Someone who felt they should be impressing somebody that morning informed us via the art of angry shouting that our transport had arrived and asked us to please make our way outside. We trudged onto the fleet of German multi-coloured buses and, without ceremony, our convoy departed Catterick Barracks for the airport. Twenty minutes into the journey on the autobahn, we passed the Bedford baggage wagons which set off two hours earlier. The plan was for our plane to depart at 0900. Because it seemed like the

RAF would actually be on time for the first time in history, they invented a problem. We were just told it was a technical problem, but we suspected the problem was with the pilot's alarm clock. At 1000 we board the plane, and I end up sitting next to Private Cheezy Cheesebourgh, who constantly smiled so much, I'm surprised he wasn't nicknamed 'The Cheshire Cat'. He pulled out a packet of Top Trumps and we played it most of the way as we headed towards our destination of Split in a newly independent Croatia.

A Mover came on board the plane wearing a hi-vis vest over his T-shirt and carrying a handheld radio. He briefly talked to the cabin crew before picking up the tannoy and announcing, "Welcome to Split International Airport..."

"Aren't all airports international?" Cheezy whispered to me.

"...Where the local time is 1347, and the temperature is currently a pleasant 20 degrees."

"This is gonna be better than a week at Ayia Napa," remarked Cheezy, rubbing his hands together.

"You will soon depart the aircraft and you will make your way to the terminal where transport will be waiting to take you to your destination. Can I request the baggage party please make themselves known to me?"

"They're the pissed off-looking ones," someone shouted from the back of the plane to a round of laughter.

"Looks like the biggest baggage party I've ever had," replied the Mover to a round of applause.

Soon after, it was our turn to get off the plane. We slowly shuffled towards the door and I saw the deep blue cloudless sky. As I stepped onto the stairs and felt the warm Adriatic air, my jumper suddenly reminded me that putting it on that morning was a bad idea. It's not like I had any choice in the matter, as this was the dress we were told to travel in. By the time I got to the bottom of the steps, I was sweating like a fat bloke in a pie shop. I saw the scrubland to the north of the airport. It was mainly yellow with the odd bush dotted about, as if they had to have a token splash of green. There was a loud cheer, and I heard it was coming from the terrace above the terminal we were heading for. It was the outgoing Regiment, who were waiting to get on the plane we arrived on to go home.

Somebody from our Regiment shouted, "Your Mum sends her regards."

"I'll give yours mine when I see her tonight," came a reply from the rabble of green above us.

They burst into laughter and carried on cheering. We knew it would be us in six months' time and that we'd cheer just as loudly, if not louder.

Due to manpower shortages at the time — the British Army always has manpower shortages, even when they are fully manpowered — I knew some of the laughing crowd would be replacing us in six months. The rule at the time was you were supposed to have 18 months between tours. However, some soldiers would come off a tour, get posted to another unit and, unfortunately for them, if said unit was about to deploy, they would be off again. Geordie Munchester had only been there six months before and wasn't too happy about it and complained to Sergeant Frazer.

His caring side came out in his reply to Geordie: "Suck it up, princess."

→» →» →»

I follow the procession of our own green uniforms towards the terminal and am glad to get into the shade and away from the happy mob. We have to go through Croatian immigration and I am expecting the heavily accented border official to say, 'Biiiizness order pleaszoor.'

I present my passport, but he says nothing. He welcomes me to

Croatia with a face which looked like he's just found out his wife has been having an affair with his dad and everyone knew except him until I arrived.

We skip baggage reclaim as our personalised baggage collectors are hard at work. Around the side of the terminal building in their jumpers, they are lumping our luggage from the baggage trollies onto a pair of six-wheeled, more modern, Bedford 14 Ton trucks. These are able to go 1980s fast, so we hope we won't have to wait too long for them to turn up.

I finally catch up with Del and Prat.

"How was first class?" I ask them.

"I'd seen the film before and the champagne wasn't quite at the suggested temperature," says Del.

"I've got yer a Blue Riband," says Prat, showing me his pockets stuffed full with them. He pulls one out and offers it to me. It's now in liquid form inside its wrapper because of the warmth.

"Thanks, but no thanks."

"Did you book the taxi?" asks Del.

"I did. Stanislav said he'd meet us out front in his T55,"[27] I reply.

The voice we heard earlier informs us again, via well-practiced angry shouting, that our transport is waiting, and if it isn't too much bother, could we make our way outside? We clock who it is, seeing that it's the newly promoted Corporal Keeling, known as 'Position'.

"Dear God," says Del. "Nothing worse than a newly promoted person trying to impress the adults. Does he not know he won't get promoted again for a few years yet so he can kick back a bit?"

Years later, I heard Position's glittering career came to an abrupt end when he was found guilty of fraud for hiding his car and claiming it on the insurance. Pity his talent at hiding cars wasn't as good as

---

27 Russian tank exported all over the world.

his talent for angry shouting. His plan was blown wide open when a Blanket Stacker[28] asked the Quartermaster why there was a dusty car in one of their shipping containers.

The buses are waiting for us outside the terminal and are driven by soldiers from the outgoing Regiment and, thankfully, not the locals.

"At least we won't potentially die today," says Del, hinting at the quality of driving in the Balkans that we will get to experience later on.

It is a 40-minute drive to our new home, and the route takes us along the coast with a view across the Gulf of Kastela to the peninsula where the city is located. The Marjan Hill dominates the view. I see a flag flying on top of it. Even though it's quite a distance away, I can clearly make out the red, white and blue tricolour and the distinctive shield with its chequerboard design. The huge Poljudu stadium also stands out from its backdrop of communist-era grey high-rise flats. It's been used for many events but is better known as the home of Hajduk Split Football Club. The buildings look quite nice until we get closer and can see they are in need of a lot of maintenance. It's pretty quiet on the bus as everyone is taking in the views of their new environment.

I don't know what I expected, but I can see no evidence of the war anywhere. It feels as if we are merely embarking on a Mediterranean holiday. Life looks like it was carrying on as normal here. There is rubbish everywhere along the route, from piles of bin bags to mattresses and even a lot of fridges. There is an enormous billboard with a picture of a pretty, smiling lady and words which don't even appear pronounceable. Old women are selling the biggest watermelons I've ever seen on the sides of the road. Petrol stations look

---

28 Anyone who is in any way involved in stores.

modern and familiar and there are a few kiosks made from flimsy tin and painted in red lead. Some are empty but others are open and selling newspapers and cigarettes. There's plenty of graffiti on walls but it is just a jumble of letters, mainly consonants, keeping the un-pronounceable vibe going. I see the Croatian chequerboard roughly painted on a wall with the letters 'HVO' in white paint below it. I recognise this from the news reports I saw in the years when the war was constantly on the telly. It stands for Hrvatsko Viece Obrane, or Croatian Defence Council, which was the official military for-mation of the Bosnian Croatians. Further off the main road, I see houses, most of which are made from concrete and look like work in progress. Some give the impression they are in a walled compound and some just seem to have been built where there was land availa-ble. The roads are in fairly decent condition and, in the parts outside the built-up areas, crash barriers previously painted a bright yellow are sun-bleached pale.

There is a noticeably large proportion of damage to the barriers along our route that can only have resulted from the obvious. Some are just lightly dented and other parts have taken a lot more force, distorting them outwards but doing their job of keeping the vehicle on the carriageway. Worryingly, there are numerous sections which have been split open, as if someone has intentionally ploughed into it in an attempt to get off the road. To add to the evidence of a country that has not quite mastered the skill of safe driving, I see countless compounds containing smashed-up trucks and cars, all of which makes me suspect the national sport must be banger racing.

The bus turns off the main road, and onto one which has no painted lines or signage. It is very straight and I can see through the front windscreen that we are heading towards the foothills. There are more of the red tin kiosks and a few newer-looking cabins sell-ing more newspapers and cigarettes. We pass a bar, well, really just a big, weathered house with the paint peeling off the wooden storm shutters and a few rusty metal chairs in a paved area under a trellis. The only clue it is a bar is the out-of-place new sign hanging on the gatepost that says BAR.

The bus slows as it approaches a huge puddle which covers almost the width of the road. It's not actually a puddle, but part of a very large swampy area the road unfortunately has to go through. We come to a stop as we wait for the traffic coming the other way. Their side of the road looks the shallower part. The Balkan 'give way' rule appears to be that whoever has the biggest balls has the right of way, as car after car just keeps coming. Our driver starts to move forward to signal that he is coming through and will soon be the right-of-way champion. A tiny Fiat 126-looking thing decides he would make a challenge for this right of way but abandons it when he realises the bus isn't stopping. He's forced over, off the road and into an extremely rough bit of ground, which does not bode well for a car the size of a shoebox.

"Winning hearts and minds one accident at a time," says Del, as the Fiat looked like it is grounded in a rut.

The smell then hits us, the unmistakable stench of foetid water with God-knows-what else floating about in it.

Welcome to your New Home

We round the corner to see our new abode. It is a concrete building in an industrial park and it goes by a name that many an RLC Bosnian Veteran will know only too well.

Dalma Warehouse.

It looks bright yellow in the sunlight and to have at least one upper floor. There is a loading ramp running down the side of it and the area opposite it has at least 30 white Portakabins positioned in the sort of neat rows that only the military can, or will, do. There is a flimsy perimeter fence and a Guardroom, which is another Portakabin, located at the entrance.

Along the adjacent side is a mixture of more Portakabins and shipping containers with a few DROPS vehicles parked up, which are being loaded by a forklift. The Guard raises the barrier to let the bus in and we have finally arrived.

"I've seen more Portakabins in the last 30 seconds than I have in my entire time on earth," I say to Del.

"They're called 'Corimecs' out here, apparently," he replies.

"They're called what?"

"Corimecs."

"What the fuck is a Corimec?"

"A Portakabin."

"So why are they called Corimecs?"

"They are made by an Italian company and they are called a Corimec because the name of the company is spelt CO.RI.MEC."

"How do you know this shit?"

"Knowledge is power my friend, knowledge is power," he says with a smug grin on his fizzog.[29]

I ended up spending such a significant amount of my time in them during the rest of my career in the British Army that I would say they were the best thing to come out of Italy since Sophia Loren.

We are led to the cookhouse and while we are stuffing our faces, our baggage arrives and is dumped outside. We hunt through a miniature mountain of bags and webbing of the same design and colour to find our own. It should have been a task on *The Krypton Factor*[30]

29 Face. From physiognomy.

30 An ITV game show that tested contestant's physical and mental attributes.

as it is bloody frustrating and would make great viewing, as a load of squaddies curse and throw kit about for 10 minutes.

Sergeant Frazer bellows at us.

"Come on, it cannae be too hard."

"He obviously found his straight away," says Del.

We are shown up to our rooms. By 'rooms', I mean 'room', as it is a hundred-man bunk on the upper floor. The walls are bare concrete with thick tensioning cables running diagonally from corner to corner to hold the building together. The ceiling is also the roof and looks like what I can only describe as corrugated asbestos. There are a few clear plastic sections and, because of the build-up of dirt, it lets in about the same amount of light as a broken torch in a cave. It looks like a plywood maze as the previous tenants had tried to give themselves a bit of privacy with individual partitioned areas, each with a bunk bed.

Prat and I manage to get one with a window, of which there are few. Some bunks have been turned into dens with their own ceilings and blankets covering the doors. It is very cosy looking, but, I'm sure, a fire nightmare to a Health and Safety guru.

There are still a few of the outgoing Regiment's guys about as they've been hanging around to do the handover with us. They view us with suspicion, even though we are there to relieve them. They probably think we will make a mess of it and cause the accidental dissolution of NATO.

I see one of them carrying a bucket full to the brim of 5.56mm ammunition and hand it to Corporal Kneeling Position.

"Might come in handy if you lose a few rounds," he says to him.

Corporal Position has a look on his face as if he'd just found out he was adopted. He likes to do everything by the book and this is way off his radar of rules. He takes the bucket nervously and looks at it.

I never saw it again and none of us heard anything about it on the grapevine, so we wondered if he took them down the beach individually and threw them in the Adriatic. Must have taken him the entire six months to get rid of every single one.

Prat picks the top bunk, and I remind him that if he lags[31] on me, he'll be going out of the window head first. We both have a battleship-grey metal locker which is soon filled up with our gear.

"I'd not get too organised just yet. I suspect this is going to change once our Regiment is in full control," I say.

We have a poly-prop chair and a small Formica table that is chipped. There's a plug socket on the wall which has many plugs running off it. This makes it look like an advert on how a plug socket should not look if a bunch of soldiers have access to a single socket. Prat pulls it out, there's a spark, a radio goes off several bunks away, and someone shouts, "Oi!"

He plugs it back in, it sparks again, the radio comes back on, and someone shouts, "Cheers."

He looks at me seriously and says, "We're gonna die in here, ain't we?"

Smeggy is on his rounds, telling everyone that there is going to be a brief in the bar.

"Is he testing the fire buckets for water quality?" I ask Prat.

"There's a brief in the Squadron bar at 1900," says Smeggy.

"We have a bar?" says Prat.

"Don't get your hopes up, it's not the bastard Copacabana."

---

31 Kind military term for involuntarily urinating oneself, or colleagues, after partaking in the consumption of large quantities of alcoholic beverages.

"Is it happy hour at 1900?" I enquire.

"Fucking pair of idiots," he mumbles as he continues on his quest to tell everyone.

The self-built bar is a testament to the innovation of British squaddies. Some of those I've visited over the years, in locations you'd not expect to find a bar, were amazing. The best ones were always produced by the Royal Engineers because building and blowing up things is their raison d'être. Their bars would put some pubs back home to shame and if they'd had table service, I wouldn't have been surprised.

The Dalma bar is a large room and could have stored anything over the years.[32] There is an actual bar against one end of the room. It has been made from wooden pallets and off-cuts. Someone had found some red PVC vinyl and covered it so you can't tell it's been knocked together with scrap wood and six-inch nails. The walls are covered with flags, some military, but mostly local ones. I would put money on the fact that they had not been donated by the locals.

There are a few acquired vehicle number plates too, some with the Croatian flag and some from the Yugoslav days. The booze is stored in fridges that are lined up behind the makeshift bar and padlocked shut. There are even some shelves to the side of them with a mirror and some bric-a-brac items to try to give it a cosy feel. An assortment of different-sized glasses, which have clearly been liberated from the local bars, make up the look. There are comfy chairs scattered about around a few low coffee tables. They aren't actually

32 I visited Dalma in 2018 during a holiday down the road in Makarska. I hired a car especially just to drive up to Split and see the old place again. The outside had changed, as the Corimecs, shipping containers and fence had long been removed. There was one Corimec remaining, and I wondered if it was still on hire to the British Army. It was back in use and a few white small trucks were parked up against the loading ramp. I took some pictures, including some of the business signage, which meant nothing to me, and sent them to a Croatian friend for translation. Turns out it had become a cheese distribution centre.

comfy, but they are better than the poly-prop ones. The only things missing are a one-armed bandit, a big telly, and an atmosphere.

Major Pippen, the OC,[33] who is the boss of the Squadron, and Edward Buckethands, the SSM,[34] who is his discipline enforcer, are leaning against the bar. Buckethands isn't his real name but one of his many hand-themed nicknames. His mitts are enormous. He is an animal and therefore I will not be mentioning him by his real name in this book in case he reads it, as I am still scared of him. I think he also has a personality disorder like Dr Jekyll and Mr Hyde. In his case, it's SSM Rational and Mr Psychotic Lunatic.

The Troop Commanders and a few other SNCOs, including Jimmy Frazer and Gunny Dawlish, stand with them.

Major Pippen greets us with, "Welcome to Dalma Warehouse, ladies and gents," and promptly goes off into a pep talk. Unfortunately, as I have no intention of writing it down, or listening to it, I cannot enlighten you as to what it might contain. He finishes with the customary, "Has anyone got any questions?" We continue the tradition of staring back at him with blank looks and in complete silence.

He nods to Buckethands and leaves the bar with the Troop Commanders in tow. We know what's coming next, and it is not for the delicate ears of Commissioned Officers. Now, this one I will remember as it is basically a pre-bollocking for the stuff that Buckethands knows we are probably going to do during the tour. He reads out a list of dos and don'ts, which was more don'ts than dos. His voice is noticeably a few decibels higher than Major Pippen's. He mentions that we have to keep the standards of dress, and anyone found not doing this will be in a world of pain. The next day's start time, mealtimes, laundry and duties are covered, but it is more about what lev-

33 Officer Commanding.

34 Squadron Sergeant Major.

el of shit we'll find ourselves in if we do mess up. He gestures to the SNCOs by him that they will be enforcing his rule of law and they have his full backing. He then points accusingly to the JNCOs,[35] indicating that, if they don't uphold the discipline, they will get double the punishment. The telling-off then takes a dark turn, and we are told of a male American soldier who has been raped in town recently. The locals hate us and the standard of driving is so bad that we might die there. Taking it back up a notch on the misery scale, he finishes on a high note by telling us they have great beaches nearby.

He informs us of the curfew at 2100, but we ware not to worry about it as we are confined to camp until the rest of the Regiment arrive later that week. There is the start of a mass groan, which is stopped in its tracks when his demeanour suddenly does a 180-degree turn. He then happily announces, throwing his hands in the air, that the bar is now open. There is a tremendous cheer from us.

Everybody gets up and moves towards the bar. A couple of the departing Regiment's guys remove the padlocks from the fridges and start asking what people want to drink.

"Can I have a beer please, mate?" I ask the barman.

"Sorry, we've got no beer."

"Oh, OK, Guinness it is then."

"Sorry, we've got no Guinness."

"Errr, how about a cider?"

"Nope, none of that either."

"Righto, what do you have then?"

"Hooch."

"What the fuck is that?"

Understandably, it turns out, the outgoing bunch haven't bothered ordering any new stock and are just getting rid of what they've left. It doesn't take a brain surgeon to work out that what is left

---

35 Junior Non Commissioned Officers. Lance Corporals and Corporals.

would be the least popular drink, a concoction called 'Hooch'.

As we are a Germany-based unit, we were not familiar with this 'Hooch'. It wasn't the local moonshine. My introduction to that would come later, but it was a lemon alcoholic brew, which was proper minging.[36] Quickly adapting to the scenario we were in, like many soldiers over the centuries who found themselves in a comparable situation, we just cracked on and drank it.

I see Corporal Rory Loughty has got himself a 'Hooch' and is merrily swigging away. He has told everyone he was going to have a dry tour and there he is, six hours in-country, off the wagon already.

"He's got the breaking strain of a Kit-Kat in a fat kid's pocket," says Del, nodding towards Rory.

"Who's got a Kit-Kat?" asks Prat, his ears picking up the only word associated with chocolate.

"I didn't think I'd be having a knees-up on the first night," I say. "On my Northern Ireland tours we were straight out on the street."

"Who's got Quality Street?" asks Prat.

"This is rather unexpected. I thought Day One would be a right old marathon," adds Del.

"Who's got a Marathon?" asks the choccy monster.

"Well, this Topic has given me a Boost knowing that it will be a right old Picnic, so we shouldn't Flake out too much. Rolo on tomorrow when we can give the job in hand a Twirl."

Del and I burst into laughter while Prat just looks confused with his bottle of Hooch.

We manage one more bottle of said Hooch before deciding simultaneously that it is time for bed, because trying to drink lemon juice is not pleasurable.

---

36 This has several meanings, such as extremely drunk, very dirty or, in this case, not particularly easy going on the taste buds.

Snakebite

The night's sleep isn't the best, even with the early start I'd had that day. The new environment, the Hooch, and the sound of 100-plus soldiers sharing the same room added to the disturbed sleep. I feel I will never nod off, but then I realise I have. I awake with the need to go to the toilet. It is still dark outside. I hear the squeaking of bedsprings and someone turning over. Faint snoring comes from the bunk next to ours. I turn over, trying to ignore the pressure on my bladder, and close my eyes, hoping I will somehow miraculously not need to pee. This battle of the wills lasts for at least ten minutes. The reason this mêlée is lasting so long is because the toilets are fucking miles away. I have to give in to the physics of pressure and time, as it would not end well for me. I get up, I swing my legs off the bed and feel about for my flip-flops. They are not where I left them and I continue hunting around the floor for them. The room is not completely dark as there is a light on somewhere which gives enough illumination, so I finally see them on the other side of the bunk. I don't know how they ended up over there. Maybe we have mice, or worse, rats.

Slipping my feet into them, I head off. I exit the room and start the long walk down the corridor to the stairs. My flip-flops make a slapping sound with each step. I pass Cheezy coming the other way on the stairs. He looks like he's just come out of a rugby scrum and has two black eyes. His normally chirpy manner is reduced to a grunt. At the bottom of the stairs, I head outside and turn left onto the loading ramp. Further down, there is a selection of Corimec toilet blocks. The first one I get to has a flooded floor. It looks about an inch deep and I guess my foam flip-flops are just over an inch, so I move on to the next one. It isn't flooded, but the urinals have orange tape in a 'X' pattern across them, which is the universal sign for "out of order". There are three cubicles, but the door is hanging off one of them and the other two are locked. I look under to see if there are any feet, but there are none. I continue my journey to release the increasing pressure of pain. The next one has a sign on the door saying it is the women's one and the next one along is for SNCOs only.

"For the love of God," I mutter to myself.

I get to the next one. It's locked.

"Arrrrgh, come on, give me a fucking break."

I approach the next one with a plan to go back to the SNCOs or women's, if it's unusable. It is open, and not flooded. It looks like it's in working order. I am nearly in tears with the relief.

I head back to the room and pass someone on the stairs. I think about telling them which toilet block is working, then the inner demon in me says, "Fuck 'em". Cheezy didn't give me a heads-up so they can find out the hard way like me.

I found out the next day from Cheezy that he just went in the women's one because he's basically lazy.

I snooze a little more before it's time to get up. The sound of waking soldiers, which is mainly shouting and laughing, rises as more arrive back in the land of the living. I hear at least two electronic alarm clocks beeping away. Nobody seems in a hurry to switch them off, so either their owners are exceptionally heavy sleepers or are away looking for a functioning toilet block. There are queues for the showers, just like the toilets. Most of them also seem to be out of action. My turn comes and I shower under a tepid dribble. I take a while to finish. This is because the water flow could be measured in thimbles-per-minute rather than litres-per-minute.

I meet up with Del and Prat in the cookhouse, which is at the back of the warehouse. There is a gigantic door which must have been used for loading larger items in its commercial days, and this lets in a rather comfortable morning breeze. It's another sunny day with no clouds, just the deep blue of the sky and a rising temperature that is rather enjoyable.

Breakfast is a choice of cereals, the usual fried stuff, and lots of fresh-looking fruit. Watermelon, oranges, grapefruit, apples, and kiwi are just some of the items that had been lovingly presented on their own table. The crockery is paper, and the cutlery is plastic, which means no washing-up duties for us. There isn't enough real estate for the Officers or SNCOs to have their respective messes so they have to share with the rank and file. However, to keep a line of authority, they maintain a space at the far end which is cordoned off badly, with a few free-standing fake wooden partitions.

"Der Sergeants' Mess doesn't look up to much," says Prat.

"Can't have our leaders mingling with us lowlife, can we now?" replies Del.

"I wouldn't want to eat anywhere near Edward Buckethands," I add. "He'd catch my eye and then probably crush my head with one hand."

"And you'd have Jimmy Frazer trying to eat soup with his false teeth hanging out," says Del.

We form up outside in a military-style rabble at the prescribed time, given to us in no uncertain terms by Buckethands. That time arrives and disappears like a SUS[37] leave pass. Jimmy Frazer turns up with a bluffboard. That's a clipboard, but soldiers soon learn that whenever you walk around a camp with one, nobody bothers you or tries to give you shit jobs. They presume you have already been tasked to do something by somebody else.

37 Soldier Under Sentence.

One by one, he calls out our names and ticks them off the list on his clipboard.

"I don't think anyone buggered off back to Germany last night," whispers Del to me.

"Delaney," says Jimmy.

"It can't be hard to get back, if you wanted to," he whispers again.

"DELANEY," bellows Jimmy.

"Sarge," he replies.

"Switch on, you fuckin' knobber," he says, pointing his pen at Del. "You've only been at work two bastard minutes."

"At least I was on time," Del again whispers to me.

"What was that, Delaney?"

"At least I wasn't on the wine,"

We laugh and Jimmy looks at us, growling, because he knows we are taking the piss, and he doesn't get the joke.

We are marched to our new place of work. It is out of the main gate and across a patch of open tarmac, which is a road.

It's a busy road.

It's a busy road populated by Croatian vehicles.

It's a busy road populated with Croatian vehicles with Croatians at the wheel.

As we march over the road, our heads are moving about, looking for a car that could be the last thing we see before waking up in the Medical Centre. We get across without too much trouble and the Guard opens the barrier for us. He is a familiar, six-foot, skinny, ginger guy. "Fucking hell, it's Careless!" shouts Del, "The Regimental grass!" He's still reeling from his bollocking from Jimmy the month before.

He was called 'Careless' because he had an unfortunate case of bad acne. Some heartless person said he looked like he'd carelessly knocked over a beehive and was then attacked by the angry bees. He had come out with the Advance party the week before. A torrent of verbal abuse heads his way from all of us. It's entirely composed of groundless facts, such as that he stank of piss and cheated at cards, which is just under the umbrella of general ginger insults.

"Yeah, yeah, yeah," he replies. "Hope you enjoyed saying goodbye to all of your girlfriends and wives as much as I did."

"He's got a pretty quick gob on him, that one," says Del.

Careless seemed to get in the shit a lot, but somehow, because of an interesting turn of events, he would curiously always get off the punishment. A year earlier, he'd been late for Guard Duty and had been given some extras by Buckethands. One of his punishment tasks was to clear the weeds from the tennis court over a weekend. He decided against the traditional method of using a trowel or other garden-based implement. Instead, Careless went for the pyromaniac technique, fetching a five-litre can of petrol from his car and emptying it over the unruly vegetation.

He then set the entire court alight, so it now resembled an out-of-control Australian bush fire. The clouds of smoke soon got the attention of the Orderly Officer who made a panic-loaded phone call to the Guard Commander, who subsequently crashed out the Regimental Fire Piquet to attend. They rushed up the main road on camp towards the tennis courts. They were pushing the big red handcart, which contained firefighting equipment from before the Crimean War, including canvas hoses that have very unconvincing water holding qualities. At the same time, The Feuerwehr[38] were called out and soon arrived en masse with sirens blaring, making a sleepy Sunday morning on camp look like a major catastrophe had occurred. The well-equipped and fully trained Feuerwehr managed, in less than a minute, to do what the Fire Piquet couldn't do in the previous ten minutes and quickly dampened the flames to a wet, black steaming mess.

38 German Fire Brigade.

Anyone else would have been looking at the mother of all bollock-ings for creating such a chaotic episode, one which involved the duty personnel on that day having to write a mini novel in the occurrence book. Careless was let off by Buckethands for original thinking.

This ability to have the luck of a lottery winner also worked out-side the military sphere of influence. He was in the UK on leave and was off to the Council Offices to either pay or contest a parking fine he'd picked up. Just outside the main entrance, he saw a man coming his way, at speed, looking 'guilty', as he put it in his own words. He made a split-second decision and clotheslined him, putting him straight onto his back and knocking him out cold. The guy could have been running for a bus but, it turned out, he was a shoplifter making his getaway. He ended up getting a Police commendation, and the Council chucked his fine in the bin.

As we pass under the barrier, some of us have to duck because he has intentionally only lifted it halfway open.

"Lift der barrier up, yer lazy shit," shouts Prat

"He'll probably get an MBE for that, knowing his luck," I reply.

As Jimmy walks past Careless, he says, "Morning, Sergeant Fraz-er." This is in a tone that could be either piss-taking or that he's after something. Knowing him, it's the former.

"Fuck off, and the answer's no," barks Jimmy.

"Charming," is Careless's smiling reply.

Later in the tour, Careless called Jimmy 'Judas', after an episode when Jimmy turfed us off a bus which was giving us a lift to the beach one Sunday afternoon. That name would stick with him for the rest of his time in the Regiment.

The MT[39] Offices, which are also the Squadron HQ, are in another concrete building that is about 80% complete. It has the name of the company who used to occupy it on the front in blue lettering: 'Jadrantrans'. Unlike the British Army when selecting real estate for use by its employees, they had maybe done a little bit of logical thinking with this one. The company must have been in the transport and logistical trade as there were offices on the first floor and a workshop around the back, where the REME[40] could fix the trucks that we broke. Fuel and GT Troop vehicles are parked out the front of the building and the DROPS vehicles are round the back. The vehicle park is just a patch of dirt and is still muddy after some recent rain.

The main door has marble steps leading up to some glass doors. In the foyer is a booth in which either the Security Guard and/or receptionist used to sit. It has a Perspex screen with an opening at the bottom, through which paperwork could be passed. The desk has a panel of coloured buttons on it, with a microphone coming out of it on a long, adjustable stalk. It isn't hard to work out that it's a public address system.

Del and I later had a play with it, as we thought it would be hilarious to make some announcements and no doubt get in the shit. It was of East European design and looked totally alien to us. After a quick inspection under the desk, we saw most of the wires had been cut and our self-entertaining plans stopped there. I bet Buckethands knew someone would think what we were thinking, and he cut the wires. That was why he was paid more than us.

39 Mechanical Transport. I always thought this made us sound like we were in the Victorian times.

40 Royal Electrical and Mechanical Engineers.

Upstairs, there is a long corridor running the length of the building, with rooms off to each side. The biggest one is at the end. It must have been the director's office, or possibly the room where they interrogated people, as it has a thick padded door covered with leather. More likely it's fake leather, to mask the sounds of punches. It is now the Squadron Operations Room, home to a staff of three. The carpet is brown, but I can't tell if that is its original colour or if it has become brown with the dirt which is brought into the building on everyone's boots. We are directed into the new Troop rest room. It won't be one for long, as our Squadron will change everything about once we have fully taken over. There are only a couple of chairs. They are the green camping ones and comfortable for at most five minutes. In the middle is a table, stacked high with newspapers and magazines.

Staff Sergeant Burton, who we haven't seen for weeks and is responsible for the vehicle fleet, appears and says, "Right, Troops, let's get to work."

The next few days are a blur. We have to inspect the vehicles we are to inherit from the outgoing unit. Vehicle documents are examined to see if servicings are up to date. Their toolkits are checked in the stores to see if they are complete. This is part of the job I find, as do many others, awfully boring. They are, as expected, in a bit of a mess because of the appalling roads in the Balkans. A fuel tanker which someone inspected underneath was found to have its gearbox held in by only a couple of bolts. The ones which were supposed to be there were not present. The outgoing unit knew that, no matter what condition the fleet was in, they would still get on the plane to take them home in a few days. If you interviewed soldiers from the different units who served in the Former Yugoslavia today, they would all say the same thing: the fleet of vehicles were in shit state when they took them over, but every one was spick and span when they handed them over six months later. It's a strange military conundrum, and I think the best brains, who are trying to solve the puzzles to life, the universe and everything, should have a crack at it.

Corporals, and a few selected Lance Corporals, go out on the convoys to learn the different routes. These include the gas run, taking empty gas bottles to a factory further down the coast to a town called Ploče. They swap them for full bottles and then take them up to a supply base in Bosnia, just outside a tiny village called Lipa.

There is a similar route with the fuel tankers feeding the thirsty NATO war machine with trips to the BFI[41], also based at Lipa. The worst of these jobs is the 'Gungy Run'. This involves taking a fuel tanker to fill up the abundant diesel generators that are being used in SNP[42] and DJ Barracks[43] down by the airport. It's the worst of the tasks and soon will become the prime shitty job for soldiers fucking up.

The best and cleanest job is driving the coaches. They are used for moving incoming and outgoing soldiers to and from the Split Airport and DJ Barracks as they are processed in and out of theatre. These are brand new, gleaming white vehicles, but only a few members of the Squadron have the licence required to drive them.[44]

The Bedford 14 Ton trucks accompany the coaches down to the airport to move the soldiers' baggage. This is a fairly straightforward task, but it involves humping and dumping the passengers' kit. I tell Prat he could at least practise his new civvy job for when he got out of the Army.

It's on Day 2 that we have our first, in theatre, traffic accident.

41 Bulk Fuel Installation.

42 Split North Port.

43 Divulji Barracks.

44 The plan was to get more of us trained to drive them. It was a chance to get your bus licence for free, so loads of us applied to the Driver and Vehicle Licensing Agency (DVLA) for our provisional licences. Mine turned up a week before I departed back for Germany. Thanks a lot, DVLA.

The CO,[45] who we called 'Mr Burns' because he looked exactly like Mr Burns from *The Simpsons,* goes ballistic. Whenever he made a speech to us, someone would always say just loudly enough, "Release the hounds." This would have everyone in fits of giggles. The SNCOs would smirk while the Officers remained completely unaware of the joke. The word on the street was that Mr Burns had made a promise to the Brigadier, which could have been a classic case study lesson in when not to make promises. He announced 7 Transport Regiment wouldn't have any traffic accidents during their tour. The vehicle accident rate in Croatian and Bosnia was off the scale compared to the figures back in Germany. It was fairly apparent there were a few more factors at play here. Driving more miles, the locals, the general state of the roads and the high marble content, which would make them extremely slippery when wet. All our vehicles were, understandably, fitted with off-road tyres. However, driving on those wet roads with off-road tyres would give you the same grip as driving on ice.

One of the younger Privates, at the wheel of an Bedford 8-Tonner, has had a slight mishap in the wet with a locally registered car on their way to the airport. The main thing is that nobody was hurt, but Mr Burns is incandescent with rage. His poorly thought-out promise has come back to bite him on the arse, while making him look like one at the same time. He wants the Section Commander to be charged immediately to make him an example. Corporal 'Sticky' Bun is in the firing line and, when he finds out he's about to be disciplined, his reaction is as follows.

"You fucking what? I wasn't even there." He had been with Staff Sergeant Burton in the Troop Office, going over vehicle documents together.

For a few days, it looks like he is going to face disciplinary action,

45 Commanding Officer. The overall boss of the Regiment.

but, behind the scenes, there is some serious diplomacy happening. Captain Haywood, Buckethands and many other SNCOs advise Mr Burns against it. The threat of Sticky being charged disappears. He is in the clear, and common-sense reality resumed in the Regiment.

Fate, it's a funny old thing though, as a few days later, a poisonous snake bites Sticky while he was cleaning up some rubbish in readiness for Mr Burns' Troop inspection. They rush him at speed, in severe pain, to the Medical Centre at DJ Barracks with a hand like a balloon. It must have been written in the stars that he was to suffer that week.

Life's a Gas

At last, my name appears on Troop Orders, saying I am to drive a Bedford 14-Tonner with Prat on the gas run to Ploče and Lipa. A bit of excitement at last. I'll just be a Driver and not the Section 2IC, which suits me fine. The Section commander is a Royal Marine named Corporal Lester. We always have a Royal Marine attached to the Regiment. I have no idea why. I can only guess it was an agreement which came about many years before so they could gain experience in a Transport Regiment, and consequently learn how not to do Military Transport. The one before Lester was Corporal Titricks, who came with a nickname. He was a hilarious guy, without intentionally being funny, and worked in the Regimental Training Wing instructing us on training courses. He was from South Wales and we really drove him to despair with our unsoldier-like way of doing things. A few years earlier, I was on a Driver Training Course and he was the main instructor. He was trying to get us to produce some presentations with the use of an overhead projector, which we were failing miserably to accomplish.

"You fucking lot have the organisational skills of a handcuffed crab," he'd say to us in his strong Welsh accent. "You bastard RLC bunch of twats make me want to... arrrrgh," as his frustration boiled over and he lost the ability to describe his irritation with us.

Corporal Lester is a grumpy old guy who's aged well before his time and we've nicknamed him 'Hannibal'. This is partly because of how close "Lester" is to "Lecter," but mainly because he has such a temper on him. We wouldn't put it past him to mutilate you in a way that would make the actual Hannibal Lecter look like a vegetarian. He'd fought in the Falkland Islands and I now realise he was no doubt suffering from PTSD.

At breakfast, we collect our lunch, which is in a brown paper bag, not too dissimilar to what the RAF served us up on the plane. Prat is happy as it contains a Wagon Wheel. The sandwiches are wrapped tightly in cellophane and their filling looks like a paste, which could be anything. They appear as if they were already sweating in the morning warmth and the thought of eating them later in the heat of the day fills me with anxiety for my wellbeing.

Next, it's off to the armoury to collect our weapons. We were issued with ammunition, morphine and body armour a few days earlier, which we've kept in our lockers. We have 120 rounds each, which means we should have been able to put up resistance for a few minutes until help arrives, should anything happen. As we didn't have radios, I think any help might be a long time coming.

There are a total of four trucks already loaded up with empty gas bottles from the previous day's run. After collecting our weapons from the armoury, we head over to the Squadron Offices to get the keys and work tickets.[46] We swarm over them checking oil, coolant,

---

46 A piece of paper that we record the mileage on and get signed by an adult to ensure that we are not joyriding or using Military Transport to move house.

fuel and lights. We clean the wing mirrors and kick the tyres. This has nothing of value and informs you of absolutely zero regarding the truck's ability to do the job in hand, but we do it anyway as it makes us feel better. This is known as the First Parade. When we get back, we are supposed to carry out the 'Last Parade' to check for faults and ensure they're ready to go for the next day's task. Realistically, we'll park up, put the gear back to the stores, chuck the keys back in the MT Office and sod off to the bar. We have to get the vehicle toolkits from the Troop Store, which is a shipping container. Each of the kits is in a couple of large green plastic boxes and is relatively hefty, as tools for trucks tend to be on the larger side. Lance Corporal 'Shaun the Yawn' is our Troop Storeman, and he is as dull and grey as the person who ends up in the stores normally is. He lays out each of the items individually on the wooden table and checks them off his list in front of me. Subsequently, he requests I sign for them on an Army Form 1033, which is an Issues and Receipt Voucher. He gives me a copy, and he keeps a copy. When I get back later in the day, he checks the items back in, and if they are all present and correct, the 1033 will be ripped up. If I am missing anything, I will be billed for the item which I lost. A new one wouldn't be ordered through the logistical chain and Shaun the Yawn will just get one of his buckshee ones off the shelf to replace the one I lost.

As we are carrying gas, which is normally classed as dangerous goods, but possibly not in Croatia, we have to get the Hazmat[47] kit from another shipping container. This extra gear includes more fire extinguishers, eye wash and orange plates to put on the vehicle so everyone knows we are carrying something dangerous. As we are on an 'Operation' in another country whose Traffic Department have more things to worry about than the carriage of dangerous goods, we apply the best rules. We work to the UK ones as the Croatian

47 Hazardous Materials.

ones probably involve just the passing of cash to the Policija [48]in a brown envelope with a knowing wink.

The trucks are lined up and ready to depart, and Hannibal calls us to the front of the convoy to brief us on the route.

"We will be following Route Gannet to Ploče."

The main routes have been given one-word names, to keep it simple, to aid us in our navigation. It isn't too hard to find your way about. Because of the mountainous terrain, the roads are limited as to where they could go and, consequently, there are not a lot of roads in Bosnia. Now and again, you might come to a junction, and it will be a toss-up which way to turn. The name of the route is normally spray painted on a house or rock with an arrow to give you a clue. The road signage seems to have survived the war, albeit with their fair share of bullet holes. I suppose the out-of-town militia still needed to know where to go to find the fighting. The routes in the British area have mostly an avian theme with names such as Parrot, Gull, Emu, or Vulture. Some areas have routes named after fish or expensive stones, while in the other areas, they just seem to have been picked from a hat, with random names such as Howdy, Eric, Skoda or Pacman.

"Basically, you want to keep the blue wet stuff on your right and the dry brown stuff on your left," says Hannibal. You can't really be more precise than that as it is 100km down the coast road.

"Remember spacings, but close up when we get to any traffic lights. Watch out for the locals. They're fucking batshit crazy and don't fall asleep. Any questions?"

There is a mixture of quiet noes and shaking of heads from us.

"Has everyone got their weapons?" he asks, pointing at us in turn, so we show him our gun to prove it wasn't somewhere it shouldn't be.

48 Local Police.

With those fine words of wisdom, we scatter off to our trucks, ready to depart on this day's marvellous adventure. I am driving first, so I go to the driver's door, reach up and open it. The climb up to the cab is a mild feat of scrambling. There is a large metal ring on the wheel hub, which is the first step, and a metal bar on the inside of the cab so you can pull yourself up. I slide my gun onto the seat as I know if I try to get up there with it slung over my shoulder, it will inevitably fall off. It will then more than likely connect with one of my more bony extremities, causing a range of reactions from taking-a-minute to watering-of-eyes to expletive-language. I haul myself up, ensuring the toe of my boot has a good grip on the hub step as I have experienced a slip here which resulted in that sickening shin pain. Military vehicles are just mobile pain-producing machines. Up I go and, grabbing for the steering wheel, I pull myself all the way up and onto the small ledge in the doorway. I move my gun onto our gear, which is piled behind the big metal box in the middle of the cab. The box is a handy place to put food to keep it in one place when bouncing about off-road, but its actual function is for the air sentry to stand on. There is a round hatch in the cab's roof, which is fitted with a fibreglass cupola cover. It can be removed and stored on a bracket outside on the back of the cab, which allows the co-driver to poke his head out and shoot down any planes who might decide we were a suitable target. We spend a few minutes making sure our gear is stowed. Webbing goes under the seats, body armour hangs over the back of the seats, ready to access. Our guns are in their own upright storage rack between the dashboard and the door. They have a clip mechanism to keep them in place, but with the flick of your hand you can get it out. We have a load of plastic water bottles which we place about the cab in any remaining spare places but always with one to hand. I plonk my arse in the driver's seat, slam the door shut, and adjust it so I can reach the pedals. Prat does the same. I adjust my wing mirror so I can get the best view down the side of the truck, as it moves when I slammed the door. I repeat the process with the help of Prat on the other one. Seatbelts are on and I go to turn the key, only to find it not there.

"For fuck's sake," I say, as I think about where I left them. I run my hands down the outside of my trousers and I feel them still in my pocket. I try to get my hand in to fish them out, but, with my seated position, my pocket is too tight to get my hand in there. Cursing some more, I remove my seatbelt, push the seat back, and straighten my body out to give my hand a chance to reach inside my pocket and eventually dig the keys out. Again, I adjust my seat, put on the seatbelt, and insert the keys. Considering the mighty Bedford 14 Ton truck is nine metres long, 2.5 metres wide, has six wheels and 6x6 capability, is powered by an 8.2 litre turbo diesel engine, has a six-speed manual ZF gearbox and has carrying capacity of 14 tons, the keys look like they are for a cleaning cupboard. They are tiny and appear as if heavy-handed vigorous starting would snap them off in the ignition barrel.

I turn the key to switch on the ignition and, as I do, a few coloured lights appear on the two big dials that dominate the dashboard. Around them, the fuel, air pressure and electrical gauges bounce into life. From somewhere behind them, a tinny, annoying warning buzzer blares away. I press the clutch in and wobble the gear stick to check that it's in neutral. The gear stick on these monsters feels like it's in a bucket of sand, giving you almost no clue to what gear you might be in. Selecting the right gears in sequence is part art form, part guess and part luck. Trying to pull away in third gear when you think you're in first or going from fifth to fourth when you actually want sixth are mistakes that happen regularly to both new and experienced Drivers. I put the clutch in anyway just in case I was in any one of the six gears available. I turn the key again and the engine cranks. I hold it there momentarily as the engine turns on and fires up with a puff of white smoke from the exhaust at the front of the truck. The cab vibrates and slightly wobbles to one side with the torque of the engine as it comes to life and I release the key. The low air-pressure buzzer continues to annoy us while the compressor works its magic, filling up the many air tanks. I slowly release the clutch, feeling for the telltale sign it might still be in gear. Not feeling the bite of the clutch, I continue to release until it is fully out. I give the accelerator a press and the RPM gauge bounces about but shows what we can hear as the engine speed increases. There's more white smoke coming from the engine. I see the air pressure gauges approaching the green arc and the buzzer tails off as if someone has just strangled it. I turn the big black knob light switch all the way to the left, to HST.[49] This switch is fitted to every vehicle in the British Military. If you turn it the other way, it will put the convoy light on, which is a tiny little light at the back that shines on a white-painted piece of metal. I always think it looks like the lid of a tin of paint. It kills the normal lights, including brake lights.

The previous year, I was driving a DROPS back to camp and as I approached a set of lights, they turned red. I had a millisecond hesitation as my brain juggled with the "stop" or "go for it" options. It chose the former and I braked harder than normal. I felt a little jolt as I brought the truck to a stop. Looking around and out the back window, I saw a Mercedes had run into the rear of me. I jumped out of the cab and met an angry, fat, bald German guy who looked like he was the record holder for drinking the most beer in his village. The DROPS had a tiny bit of paint removed from the tow hook, but his Merc came off worse with damage to his grill and bonnet. He called the Polizei, who must have had a slow work day as they turned up within minutes. Normally they favoured their own countrymen and Johnny Foreigner squaddie got the fine. He was jabbering away in German at 200mph

49 Headlights, Side and Tail.

to Das Fuzz and pointing accusingly at me. "Kaput" was the only word I picked up. The coppers wandered over to me and conveyed the accusation from the guy that my brake lights weren't working. Eager to check, the copper prompted me to jump into the cab, where I realised I'd mistakenly moved the switch one click too far, unintentionally activating the convoy setting. A quick click back to the left and a press of the pedal, illuminating the fully working brake lights and the bewildered guy got the fine. One-nil to the British Army.

Hannibal comes down the line of trucks to check if we are ready to go and we give him the thumbs-up. I see the front truck move towards the gate and then the red and white barrier rises to point to the sky. The truck in front pulls away and I follow in turn. We turn left onto the long straight road, and I keep one eye on my mirrors to see if the last one is following me. At the huge puddle ahead, Hannibal goes straight through without slowing, creating a plume of manky water as high as the truck. The Croatians, coming the other way and not wanting to drown in filth, wait for us as we thunder past. At the end of the straight road, we turn left, as per Hannibal's brief to keep the water on our right and the mountains on our left.

After we leave the urban expansion of Split behind, the coast road becomes exceptionally scenic. It winds along the rugged rocky landscape, cutting into the cliffs and around headlands jutting into the sea. One minute we are so close to the sea, I could stop and jump off the truck into the water. The next, we snake up and into the hinterland.

This road was some feat of engineering in its day. The locals are eager to get past us, and I see them bunched up behind the last truck. They are waiting for the road to straighten so they can overtake, pulling into the gap in our small convoy. Some are super impatient or have nothing to live for as they overtake on blind bends. I see one in my wing mirror coming along the side of the truck and I realise another car is approaching from the other direction. "Fucking hell," I say, with a mixture of disbelief and admiration for their lack of fear.

"Watch him, WATCH HIM," shouts Prat, as a car comes the other way. There isn't a lot I can do, as there is nowhere to go other than off the edge of the cliff. I feel like we are on a mad fairground ride with no ability to stop or get off. Some cars relent and fall back behind us, while some just keep going. I can only pull over a tadge more as they squeeze between us and the car coming the other way. Its blaring horn rises and falls from the Doppler Effect as it flies past. This chaotic sight is replicated along the rest of the convoy. Sometimes, a mile or so down the road, we see the car who had risked a journey to the underworld. It has now pulled over and the driver, cigarette hanging from his mouth, is casually reading the morning paper at a kiosk.

"Ders a lot of Germans on holiday," says Prat, noting a lot of the cars have German number plates.

"Yugoslavia was a very popular holiday destination with ze Germans," I reply, "and quite a few Croatians live and work there, so maybe that's why."

Later on, someone tells me the reason why there are so many German cars is because the Government struggled to pay their soldiers for their time serving, so they were allowed to import a car from Germany with no importation fees. I guess they just drove them back and continued to drive around on the German plates. I'm speculating that being legal on the road was an optional thing then.

We go through picture-postcard little fishing villages, past empty white painted hotel complexes and even deserted campsites with their sun-bleached hand-painted advertisement boards. We pass yellow road signs with names of towns I've never heard of: Omis, Brela, and Makarska. The only ones I know are Ploče, our destination and

Dubrovnik, which is 200km away. We continue to make our way along the highway and, at one point, the road is cut into the cliff as it starts the climb up and up. It disappears around a corner and, as we follow it, we can see it continue to ascend parallel to the coast up to at least a thousand feet above the sea. The truck is a left-hand drive, so Prat is looking nervously out of his side window down to the water, which is further and further below us. The only things between us and falling to our deaths are my driving skills and small brick-like structures dotted along the edge of the road. They might stop a Fiat 126, but I wouldn't put a lot of money on them stopping much else.

Prat is looking even more uncomfortable as we gain height and says, "Fuuuuucking helllll, dat's a long way down."

He is now sitting bolt upright and has one hand holding onto the door and the other against the dashboard.

A truck coming the other way is straddling the white line in the middle of the road. He sees us and moves over, but it's a tight squeeze as we speed past one another.

"FUCK, FUCK, FUCK," shouts Prat. His view must be worse than mine.

"Look at that," I say, excitedly, pointing at a large rocky overhang.

The inside section has been squared off with the violence of more than one truck hitting it. I notice scuff marks and fragments of scattered rubble along the side of the road.

"It must have been DROPS truck carrying shipping containers," says Prat.

"Can you see anything below?" I ask Prat, thinking there might be a load of smashed-up trucks at the bottom of the cliff.

"I'm not looking anymore," he replies.

I'm sure he has his eyes shut, but I don't want to take my own off the road at this point to check. After a momentary pause, I suddenly shout, "JESUS CHRIST!"

"WHAT, WHAT IS IT," shouts back a very panicking Prat.

"I didn't pack my swimming kit."

"I'll be tying big fuck-off bricks to yer ankles when we do get to der beach," he says threateningly.

As we reach the top, the road continues its parallel track along the coast and starts its descent back to sea level. I ease off the gas as the weight of the truck carries us down the hill. Hannibal has slowed the convoy and I change to a lower gear. I let the truck coast down, trusting the engine will reduce our speed without having to apply the brakes too often. Truck brakes can easily overheat, consequently leading to something known as 'brake fade'. You'll then have the same braking force as if they were made from toffee. I let the truck roll under its own momentum but, due to the steepness of the road, I need to press the brake pedal now and again as the engine RPM increases and is struggling to hold it back. It's a trade-off between trying to minimise the frequency of braking and keeping the RPM in the green part of the dial. The road levels, and the convoy picks up speed again. I feel a little bit of relief and I notice Prat has now relaxed in his seat.

We pass more villages which we spot down by the shoreline with the names Baska Voda and Igrane. *[Looking back, I still find it peculiar that a few places we passed would be where I was taking holidays two decades later.]* Hannibal turns his truck onto a fairly big patch of ground off to the side of the road. The trucks kick up clouds of dust that moves with them until they stop and the cloud carries on moving.

"Break time," I say, coughing as the cab fills with the dust from the truck behind us.

"I'm ready for a stretch and Geoff Hurst,"[50] replies Prat, as he unbuckles his seatbelt and straightens his body to remove the per-

---

50 Geoff Hurst – Burst. To relieve oneself.

manent bend from his spine.

"Don't piss on the tyres, you minger," I remind him.

The Army like to call this a Halt Parade, so, while Prat scurries off to find a bush, I take a quick walk around the truck to Parade it at the Halt. There are eight metal pallets with gas bottles, and a ratchet strap goes across the width of the truck over two of the pallets. The metal sides of the flatbed are still fitted, so the straps just keep them from potentially bouncing out should we hit a large pothole. The bottles are loose in the pallets, so they would go everywhere, but at least we'd still have the pallets in place. I check if they are still tight and tighten up any that have become loose.

Prat returns from his call of nature.

"I can see the Croatian headlines now: Tiny Maggot Seen Puking Into The Adriatic," I tell him.

"More like: Sea Monster Spotted," he says, picking up on my joke unexpectedly quicker than normal.

Hannibal arrives.

"Well, that was a bit brown trousers going up the hill, eh, lads," he says. "I've done this route a few times now and that is as bad as it gets. Well, apart from the border crossing back to Split."

I break out one of my sweaty sandwiches from their cellophane prison. The cheap white bread is looking limp, like it's just died. I peel the bread apart to inspect what delight I have in store today, but I am none the wiser as to what the actual filling could be.

"Looks like mystery paste," I say disappointedly, sniffing at it.

"Fuck eating that shit," says Hannibal. "There's a cafe we'll stop at on route for some grub. Does a lovely meat platter. No idea what it is, but it's better than the crap from the galley."[51]

My sandwiches are then unceremoniously flung towards the Adriatic.

---

51 Royal Marines are Navy, so the cookhouse to him was called the Galley.

"You'll have Greenpeace on your case for poisoning the sea life," says Prat.

We depart in another cloud of dust and I am again at the wheel. Prat will take over for the Ploče-to-Lipa leg.

→» →» →»

Ploče isn't the pretty little town I expected, but a dirty looking industrial port. It reeks of something awful burning, economic stagnation and I don't notice any vaguely modern-looking buildings. I bet the last time something new was built here, Gerry Marsden, of Gerry and the Pacemakers, was on the Mersey Ferry and thought, "I've got a great idea for a song." We arrive at the gas bottling plant and wait at the main gate while Hannibal disappears into the gatehouse.

"You know he could either be dealing with the paperwork like a normal person or have all the staff up against the wall threatening to shoot them," I say to Prat.

"Whichever scenario played out, it has worked," he says, pointing at the now-lifting barrier up ahead.

I follow the truck in front and see Hannibal with his gun waving at me as I drive past him at the gatehouse.

"Just follow on," he shouts.

As I drive past I try to look inside the door to see if there are any staff with their hands above their heads.

The factory is exceptionally shabby in a way only an ex-communist factory could be. There are several large buildings that are painted a light green and, like all the painted things I've seen so far in Croatia, they're all rather faded. They have lots of big heavy metal-looking double doors which are unpainted and are grey. I continue to follow on and we turn down in between these buildings. The ones on our left have the big metal doors, which are open. Hannibal reappears from his staff team-building session and gestures for us to get as close to the building as we can. We pull up next to an opening and I see inside there are hundreds of gas bottles. There is a cranky conveyor belt squeaking away, carrying more gas bottles around the building. There are big red signs everywhere and even though they are in Croatian, it's not hard to deduce they're strongly suggesting we don't spark up a cigarette. The place reeks of gas and a prospective explosion, and I am not looking forward to hanging around here too long. A workforce of middle-aged women dressed in white coveralls appears, and these are the first locals I have seen who haven't got cigarettes in their mouths. One lady reaches over onto the truck, grabs one of the gas bottles, and hauls it out of the pallets like it weighs a few grams. These are industrial gas bottles, are about 4ft in height and probably weigh about 30kg empty. She then carries it to the conveyor belt and drops it into its slot, standing up. They take turns grabbing a bottle as if these things are made of paper. One of the women points at Prat and me and speaks to us, expecting us to be fluent in Croatian. Prat looks at me and says, "I've pulled, but I don't fancy yours much."

She again points at us and we work out she's ordering us onto the back of the truck to start passing the other bottles to them.

It's hard going and the Croatian ladies put us young lads to shame. They laugh as we struggle to move the bottles towards them. It's not made any easier as we have our guns slung over our backs because we didn't want to leave them in the cab unattended. The sweat is now dripping off our foreheads and my T-shirt is feeling damp. As I pass the last one over to Madam Butane, I am looking forward to a breather. As she toddles off with the last one to the conveyor belt, I see the others now bringing full bottles back to us for loading. The laughing ladies don't relent as they are now literally throwing the bottles at us.

One of them says, "Schnell! Schnell! Faster! Faster!" and they laugh and cheer at this remark. They continue to talk and giggle amongst themselves.

"Der probably asking if we are d'best NATO has to offer," says Prat.

"Maybe they are slagging off our manual handling skills," I reply.

In a generic East European accent, I say, "Look at him not keeping his back straight and bending at the vaist, he's gonna suffer in later life the veak, vestern imperialist."

"Maybe day are dose ex-shot putters who were actually men," he replies laughing.

"Or employed to push start tanks."

We need to stop for a second, as we are both now laughing.

As the last bottle is dropped into place on its pallet, the ladies vanish back into the dark of the building. We put the ratchet straps back over, tighten them up, and jump into the cab. We scrabble round for some water and in silence we gulp away after our gruelling workout with the Croatian mothers of back pain.

Prat jumps into the driving seat and I settle into mine. We follow the others round to the gatehouse and wait for Hannibal to do his thing.

"He's now sorting the paperwork out or telling them not to call the cops because he knows where they all live," I say, as my imaginative mind continues to run away from reality.

We see him come out. He shouts something unintelligible and waves at us with a piece of paper in his hand.

"That's probably his list of demands for the negotiator," I say to Prat.

We leave the industrial Ploče behind us and start following Route Pacman. The road climbs as we go up into the hills towards the Bosnian border. With each ascent, the road creates the illusion of a never-ending climb, and I anticipate a panoramic view of the landscape as we reach the peak. However, the road simply continues upward. The scenery is a rocky scrubland dotted with a few stone walls and a few buildings. These could be dwellings or just shacks. We arrive at the town of Metković, which is on the border. I am excited, but partly hesitant as to what it'll be like on the other side. We are stopped at the crossing point, which is just another Corimec manned by a few bored-looking officials dressed in blue military-style uniforms. I notice a brand-new metal sign, which is the first one I've seen since arriving in country. 'Welcome to Bosnia and Herzegovina,' it says in English and a few other languages that are alien to me. Hannibal is in the front truck and is showing his IFOR ID card to the soldier. We have also got IFOR stencilled on all sides of our trucks in white paint just in case anyone's in doubt who we are. We are quickly granted access and roll across the border into the country, which has dominated the news so much over the last four years on its journey through civil war and now towards peace.

"Here we go," says Prat.

"Right, keep your eyes peeled, stay on the road and don't stop for anyone," I say mockingly.

"Should we, errr, you know, like, errr, load our weapons or what," says Prat with a tone of seriousness.

"Hannibal is our loaded weapon," I reply. "He'll keep us safe."

I'm not too sure what I was expecting, but Bosnia looks exactly the same as Croatia.

The road continues its ascent as it snakes through the countryside, following the route of least resistance for the road builders. I see my first sign of the war as we drive by an abandoned house pockmarked with the unmistakable signs of bullets striking the exterior. We pass more and more houses. Not all of them are showing the same level of damage. A few of the heavily damaged ones looked lived in, and a few of the undamaged ones look empty. I guess they have either repaired them quickly, or what I am seeing here is evidence of ethnic cleansing. The news made it seem like only the Bosnian Serbs were involved, but the red and white chequerboard flags suggest we are in a Bosnian-Croatian area.

We still must endure cars cutting in and out of our convoy. The road eventually gets to a plateau and straightens out. It's a relief as they can now overtake in relative safety, but there are still a few who cut in front of us at the last minute. We even have the odd dilapidated coach have a go at getting past. These are also from Germany, but, judging from the missing lights, bumpers and, in some cases, windows or doors, I suspect they too are local.

We see the sign for Tomislavgrad, or TSG, as is it is known to us military types, and the kilometres count down. Lipa is not too far from TSG, so we know we'll soon be arriving at our drop-off point. Hannibal's truck pulls over on the outskirts of a village and we follow. Nothing happens for a few minutes. "Is this the lunch stop?" says Prat?

"Dunno, I hope so," I reply. "I'm getting hungry now."

Then the truck in front starts off, so again we follow on. As we pass by where Hannibal was parked, there's a small house with wooden benches outside, which is clearly a restaurant — it has the word RESTAURANT above the door — and it's just as clearly closed.

"Nooooo," I say. I'm now regretting chucking my sandwich away, even if it did have a tasteless filling.

TSG gets nearer and nearer and soon we are approaching the outskirts. As we turn off Route Crow and onto Route Kite, there is a strange-looking vehicle parked up. It's painted in light green and brown camouflage colours, has six wheels and is very rectangular. It looks like it hasn't moved in a while. Here is the proverb 'Necessity is the mother of invention' in its physical form. It's an improvised armoured battle bus and has become a local attraction. There is a high round turret on the top and a small slit at the front for the driver to see out of. The front is angled, which I suspect is nothing to do with improving its aerodynamics. It has a couple of headlights mounted on brackets down low and on top to give it a sporty rally car look. The armoured plates on the side come right down to the ground with little clearance and you can see just the bottom of the tyres. Along the side are little circular gun ports that are covered by a round metal plate and can be swivelled out of the way from inside. It looks almost futuristic, but the couple of flat tyres that it's sporting makes it look like what it actually is: a pile of junk.

We're on the last few miles to Lipa camp and the road has reduced in size, but thankfully, so has the local traffic. Lipa village is a smattering of houses spread out so thinly that the closest two could be classed as the village centre. We turn left off Route Kite and up a dirt track that leads us to the front gate. The camp was formerly a patch of ground with nothing there until the Royal Engineers arrived, and now it's a patch of ground with a barbed wire fence around it. We drive in and wave to the bored-looking guard who is holding the barrier up for us.

We go up a slight incline past rows and rows of Corimecs, and through another gate into the stores area. There are shipping containers everywhere, piles of boxes, rolls of matting, and forklift trucks bouncing over the rutted ground. We stop and Hannibal comes down the line, telling us the drop the sides of the flatbeds. Prat and I remove the ratchet straps and then drop the sides. The forklifts swarm around us like flies, offloading the pallets of full gas bottles in a matter of minutes. Just as quickly, they load identical pallets, but with empty ones that we'll take back to Split. They'll do the same round route again tomorrow. Oh, the glamour of logistics. We put the sides up, put the straps back on, jump back in the trucks, drive back down to where the Corimecs are, and park up.

"I think it's lunchtime," I say to Prat.

"I'm just having a starter," he says, as the back end of a Wagon Wheel disappears into his gob.

Hannibal shouts to us, "Come on, lads! Let's go and see what we can scrounge from the galley."

"Cookhouse," shouts someone to remind him he's currently with the British Army and not the Royal Navy right now.

"I guess the restaurant was closed," I say as I catch him up.

"Yeah, we pulled in and the fuckers were shut. I've been there a few times in the last week and it's bob on."

"Maybe they were closed for lunch, or Friday is their half day," I say. The cookhouse is a bunch of Corimecs welded together with the interior walls removed. It is rather quiet in the dining area, which is a telltale sign lunchtime has been and gone. Hannibal wanders off to find a Cabbage Mechanic and will hopefully work his magic, which could involve a threat of violence. We pick a table and sit down around it to wait, and I'm half expecting Hannibal to come back out of the kitchen with the poor chef in a headlock. They appear together, but not how I was imagining it. The chef is smiling and Hannibal walks over to the table we are sitting at and says, "How about some egg banjos, lads?"

"Get in," says Prat.

→» →» →»

The egg banjo, the bringer of morale, the king of military cuisine, the best thing you'll ever scoff. It's best enjoyed when you're cold, wet, exhausted and on your last legs, so that you're most prepared to savour the unadulterated joy that it has brought to so many squaddies over the years. It's astonishing that no celebrity Egg Technicians[52] have adorned it with a garnish, considering how straightforward the design is. Maybe they'd try a wee bit of balsamic glaze around the outside edge of the plate, then sprinkle some parsley on it and claim

---

52 Yet another nickname for an Army Chef.

it as their own. If they ever claimed the idea was theirs, I would like to think the British Army and about a million veterans would march on their kitchen. It's a straightforward fried egg sandwich. The egg must be fried in fat, the more the better. The bread must be white and cheap. For it to truly be called an egg banjo, the yolk must be intact. The soldier will take a bite and close their eyes as they feast on the hot egg and bread. At some point during the consumption, they will bite into the yolk, and it will spill out and down the front of their filthy combat jacket. Upon noticing they have spoiled their filthy jacket with the yellow yolk, they will immediately move the offending sandwich away from the front of their body. This is normally to one side, either left or right, depending on their hand dominance. With their other hand, they will frantically try to wipe off the runny yolk in a downward movement, thus giving anyone watching from afar the impression they're playing an invisible banjo.

Life's a Gas, Part 2

It's back to the trucks with our satisfied bellies we go. There's the quick check of oil, loads and lights before Hannibal gives us his brief for the final leg of today's journey, that will see us head back down Route Kite to TSG. Then down Gull back towards the Kamenško BXP[53] and finally home to Split in time for Hooch and Pot Noodles. We mount up and it's my turn to drive again. We bounce out of Lipa camp and down the familiar path, turning left at the TSG battle bus onto Route Crow. A few miles down the road, we pass the sign for Split that'll take us back down Route Gull.

TSG disappears in my mirrors as we climb again, up a winding road which has abandoned battle-scarred buildings along the way. There is still filthy-looking snow on the sides of the roads that is

53 Border Crossing Point.

stubbornly melting. Further up the mountain to my left, I notice cleaner-looking snow that hasn't been splashed with dirty melt water from passing trucks. The road levels off and bends around to the left and before us we see an immense lake and the harsh landscape stretching off in to the distance. The lake is called Buško Jezero, but we will just refer to it as "the big lake" on the way to TSG during our time in country. (I only learned its name years later when I was bored one day, after Google Earth had been invented.) The road now winds down the hill towards the lake and we use the low gears to keep the truck's speed under control. The road follows the edge of it for a while before it snakes off into the rocky scrubland. We pass more dwellings. These are untouched by the conflict but still look rundown. It has a feel of economic decline and I can't imagine what the locals do here for work. The landscape is covered in hardy-looking, wild, growing bushes, which give the impression farming would be impossible. The only attempt I observe of anyone trying to grow anything is in the small plots of land around those few houses. I pass the sign for Kamensko, which isn't too far away, so at least I have something to measure this bit of the day's driving by. The BXP is again a collection of Corimecs and I see one with the sign of the RMP.[54] I follow the trucks ahead onto the edge of the road. As I come to a halt, Hannibal scurries off to the RMP Corimec to book in and then book out as we are not planning on hanging around. Just as I've climbed down from the cab, I hear the call from Hannibal.

"Let's get the fuck out of here."

I climb straight back up into the cab.

The border guards lift the barrier as we steam through back into Croatia, leaving them with our clouds of dust as acknowledgement because a wave would seem too friendly. The road descends now

---

54 Royal Military Police.

with some long stretches where you could really get some speed up. On the right of the road are jagged rocky outcrops about the same height as the cab. On the left, a deep ravine with a rusty barrier that looks like it wouldn't stop a bicycle. The barrier is only installed at intervals because someone must have deemed the way dangerous but only had a budget for a fraction of the length of the road. The downhill part seems to go on forever, and the high RPM of the engine is loud as it struggles to hold us back. I press the brakes, but it's a juggling act. I can apply them harder to slow us down more so they have time to cool between applications or use them less hard, but more frequently. My hearing becomes muffled. I swallow a few times and I feel my ears pop. My hearing becomes clear again for the time being.

There is a notable rise in the temperature as we continue and in the distance I see the plateau on which the road will soon level. The scrubland has given way to green fields that are being farmed. We travel through numerous villages, and the houses are now devoid of any battle damage. Route Gull continues to wind around the hills and in places, going back up occasionally, but ultimately having a downward trend. There are more cars on the road, as impatient as all the others to try to become an In Loving Memory plaque. Along the route, I see flowers on the verge of the road, which denotes someone's demise that wasn't war-related. There were modest flowers arranged neatly in a vase, while others were much grander, with elaborate wreaths. A few were big stone plaques, more like a headstone, with a picture of the deceased etched into the marble. I see a few more further along that have steering wheels attached to them. It was as if to emphasise the fact they'd enjoyed driving but weren't very good at it in one bold statement.

We turn a corner and at last we spot the Adriatic through a gap in the hills and the haze. I hope it's the Adriatic and not another massive lake, as the day has been long and I am keen to get back to

Dalma. We reach the last downhill leg, which is known as Split hill, and the road is now the busiest I've seen it all day. I presume it's the Croatian rush hour. The increased traffic has stopped the kamikaze overtaking, and the locals are now resigned to their fate that they will live to see another day.

I can view the entire peninsula which Split is built on as we reach the crest of the hill. The traffic up and down the hill is a slow procession but some feel it necessary to beep their horn at the car in front, for God knows what reason. We pass the medieval Klis Fortress high above us on our right. Its strategic location is evidently chosen because it dominates the gap the road runs down between the mountains of Mosor and Kozjak. On our left, further in the distance, following the contours of the hill, I notice a partly constructed motorway. The lack of anything that looks even slightly to do with road construction tells me it's a suspended project for now. I think when it eventually opens, it'll be chaos as you'll have three lanes for the fast, faster and even faster lunatics. As we get to the traffic lights at the bottom of the hill, I spot the sign denoting we are about to turn back onto Route Gannet. I recognise where we are from last week's bus journey from the airport. I feel relieved again to have made our way down those hills without incident. It's not too far along Route Gannet until we turn left up the straight road to Dalma and back towards the huge puddle of filth. We are not hanging about as we can almost smell the finishing line — and the puddle. The deepest bit is on our side of the road today and a few feet of liquid isn't a problem for our mighty 14-Tonners.

I can't quite spot Hannibal's truck up ahead, but I do see the wall of water on either side as he ploughs through at speed. It almost looks biblical, as if we were parting the Red Sea. A formerly white Fiat 126 passes me, its windscreen wipers going at full speed, as its driver tries to clear the deluge of water that is now running off his car. I have a good view now as the truck in front of us repeats, and there are again walls of water thrown high in the air on either side. I see another car come out of what looks like a vertical lake, the windscreen wiper going at full pelt. Then it's my moment to contribute to the Croatian car washing industry. The car that has my name on it suddenly halts before the puddle as he realises he's about to get swamped. I realise the reason why he's had a change of mind. It's because of his open window. I notice him with a cigarette in his mouth, frantically trying to wind it up as I bear down upon the now calm, but soon to be sea state 9, puddle. I thunder into it and the waiting driver is wise to have chosen to remain on land. He still gets a nice rinse from the water that our big off-road wheels have dragged along with us. I look down and see him looking back at me with a face of rage and his cigarette-free mouth moving as it produces a torrent of Croatian insults.

We pull into the camp on the right. Careless gives us a wave as he holds the barrier up with one arm and cradles his gun in his other. "Looks like Careless fucked up again. He's on guard," says Prat.

"He'll probably have won the German lotto and the Military Cross by tomorrow, knowing him," I add.

We go straight to the POL[55] point to fill up the trucks for their carbon copy jaunt in the morning. We then park them up in line and unload our kit from the cabs and record the end mileage on the work ticket. "That was 250 miles today," I say to Prat.

"All on bastard back roads. No wonder I'm fucked," he replies.

"Is that a summary of today's anecdote?" I ask him.

"Dat's about der size of it, I reckon. Me fucking leg is killing me."

"My leg is killing me too," I say. "You need about a thousand PSI pressure to keep the bastard accelerator pedal down."

This is a design flaw with some of these vehicles. The manufacturers did not incorporate ergonomic design into these trucks. All

---

55 Petrol, Oil and Lubricants. Or the petrol station to non-military people.

of them have a squeak that emanates from somewhere in the cab. We are oblivious to it, in the same way as someone who lives next to a train track never hears the trains. The tool kits are returned to Shaun the Yawn. "Took your time, lads," he drawls sarcastically. "Did you leave the handbrake on or what?"

"If they had more than four gears, we'd be able to go faster," Prat comments. "They've got six, er," Shaun replies, stopping mid-sentence, realising he's just bitten the lure of the bleeding obvious statement. We cheer at his insatiable need to correct us. I sign everything back in and check off the 1033 to ensure I am not missing anything. Once we're both content, he tears up his copy of the 1033, symbolising the termination of my responsibility for the tools provided by the Queen for the day. I keep my copy and, years later, I hope, I'll auction it at Sotheby's for £16,000 to a military collector who was a former Storeman.

We dump what we don't need to take up to the office outside the front door of the building. We're taking just our guns, ammo, work tickets and keys upstairs. We hand over the work tickets and ensure we hang up the keys in the key press.

Staff Burton appears. "Make sure all the keys and work tickets are back and the trucks filled up and ready to go for tomorrow. Any faults with the trucks I need to know about?" he says, in a tone that tells me he dislikes his current job.

"Sergeant Frazer has done Troop Orders, so make sure you check for tasking tomorrow," he adds.

I check and I'm on the same run again in the morning with Prat.

"Same for us again tomorrow," I say to him.

"Better than hanging around here servicing trucks or waiting to get spammed for shit jobs," he replies.

I ended up on the same run the whole of the following week and at the end of it I could bench press 300kg.

"We have Sunday off though," says Prat, looking at the Troop

Orders. "There's a Church Parade but it's not a three-line whip."[56]

"It'll be the Padre talking to himself, then," I add.

Jimmy Frazer makes an appearance from his office next door and his caring side comes out. "There's late food on at the cookhouse for yiz all and if ye fook aboot tae lang, the slops will bin it. Dinna say I didn't warn ya if yer go hungry."

He dips back into his office and then back out, but now with a smile he's trying to conceal.

"The confined tae camp restriction is tae be lifted taemarra too."

We cheer. Being stuck on camp for the last weeks has become monotonous in the evenings. as there isn't a lot to do.

"No more fucking Hooch," exclaims Prat.

"But, be warned," Jimmy pipes up.

"Here comes the riot act," I say.

"There is a curfew at 2200 and anyone coming back late will have untold misery dumped upon them."

"Ah, 2200 isn't too bad," remarks Prat.

Gone to Pot

Prat and I run under the barrier, which is the official line that denotes you're back on camp.

I expect the Orderly Sergeant to shout, "SAFE," like a baseball umpire as we reach the base. "2159," is all he says whilst looking at his watch and pulling a face to underline how close we were.

"Make sure to book back in at the Guardroom," he reminds us.

There are a few more stragglers coming down the road, but they still have a good hundred metres to go. As they near the barrier, the Orderly Sergeant suddenly booms, "2200, that's it," and as

---

56 Compulsory attendance.

they cross, he instructs them to move to the other side to us. "Your names will be passed to your respective SSM's in the morning," he tells them.

It's like the end of a fitness test, with everyone panting and sweating from the final dash for the line, except for the fact we're wearing jeans and shirts.

→ → →

Earlier in the day, there was a noticeable air of excitement in the warehouse. Everyone was finally glad to get off the boundaries of the warehouse and away from the military. I, Prat, Del and a few others wandered down the road to see what the local vicinity had to offer. We skirted around the puddle, looking out for any military vehicles that may be imminent or Croatians bearing a grudge. Even though there was nothing coming in either direction along the road, we still walked past it at a hurried pace. We came upon the bar that was closed as we passed it on the first day, and, to our surprise, it was open. The shutters on the weathered house were flung open, the tables had tablecloths on them and even the chairs had cushions, which hid the rust. There were a few people already sitting around the tables, and it was a mixture of locals and out-of-place soldiers from the warehouse. There was a gigantic table under the trellis with a couple of benches made from thick wood which had been painted an artificial brown on either side.

A man appeared from nowhere, by which I mean the door, and, judging by his age, he wasn't one of the waiters, but the owner. He motioned to us to sit down at the bench next to which we were awkwardly standing. He had curly black hair which I couldn't discern if it were wet or greasy. His skin was pitted and dark. He had wispy whiskers above his top lip and a chin that appeared groomed.

"I think he's Colonel Gaddafi's stunt double," said Del.

We giggle like school kids, knowing he'd probably heard what

Del said. Predictably for us and like the ignorant British holiday makers we sort of are, he said in perfect English.

"Welcome, what would you like to drink?" And predictably, like the British soldiers that we actually are, we ordered beer.

"In Croatia, we call beer pivo," he informed us.

The local popular brew seemed to be a German beer, or pivo, called Kaltenburg. It's made under licence in Split. *(We found out later in the tour that the brewery was situated across the water from the quayside at SNP and has a big yellow 'Kaltenburg' sign on the side of a building.)* German beer doesn't normally give you a raging headache, unless you drink your own body weight of it. A couple of glasses of the big 'K' and you feel like someone's kicking a football around in your head the next morning.

Colonel Gaddafi turned up with pivos for us all, disappeared, and quickly returned with a gigantic silver platter piled high with chips.

"We didn't order these," exclaimed Prat.

"They're a little bar snack for you," said the Colonel.

There were 'oohs' and 'ahs' of approval all round from us all as we tucked in. "It must be a Croatian custom," said Dave Ponder, who tagged along with us this evening.

All I remember about Dave Ponder to this day is that he was infamous for chucking a local kid in the harbour a few weeks later. He was down there one Sunday and this kid cycled up to him on his bike and started talking in broken English.

"Hello, fuck you, English soldier[57], bastard, hello, football."

Dave laughed for a while, but the kid kept talking while cycling slowly next to him. "Hello, Spice Girls, football, fuck you, Mercedes, bastard, bastard, Liverpool."

---

57 Foreigners think everyone from Britain is English.

Either the kid had touched a nerve or Dave had quickly become fed up with this perceived torrent of abuse. Suddenly he grabbed the back of the kid's bicycle seat with one hand and the handlebar with the other. He then ran along the edge of the harbour, taking this kid on a journey of increasing speed. Dave then moved to the left and launched him off the edge into the water. The bike nosedived into the water with the kid hanging on like a crap Evel Knievel. After an age he surfaced, as thankfully he could swim, but his bike was heading to the bottom of the harbour several metres below him. He continued with the insults while Dave carried on like nothing has happened. How he wasn't lynched by any locals we don't know. I often wonder after all these years, if, aside from lots of Croatian older guys who understandably disliked us for constantly soaking them at the puddle, there's one middle-aged guy who despises us. This animosity stems from a British soldier dunking him in the harbour while he was simply trying to practice his English skills gained from watching TV.

The bar itself will become known by everyone simply as the 'First & Last'. We will frequent it regularly on the way out to, or back from an evening out. Each return visit we'll expect the enormous silver platter of free chips. This must have been his marketing ploy to keep us coming back as we are never going to be offered them again.

"Another pivo?" said the Colonel, as the first round of drinks had been quaffed by us.

In due course, we have to stop his efficient service as we wanted to see a bit more of the local area and not fail by spending the entire evening in the First & Last.

"Can we get the bill please," asked Del.

"Another pivo?" he enquired, ignoring Del's request

"Sorry, but we have to go," said Del. "We want to see the local town."

"It's no good," he said, trying to persuade us to stay. "Here is better."

"Just the bill please," reiterated Del with a forced smile.

He relented and said, "Of course, Kuna or Deutschmarks?"

We paid in German currency, which was kind of handy, as it was all we had on us.

The local seaside village is called Stobrec and, like most of the other villages and bigger towns on the Dalmatian coast, it's built on a peninsula. There's a pretty little harbour, currently with no kids floating in it, and a stony beach. The main road – or the only road – follows the waterfront and curves around to a small harbour where a few small fishing boats are moored up. On the side closest to the water is a white stone pavement with small trees lining it to offer anyone strolling some shade from the midday sun. At the end is the harbour with a small car park which uses the 'park at will' method. Overlooking it are a couple of bars with big open patio doors and seats outside and in. The road continues around a corner, but a sign denotes it's a dead end. We wandered about with our hands in our pockets but flocked back together to peer off the edge of the harbour into the crystal-clear water of the Adriatic. It was a very calm evening, the sea is glass-like and the Croatian flag at the end of the harbour arm hung limply. The sun was setting out to sea and turned the towering mountains behind us a light shade of pink.

"I might come back here on holiday," I said.

"I wasn't quite expecting this," exclaimed Del. "I can't believe we are getting paid to be here right now."

"Say that again tomorrow when you're humping and dumping gas bottles down at Ploče," I replied.

"Some civvies would pay thousands to drive trucks around here," he added.

We picked one of the two bars and hoped for the best. I saw quite a few faces I knew or recognised from the warehouse who were also making the most of the Saturday freedom. As soon as we sat down, a waiter was upon us taking our order and, within a few minutes, we had a round of pivos in front of us.

"Dis is better than Germany," said Prat. "Dey take ages to pour a beer back in Bielefeld."

This is true. As connoisseur beer-drinking Brits, we get mildly frustrated when Germans pour a beer straight into the glass and unsurprisingly it ends up with a massive foamy head. You then have to wait an age while it slowly settles down before they again top it up using the same foam-producing method and you have another prolonged wait on your hands. This normally takes place at the bar, so you end up drooling like Pavlov's Dog watching the foam reduce slower than coastal erosion. You just want to barge around the back of the bar, grab a glass and say, "Fucking hell, Herman. Have you ever considered tilting the glass to one side when you pour it?"

We looked nervously at our watches as it passed 2100, knowing we had the Sword of Buckethands hanging above our heads. Doing the mental maths, we worked out it was about a 20-minute walk back, and we had just ordered another round. We finished up and paid and headed off in good time. The walk should have been a gentle one, but the pace was enough to get a bit of a sweat on and we knew the clock is ticking.

At we passed the First & Last, Prat said, "One quick one 'ere?"

Del, Dave and the others declined and carried on up the road towards safety from the threat of disciplinary action.

I caved in and said, "Just a quick one," looking at Prat for reassurance. The Colonel took our order and then decided to chat to some of his friends at another table. We nervously tapped our feet and glanced at our watches while fooling ourselves by saying, "We've ages yet."

Finally, he arrived with our beers and we asked to pay straight away. We gulped them down like a thirsty shipwrecked sailor who's just been rescued, checked the time and sprung out of the chairs towards the long, straight road. "It's 2153, therefore we have seven minutes to get back," I said.

"Eight minutes. Ish," said Prat.

"Nah, it's seven minutes to 2200."

"Curfew is at 2200, so we have until 2200 and 59 seconds, because then it'll be 2201."

"I think if we try to reason this with Buckethands, we're pissing in the wind."

As we cast our eyes upward towards the warehouse, I commented, "Was it genuinely that far on the way down?" We were walking as fast as we possibly could before it became a run. "Four minutes to go," I said to Prat.

We broke into a gentle jog. The warehouse was getting closer. I couldn't see the Guardroom as it's around a corner and off to the left.

The pace quickened and, as we rounded the corner, I checked my watch.

One minute to go and it was now a do-or-die sprint for the finish that would have made Usain Bolt look slow. The barrier was up for us and we crossed into camp, and we only knew we would be free from disciplinary action when I heard the Orderly Sergeant say, "2159."

→» →» →»

We wander towards the door to the accommodation block.

"I could do with some snackage, you know," I say to Prat as the pivo sends a message to the food part of my brain.

"Me too."

We resign ourselves to not having a bite before bed when we notice quite a few of the lads sitting about in the smoking area eating Pot Noodle. "Where did you get them?" I ask one of them.

"That container over there," he says, pointing with his white plastic fork, "It's not locked, so just help yourselves."

We go to investigate. It's unlocked, and it's full of Pot Noodle. Not being greedy, we take one each and close the container as quietly as we can.

We head back to the smoking area to enquire where they got the hot water and cutlery. The same guy says, "In the cookhouse, mate. It's not locked, and the water boiler is on all night for brews."

We find a quiet nook away from the Orderly Sergeant's naturally inquisitive nose to eat our stolen nosh. We're still damp from our evening run and I still feel bloated from the last pivo I drank far too quickly to enjoy. In complete silence, we scoff the contents of the mini plastic bucket and I have a moment of contemplation as I blow on my steaming noodles. I think of my journey from the Army Recruiting Office in Birkenhead seven years earlier to how I got to be sitting here right now. I remember the Sergeant with the porn actor moustache, which was fashionable in the military back then, asking why I wanted to join up.

"Adventure," was my excited reply.

He scoffed at my answer and then told me about the brand-new car he was going to buy when he retired from the Army next year.

In my short career I've hiked in the Canadian wilderness, stomped the streets of West Belfast and climbed a few mountains in Germany, Austria and Malaysia. During my leave, my pay has funded several road trips around Europe, a jaunt on the Trans-Siberian Express, and a few weeks in China. I've met the most interesting people of different nationalities and also some of the biggest dickheads ever conceived. The journey isn't over yet. I know I will one day look back on that moment sitting there in Croatia with fondness, and it will become another chapter in a book.

Diesel Do, Mate

By the end of the week of doing the gas runs, I am dreaming about Route Gannet, Kite, Crow, and Gull. The hand balling of the gas bottles has become easier, but we are still the laughing stock of the Ploče women's body building club. I have managed to body swerve any duties so far, but one has finally caught up with me. Tonight, I am the Duty POL. There is a 12,000-litre TTF parked outside for anyone who needs fuelling up. I have a cot bed in one of the spare rooms in the MT Offices so I'm on hand to spring into action throughout the night. My duty starts at 1800 after I have had my evening meal. I've also collected the standard brown bag of sandwiches with their contents of unfathomable origins or flavour. I make my way over to the office to relieve Cheezy, who's covering the day shift. "All good, pal?" I enquire.

"Yeah, the keys for the TTF are in the truck and the paperwork is on the passenger seat."

"You off out tonight?" I ask him.

"Fuck, yeah," he says, smiling. But even if he were about to receive the mother of all bollockings from Buckethands he'd still be smiling.

I settle down in Jimmy Frazer's office with my feet on the desk with a magazine about making model airplanes which I found in his drawer. Just as I'm reading about the techniques on how to achieve the best weathering effects when painting your Lancaster Bomber, I become aware of footsteps coming up the stairs. I quickly drop my feet off the desk and put the magazine back in the drawer in case it's Jimmy coming to check I'm not sitting at his desk with my feet on it whilst reading his magazine. I hear someone say hello down the corridor. I pop my head out of the office.

"Hello..." I look for his rank and see he's a Lance Corporal, "...

mate, what can I do for you?"

"Are you the Duty POL?" he enquires.

"Sure am," I say,

"Can I get some fuel?" he replies.

"No probs," I tell him.

We walk down the stairs and out to the truck, and as we go I ask, "Where are you from?"

"Well, I was born in Newcastle but I was brought up in High Wycombe,"

I laugh. "Nah, who are you with out here?"

He laughs at his misunderstanding of my question.

"I'm Royal Signals based down at DJ Barracks. I've come back from Banja Luka and didn't think we had enough gas to get home today, so we thought we'd pop in for a top up."

His mate is asleep in the passenger seat.

I jump in the TTF, fiddle with the keys and fire it up, producing a big plume of white smoke. The engine sounds a bit rough as it ticks over. I then engage the PTO,[58] which will drive the pump for the fuel delivery, and it now sounds like a bag of broken spanners. I jump back out of the cab and hand him the hose. He drags it over to his Lanny,[59] pops the cap off and starts fuelling up.

With a full tank of diesel, he hands me back the hose, and I lay it down on a drip tray. It's full of light brown absorbent granules that will soak up any drips of fuel from the nozzle. I grab the paperwork from the cab, take his name and unit and the amount he took, and get him to sign. He may as well just put an X as it's simplified accounting and nobody cares.

"Cheers for that," he says, jumping in the driving seat. As he slams the door shut, his passenger wakes up and looks in a slight-

58 Power Take Off.

59 Land Rover.

ly confused state. The last thing he probably remembers was leaving Banja Luka camp some six hours earlier. One skill some say the military teaches you is the ability to sleep anywhere. They don't technically teach this skill, but it is gained through the nature of the job, which requires enduring long hours in uncomfortable environments such as the front seat of a Lanny. I just get my feet up and the modelling magazine open when I hear more footsteps coming my way. I carry out the 'feet back down, magazine away, in case it's Jimmy' drill.

"Hello," comes the voice.

This time there's not a uniform but a guy in civvies. This could be anyone, so I go for the default setting of, "Yes, sir, what can I do for you?"

His hair is too long to be military, but this could be a trick employed by Buckethands to catch me out.

"Are you the gentleman I need to talk to about getting some fuel?"

He's not military.

"I am indeed," I reply to him.

As we make our way to the TTF, I enquire who he is.

"What are you doing out here?" I ask him.

"I'm a photographer for NATO," he replies.

"That must be interesting. I thought you were someone on holiday after free fuel."

He laughs, but a little bit too nervously.

He's got a Lanny too, but this one isn't military looking at all. It's light in colour and has a roof rack. The only thing to remotely suggest its military are the words 'NATO' written on the number plates. I start the truck, engage the PTO, jump down and pass him the hose.

He pauses for a second, as if he was expecting me to fill it up for him. "Oh yes," he says awkwardly, taking the hose from me.

As he gets to the back of the vehicle he says, "Dear me, I've left the keys in the ignition."

I take the hose from him and he opens the door, looking for the keys.

"I'm sure they were here," he exclaims, fumbling about.

Patiently waiting for him, I have to stand and stare at him while he keeps looking. He pats himself down and realises they are in his pocket. Identifying hopefully the correct one, he inserts it in the fuel cap and turns it to the right and left without too much expectation of the cap being removed. With some more jiggling of the keys, it relents, and he gets it off. I slide the nozzle in and pull the lever. The engine tone of the TTF changes slightly as the fuel pump starts working, as it's under a slight load.

I continue to fill his Lanny up for him and ask about his job out here. He tells me he's out here recording NATO's mission, and he's experimenting with new technology which uses digital instead of physical film. It's fairly new, and you basically put your pictures straight into a computer and send them anywhere in the world. It's ground-breaking for the media industry, he goes on.

"You think it'll catch on?" I ask him.

"It is the way ahead for photography," he adds.

He pulls out a small flat bit of plastic from his jacket pocket.

"That's a memory card, and it has over 200 pictures on it."

"I'd lose that, to be honest."

The fuel nozzle clicks off, I give the lever another press and it clicks off again so I know he's full up. I give it a rattle in the filler cap to get rid of the dregs before I drag it back over to its resting place in the diesel-soaked drip tray.

This continues throughout the evening as passing troops drop in for fuel and I am up and down the stairs like a forgetful postman. I never find out the best way to paint a Lancaster Bomber so that it has a realistic look. I do have a quick chat with everyone that evening.

From some I only get one-word answers, while others give me their life story, and their entire family's life story too. After midnight, it quietens down and I have a chance to stretch out on the cot bed, hoping not to be disturbed. It's a still night. I've got the window open, and the sounds of dogs barking far off in the distance reach my ears. My hands now whiff of diesel, even though I've washed them several times. I've probably got it on my clothes, so I'll have to get some laundry done in the morning.

I'm sitting in the truck. I've broken down on Route Gull and I smell gas. In the distance I see a convoy of Fiat 126's coming towards me and they have someone standing up through the sunroof holding a hose spraying water. They are getting closer and I realise my window is down and reach for the winder, but, no matter how much it goes around and around, the window stays down.

"Oi," I hear someone shout.

I shift my eyes to the passenger seat and there's nobody there.

"Oi," I hear it again.

I look behind me out the small rear window, but I can't see anyone. The cars get nearer and the winder still doesn't work.

I close my eyes, ready for a soaking, and I then see Jimmy standing at the end of the cot bed. "Git up, yer lazy barstard," he says, as I realise I'm still in the room at the Squadron Offices.

With slight euphoria that my impending payback soaking will not happen, I sit up.

"I'll cover the POL until Cheezy turns up if ye want to go and get some scram," he says, showing his caring side.

I grab my few belongings and head back across to the warehouse to get ready for the day ahead.

Float like a Butterfly, Sting like a Beer

I've still not been tasked to drive anywhere, so it's going to be a day checking over the trucks that are not out on the roads and skiving and hiding. Mainly, it'll be hiding from any crap jobs which may filter down from higher, better paid SNCOs. The afternoon has been declared a sports afternoon or 'sporty' as we soldiers say. It could take the form of volleyball or a five-a-side or even a nice relaxing game of badminton. It could also be a right old beasting in the shape of a run that would have been described as gentle. At the start it might be, but invariably it'll end up with us going up the nearest hill while the Squadron racing snakes set the pace.

Just before lunch, those of us still on camp pile into the Troop restroom for the obligatory "I've git nuttin' for ye, see ye after scoff" talks from Jimmy. Today's talk is a little different.

"Right, be at the Guardroom wi' ye swimming kit at 1345" is today's notification of what the sporty is going to be.

"Are we havin' darts tournament at the First & Last, Sarge?" asks Prat.

"Aye, don't firget tae bring yer face as we'll be usin' it for the dartboard," says Jimmy quick as a flash. He cracks a smile as we laugh.

I have a very light lunch as I am still unsure how this sporty is going to turn out. I don't want to be puking it backup in case it turns out not to be the gentle paddle we are hoping for, but instead a vigorous swim to the Italian coast and back.

We gather at the Guardroom five minutes before the five minutes before the acceptable time we were told to be there. There were already a few there who didn't want to take any chances by deciding to be there five minutes before the five minutes before the acceptable time that was five minutes before the actual time. This would sometimes get out of hand and soldiers would be there hours before the time they were told to be somewhere, just in case.

Corporal Ish Oldman, the troop PTI,[60] turns up.

"You taking this sporty, Ish?" I ask him.

"I certainly am," he says, nodding.

"Result," says Prat.

Some PTIs thought every session they took had to end with us all looking on the cusp of passing out from over exertion. Ish was always up for a laugh and always made his PT sessions enjoyable.

"I can't swim," declares Del, "I can drown very well, though. I've always been able to do it as it comes naturally."

"Don't worry Del, I'm lifeguard trained," says Ish. "So, if I see you going under, I'll put some more sun cream on."

"Right, fall in, three ranks," he shouts.

There's the usual confusion of forming up into a squad as someone becomes the fourth rank thinking they are in the right and the person in the first rank is in the wrong. Eventually, we sort ourselves out. Ish says, "I need a couple of volunteers for traffic marshals."

I'm in the middle rank behind Del, so I push him violently forward. "Well volunteered, Del," says Ish, chucking him a hi-vis vest. "Can you take up the rear please?"

"I'll try, but it might make my eyes water a little," replies Del.

"Right, let's get out of shitsville."

"Byyyyyyyyy the left, off to the beach for a dip," he yells like a stereotypical Drill Instructor.

Then talking from the side of his mouth in a quieter tone, "for maybe a pivo or two."

"Quuuuuick, march," he yells again.

As we depart past the Guardroom, he turns to me, winks and says, "you never know who's watching."

60 Physical Training Instructor.

As soon as we are out of sight of the warehouse, he mockingly shouts, "For security reasons, troops will cease to march in a squad and now walk in a rabble, quuuuuuuick walk."

We burst out laughing.

After managing to navigate the 'puddle of Hepatitis A', and crossing Route Gannet, we safely arrive at the beach. "Right," says Ish, asserting his control that this is an organised swim with a purpose.

"Two at a time I want you to swim out to that orange buoy and back and then" – he pauses – "do what the fuck you want."

We spread our towels out and take off our trainers and T-shirts. The beach is all small stones and no sand, so it makes the ones who forgot their flip-flops look like zombies walking as they head to the water's edge. As we dip our feet into the sea, the winter chill still lingers, prompting countless expletives from us. The deeper we go, the more the profanities increase in their crudeness until we dive into the water and they cease. Some stand still, continuing to swear with the water just below their testicles, trying to muster up the courage to fully immerse themselves in the freezing Adriatic. We don't stay in for too long, as it's far too painful to endure. Some of the more resilient members of the troop remain in the water, splashing around and swimming so poorly that they appear to be drowning. There is zero reaction from any of us on the shore and Ish, taking his responsibilities seriously, says to us, "There's a bar over there. Shall we check it out?"

The bar is not much bigger than a shipping container, but size doesn't matter as long as it has cold beer. There is a wooden-decked area in front of it that looks like it's been made from pallets. We order a few bottles of Kaltenburg from the friendly barman, who fishes them from the cooler below the bar. There are some bits of memorabilia on the back of the bar, including a few pictures. In one of them there are soldiers posing on and around a tank. I can't quite work out if it's theirs and in working order or if it's one they have knocked out. They all have their AK47s pointing in the air and the two of them in the middle hold the Croatian flag. It's not too dissimilar to ones I have at home which were taken on a training area in Germany, where I'm photographed next to some piece of large military hardware.

Ish, Prat, Del and I sit down at a table, which is a wooden cable drum.

"This is the sort of sports afternoons I prefer," I say to Ish.

"Buckethands would have us running up and down those mountains over there," says Del, pointing at the high ground that is always overlooking us. "Where is he?" I ask. "I've not seen him for days."

"I think he's been busy with Pippen the Chicken this week," says Ish.

"Pippen the Chicken?" I say, laughing. "What's that all about?

"This is his first operational tour," replies Ish.

"What?" says Del. "He's like pushing 40 and must have done at least a few tours."

"Nope, he must have called in sick when he was a young subaltern and then he's been in staff jobs most of his career."

"He'll look der business on der Medal Parade when we get back," says Prat, referring to his lack of medals. "Especially when he has to present Private Greengrass wif all his."

Private Greengrass is an exceptional soldier in two ways. Exceptional in that he has a load of medals, pretty rare in the mid-nineties. He just seemed to be in the wrong place at the wrong time and was always picked to deploy somewhere, mostly for short periods, but long enough to qualify for a medal. The other reason why he is exceptional is he is not exceptional at all. He's a very quiet lad who has a polite demeanour and fades into the background. He is probably not going to go too far in his Army career because being loud and noticeable gets you promoted.

"Who wants another pivo?" asks Ish.

We all nod or raise our hands to confirm we will continue to partake in Ish's sports afternoon. He comes back from the bar with our beers on a tray and says in the style of a boxing commentator.

"Innnnnnn the red corner," he shouts.

"The Git from Split, the wrecker of heads and overall bad boy, who is yet to be defeated by anyone from the cream of the Royal Logistic Corps, I give you Misterrrrrrrrrrrrrrrrrr Kaltenburg."

We laugh as he puts the tray down, picks up a bottle, pretends it's a microphone, and continues his impersonation.

"In the blue corner. All the way from Bielefeld Deutschland, coming in at four hundred Pounds Sterling, one hundred and fifty Deutschmarks and a few odd Kuna. It's the pride of Liverpool, the Garston Gimp, Scouuuuuuuse Prat."

We're all laughing raucously now as Ish carries on.

"In the yellow corner, with his inability to outwit a drugged rabbit, we have the best thing to come out of the Republic of Ireland since Guinness was invented. Its Deeeeeeeeeeel Delaney."

The Croatians, who are all smoking, are also sharing our sports afternoon, look at Ish with total confusion as to what they are actually experiencing.

"In the grey corner, a man the less said about the better. From boreman to future bedding Storeman. It's Scouse Leeeeeeeeeeeeeeee."

"Finally," he pauses. "In the cool corner, it's the PTI without an STI but has a GTI and the FBI looking for him to help them make a record with EMI. It's Ish Oldmannnnnnnn."

"Ding, ding, round one," shouts Prat.

Ish takes a big swig from his beer and comments, "Mister Kaltenberg comes out swinging and Ish is on the ropes already."

We spend the rest of the afternoon laughing away, puzzling our cigarette-toting Croatian neighbours while getting drunker by the round. By now nearly everyone has joined us in the bar and the owner thinks his Christmas has come early, if the amount of pivo we are buying is anything to go by. We're all in good spirits and we want to stay at the beach bar until late, but Ish concedes we need to head back. He announces we need to finish up our drinks and then rounds up those still sunning themselves on the beach. We stagger the gauntlet back to the warehouse, laughing and shouting as we go. The First & Last is closed, but, in hindsight, it's for the best that the temptation wasn't dangled in front of us.

I am asleep by 1800 but I wake later in the night with a raging headache, a mouth like a dry shammy leather and I'm busting for a piss. I stand up to ready myself for the long trek to the toilets and I see Prat face down, snoring, with one leg hanging off his bed. Mister Kaltenberg has knocked us out and remains the undefeated champion. For now.

3

Suits You, Sir

FTER COMPLETING the previous month with a few more gas runs, I see my name down to do the 'Gungy Run' on Troop Orders for the next few days. I'm not aware that I had fucked up and I would have surely been told I had, if I had. I'm down to do it with Zero, who is equally perplexed why she's also tasked with doing it. Zero is called Zero because of one legend-level incident which happened many years before and, like most Army nicknames, if it's a good one, it'll follow you around for your entire career. Her actual name is Siobhan O'Grady and on that fateful day during the early days of her basic training, an angry-looking Sergeant accosted her.

"What's your number?" he enquired in a stereotypical training-depot angry manner.

"Two, five, eight, oh, three, two, three, oh, Sergeant," she replied.

"Oh?!" he said in shock. "BLEEDIN OH?! There's no bleedin oh-s in the British Army, only zeroes," he shouted at her angrily. "What's your name?"

"Zero Grady, Sergeant."

We go to see Jimmy, who we know will provide a reason for why we were tasked and, even if he doesn't, he'll probably inform us we're doing it, anyway. "Sarge, neither of us has fucked up," I say to him adding a "have we?" just in case in missed something. "Naah, ye havnae, in fact nobody has recently, so I had to pick a couple fir a few days and ye tae came tae mind," he replies. "Dinna worry, someone will fuck up in the next 24 hours, so you'll be free."

True to his word, someone does, and we only do it for one day, but what a day!

→» →» →»

After the morning meet-up in the Troop Office, Zero and I get ready for the day. We agree that I'll go and First Parade the truck while she signs for the tools and Hazmat gear. I find the tanker down the bottom of the vehicle park against the perimeter of the camp, which is a British Army high-security fence, built on a budget. On the other side of our formidable barrier is a busy wholesale fruit market. There are a few skips near the fence and, from the smell, they must dump in any unwanted fruit, leaving it to rot away in the heat of the day.

I have to dip the tanks on the back of the truck and check off what the paperwork says we should have compared to what we actually have. It's acceptable, implying that the locals haven't been syphoning off any yet. Our high-security fence must be working well as they've not realised that if you give it a hard push the entire length of fencing will flop on to the ground.

We are using the smaller Foden 12,000-litre TTF, which has six wheels and a lower fuel tank. The other TTF we have in the fleet is the 22,500-litre version. It has eight wheels and its tank on the back is much larger and worryingly taller. This extra elevation gives it a higher centre of gravity. So, when the fuel sloshes around inside the tank, the truck will wallow about and I'll get to see an eight-wheeled truck go around a corner on only four wheels later that month.

With the levels checked on the TTF, I start it up. It fires and produces a smokescreen of white, which comes into the cab stinging my eyes. The low-air gauge continues to shout its warning, so I press the accelerator to get the revs up, which produces more clouds of white smoke. That day's wind favours the clouds of diesel fumes to envelop the market. I don't hear any shouts of protest from the locals. It's doubtful they'll be able to smell the diesel from the amount of cigarettes they smoke. More likely the greengrocer will attribute the hint of fuel to the "that's what we wash them in to keep them fresh" excuse. I bounce the TTF across to the Troop Store, so Zero hasn't got to carry the gear to the far end of the vehicle park. The ground has now dried out in the spring warmth, but it still holds the shape of a pile of churned-up mud as if an entire Squadron of tanks has driven through it a few weeks ago. It's so rough that some trucks are losing their loads, wing mirrors, lights, and, in one case, their door before they even get off camp. The toolkit goes in the tool bins at the rear of the vehicle. The Hazmat kit has to squeeze into the cab with us, as "Hazmat" wasn't even in the dictionary the decade that this truck started production. They did fit ashtrays though, in case the driver fancied sparking up a quick cigarette in-between delivering his 12,500 litres of fuel.

"We have to wear the sodding Jackson suits today," Zero says. "Shaun the Yawn said it's come down from RHQ."

The Jackson suit is a pair of coveralls designed for use around fuels by having a rubber fuel-resistant coating on them. Donning them in a cool environment is bad enough and so it's not something we'd wear willingly in the Balkan heat.

"They'll give us Jockey's Bollocks," says Zero, referring to the increased possibility of a sweaty heat rash in the groin area.

"You don't know what it's like to get Jockeys Bollocks," I say to her.

"Not having any dunnage doesn't mean we don't suffer, you know?" She looks at me like I'm stupid.

"Well, you think you know everything and suddenly someone drops that nugget of information in your sweaty lap," I add.

We manage not to harm Anglo-Croatian relations that morning by allowing the local traffic at the puddle to pass before we take our turn. Zero is at the wheel and gingerly moves through the small inland lake, not wanting to cause a tsunami. "If we go through it at speed, this museum piece will conk out, and the Navy will have to come and winch us off with a helicopter," she says.

I laugh and say, "This bloody puddle is getting bigger. Why isn't it shrinking now that it's getting warmer?"

She knows the way to SNP, which should only be a 10-minute drive from Dalma. The morning traffic is heavy, and, when we get to the roundabout at the bottom of Split Hill, it's hardly moving. We see the reason for the delay, which is an accident up ahead on the junction at which we want to turn. A car has gone into the back of another, with a lot of force, and the road is littered with bits of glass and plastic. The drivers are both scratching their heads while smoking cigarettes as they wait for the Policija to turn up. I hear screeching brakes and then the unmistakable accompanying sound of the violence of metal on metal. Behind us, someone else has decided to join in the morning's chaos.

"Fuck me, is it National Car Accident day today?" I ask.

"Maybe it's just an excuse for them to light up a cigarette," replies Zero.

"Just being awake is their excuse for having a smoke."

We pass the first accident, and there's an overpowering odour of petrol. This doesn't seem to register as a potential problem to the drivers during their quest of smoking a pack of cigarettes before you can say, 'Bye-bye, No Claims Bonus'.

"Don't hang about," I say to Zero, as it is a potential problem for us with our thousands of litres of fuel behind us.

We're waved into SNP 30 minutes after leaving Dalma by the diligent Croatian guard, who has the obligatory cigarette hanging out of the corner of his mouth. I also suspect he has a repetitive strain injury in his right arm from waving everyone into the port. He either knows everyone or he doesn't give a crap about his job, and I suspect it's the latter. Zero has done the Gungy Run before because of breaking the curfew by "one bastard millisecond." Her words, not mine, or Jimmy's.

There's an RFA[61] vessel parked up alongside the quayside and opposite it are large storage sheds running the length of the port. Inside some of the sheds are offices and accommodation which are used by the unit manning the port. At intervals outside the sheds are big green generators that are noisily supplying the power which the troops need to work and live.

"They all need filling up, so it's quite a long task," says Zero.

I pull a face, saying nothing, as my face expresses more than my current vocabulary.

We put on our Jackson suits. They feel and look horrifying. The rubber coating is only on the front, but within minutes we are sweating as expected.

We have been taught a set of procedures to follow every time we pump fuel. We lift the sliding door of the compartment which houses the fuel pump gubbins. There's a tiny switch that will automatically put the handbrake on if it's open. One of the checks you always do on a First Parade is to make sure the pin holding down

61 Royal Fleet Auxiliary.

the compartment door is in place. We'd been told horror stories by Instructor Pool Cue of them popping open on the Autobahn, resulting in an emergency stop that a crash test dummy would find hard. We have to earth the truck with a metal spike that is attached by a long wire to the vehicle. This is supposed to be hammered into the ground, but we're on the concrete floor of the port, so we jam it as best as we can under the back wheel.

There is also another earthing wire which has a clamp on it which we have to attach to the thing we are refuelling. Next, we connect the fuel nozzle to the outflow pipe and engage the PTO. We get our drip trays and the absorbent granules for any spillages. We make sure to have the fire extinguishers to hand, just in case. We have more than 20 generators to fill up, so, being safety orientated, we ignored all of it.

Zero has a method that uses a bulldog clip to keep the safety switch down on the pump compartment so the tanker could be driven the few metres between each of the generators. We tie the earthing clamp and spike on to the vehicle somewhere, ensuring the loose cable isn't going to get caught under the wheel and ripped off. Zero disengages the PTO and I walk alongside the tanker carrying the nozzle to the next generator. I hook the pipe over the front bumper and then attach the earthing clamp to the generator and jam the spike under the back tyre. This reduces the time spent at SNP by a good hour, but we know if we get caught, we'll be doing the Gungy Run for the rest of the tour. By the time we finish, we'll have lost about 100lbs between us.

A passing Sergeant exclaims, "You must be warm in those gimp suits?"

The next person who passes us is a Corporal, and he says, "You two must have right old Jockey's Bollocks." He turns bright red when Zero turns round and he realises.

"They're so sweaty, they fell off," she says, simultaneously grabbing her groin. He hurries off in embarrassment.

Next stop is DJ Barracks by the airport. It's only half an hour's drive from SNP, so I presume there has been a pause on National Traffic Accident Day.

"It's now National Smoking Day," says Zero. "Every fucker has a cigarette in their gob."

She's right. Every driver, pedestrian, newsagents in their tiny kiosks, school kids, Policemen, are all smoking.

"I'm surprised the country hasn't got a pack of Benson and Hedges on their flag," she adds. We turn into DJ Barracks. Two soldiers — one British, one Croatian — manning the gate wave us in. IFOR rents part of the camp from the Croatian military, who still use the other part. The generators on the barracks are too spread out for our time-saving trick to be of much use here. They are dotted around the camp and usually tucked away behind Corimecs, so they're hard to find and harder to get the tanker close enough to. At the first one, we don our torture suits and carry out the taught fuelling procedures.

It takes longer at the barracks and at 1230 we go looking for the cookhouse. We leave the tanker at the last generator we filled up, which is down a little rough track. Taking off the gimp suits is such a relief, but our T-shirts are sopping wet with sweat.

"God forbid should we get a drop of diesel on our uniform and go man-down with dermatitis," says Zero.

"The choice between that and heat exhaustion is like asking which half of a dogshit sandwich we want," I add.

Lunch is in a very well-presented cookhouse with a fine selection of offerings which wouldn't be out of place in a posh hotel. This camp is some sort of HQ, so they seem to have better things than anywhere else I have visited so far. Afterwards, we head back to the tanker to fill the last of the generators. We see someone lurking by our tanker as we walk along the track. A tall, thin Sergeant, with an out-of-fashion porn moustache, immaculately shaped beret, and a cap badge that I'm unfamiliar with, turns and faces us.

"Is this your vehicle, gentlemen", he enquires?

"Err, yes it is, Sergeant."

I have to look twice as I think for a minute it's the same Sergeant who told me about his new car in the recruiting office many years before.

I glance again, and he's a very close likeness, but it's not him.

"Well," he remarks, rubbing his hands with glee, "you can't park there."

We don't know what to say and don't want to say anything obvious, otherwise it might aggravate the situation with this Sergeant from the 1980s.

"Your vehicle is blocking the track," he says.

I ponder over for what we may be blocking it, and I still don't want to say anything.

"Down the end of this track is a generator," he continues, and again I'm holding back from saying something.

"That genny powers these Corimecs."

He's now loving this. I now have an inkling as to what is coming, but I still can't believe it.

"And if the fuel tanker..." Bingo, he's said it.

"We are the fuel tanker," I mumble.

"And if the fuel tanker" - he repeats himself, emphasising the word 'tanker' - "can't get to the genny to fill it up. Eh, what did you say?"

"We are the fuel tanker," I say a tad louder.

He looks at our vehicle and then back at us a few times and then the penny drops as to who we are.

"Ah, err," he mutters. He's now looking for a way out to save face.

He's got nowhere to go other than past us.

I'm half-expecting him to suddenly point and shout, "Look, there's Slobodan Milošević," then sprint off as we are distracted.

After what feels like an age, he smiles and exclaims, "Well, it's a load of shit, isn't it?"

His body language is one of defeat as his shoulders rapidly droop. We are unsure if this sudden confession is real or a trap?

"The RSM has me out policing the parking on this camp. Everyone's got a job to do, and it's not like they are parking illegally, and it's not like you have to pay a parking fine," he remarks in a dejected tone.

"I have been in for 15 years, been all over the world, done tours of Northern Ireland, took part in the Gulf War... I then volunteer for a job out here thinking it'll be exciting and I end up as a fucking car park attendant."

His depressing confession leaves us unsure of where to direct our gaze and how to cope.

"We need to get going," says Zero, smiling awkwardly.

Gradually, we move closer to the tanker, and he responds by moving. He walks past us with his head bowed and back along the track, looking like a beaten man. "That was spooky," says Zero.

I swear I saw him months later up country somewhere. I had a flat tyre and I was dealing with it off to the side of the road when a Lanny screamed past at an incredible speed. There was a guy behind the wheel who looked just like him and he was laughing his head off. I was half-expecting a fleet of RMP vehicles with their lights blazing away to follow past in pursuit. I thought to myself, as the 1980s porn moustache was still a look favoured by some, that it made a lot of soldiers look almost identical.

We finish up filling the last few generators and are back at Dalma by 1500. With the tanker fuelled and parked up, and the gear handed back to Shaun the Yawn, we head up to Jimmy's office to see who's fucked up today, thus relieving us from having to repeat the Gungy Run again tomorrow.

"Aye, someone's fucked up. Dinna worry," he tells us. "But it's only the one, so I'll need one of ye fir tomorra."

"I've done it a few times now," says Zero.

"Aye, but you fucked up, and I didn't," I reply, "so technically, it should be you."

"It was one bastard millisecond," she says.

"A crime is a crime," I say, smiling at her.

"I've done my fair share of penance for it."

"You're still a criminal in the eyes of Sergeant Frazer here," I say, hoping for him to at least back me up.

"Why don't yez just flick a coin for it, fir fuck's sake?" he diplomatically interjects.

The gods of chance are smiling on me today. I won't be doing the Gungy Run ever again.

Port to Account

There is a ship due in at SNP bringing in more vehicles that belong to the constant influx of troops who are arriving daily. We have been tasked to supply some fuel trucks for them in case they need topping up, as they are going straight up country. There are five of the 22,500-litre tankers ready to go this morning with the British Army's finest Drivers, namely The Prat, Del & Me Gang. Hannibal will be running the show today but the TC,[62] Lieutenant Barton, is coming along, thinking he's in charge. Hannibal is an experienced Corporal so he will run things but will manage to make the TC

62 Troop Commander.

feel as if it's all his doing. It's the usual out-of-camp-and-turn-left, through the puddle, soak the locals, turn right onto Route Gannet to the roundabout at the bottom of Split Hill, observe an accident, turn left towards SNP, and get waved in by the diligent Croatian guard with a freely movable arm.

We park up in a line next to one of the sheds and are summoned to the front vehicle for the brief from the TC.

"Right, boys and girls, pin your ears back," says Hannibal, getting his notebook out.

I look around and, not seeing any females with us, I dig Del in the ribs and say, "You're the token girl today."

"Lieutenant Barton wants the tankers at intervals along the sheds here. At least a 20-metre gap between them. You'll need every hose out with drip trays and nozzle stands. Jackson suits will be worn."

We groan at the last sentence as it's already warm and only going to get hotter.

Hannibal displays a sense of discontent as he examines his own notes again, suggesting he is also dissatisfied with it.

"Unloading of the ship will commence at 0900, or so I've been told. You've got lunch bags, but you can get brews from the cookhouse in the shed over there and the CO will pay us a visit at some point. So, no fucking about."

He flips away his notebook, turns to the TC and says, "Sir, do you want to add anything I may have forgot?"

"Err, no, I think you covered everything for me. Thank you, Corporal Lester."

"Questions, anyone?"

There's the customary bout of silence and glazed-over-eyes looks from us. "I have one," says Del, raising his hand.

"Fuck off, Delaney, knowing you, it'll be about how do you grow seedless grapes or what's the difference between a boat and a ship or something similar," replies Hannibal.

"Right, get to your vehicles," he tells us as we disperse, leaving Del standing on his own with his arm still raised.

We set the tankers up as directed and guesstimate the 20 metres we were asked for. The TC, clearly feeling the need to get involved, declares our 20-metre guesstimate to be not good enough and insists we increase the distance.

"Do dee do measuring at Sandhurst?" asks Prat.

"Dunno," exclaims Del, "but I bet they do interfering with shit."

The TC runs along the line, moving the trucks. This involves putting the hoses away, as we have to be seen to be doing it correctly.

"Fucking hell," says Del. "Where's Hannibal?"

"He'll have us doing this all day long if he's left alone," I add.

Hannibal appears from the shed with a brew in his hand and instantly clocks what's going on with a look of astonishment. I imagine he's currently thinking something along the lines of: "For fuck's sake, I leave him alone for two minutes and he's putting his oar in."

He walks over to the TC and distracts him by offering him his brew, "Sir, I've got a wet for you."

He gets him away from us so we can set up again and we're left in peace.

Hannibal comes down the line telling us, "There are brews inside the shed when you're ready, lads."

"Where's the TC?" I enquire. "Did you chuck him off the quay by any chance?"

"I've given him a task of getting in contact with the Squadron and to get someone to bring more absorbent granules to you. Not that we need him, but I can't have him thinking he's in charge."

Now the calm has returned, we can go in the search of a brew. Inside the shed are the Norgie containers which contain the liquid delight. We stand around chatting in the shed that is slowly becoming a sauna while we drink our hot tea-stew from paper cups. These cups are so thin you need five to insulate your fingers from the heat from the hot liquid. I wander outside to get out of the furnace and find a spot in the shade.

Del follows me out and says, "Did you know a guy fell off the quayside last week? They fished him out, and he's still in hospital now."

"Really," I exclaim, waiting for the punchline. After a long pause I say, "go on."

"They had to pump his stomach out and give him God knows how many shots because of the crap that's floating in the filthy water."

I wait again for the punchline and prompt him with a "go on."

"Yeah, you don't wanna fall in there, do you?"

He wanders off with his brew, tutting, and I grasp that it wasn't a joke and someone must have actually fallen in.

The TC has us suited in our Jackson suits at 0900, ready to dispense fuel as required, even though the ship still has its ramp up and there is zero activity happening anywhere. While we wait for the military machine to spring into action, I feel the sweat dripping down my back and arms. The arms experience is a new one, but then again, wearing rubber overalls in a rather warm environment is also new to me. The sun is on the vehicles now and I try waiting in the cab but can't get any shade as it's shining right through the windscreen. Grabbing a bag of absorbent granules, I put my shirt over it to make a rudimentary pillow. I slide it under the tanker between the front and back wheels. I lay down and roll under the vehicle to get some respite from the direct sunlight. Laying on my back on the hard concrete floor, finding the sweet spot for my head on my homemade pillow and trying to ignore the unremitting smell of diesel, I close my eyes. Not trying to think about the rubber suit I'm in or the 22,500 litres of fuel above me, I manage to have a kip.

Even now I am amazed I achieved any sleep in what was such an uncomfortable environment. Sometimes when I was visiting civvy mates years later and they would ask if I'd be comfortable enough on their sofa, I'd laugh and say, "I've slept in worse places." I don't think they would have imagined that day at SNP.

A pair of talking feet standing next to my head wakes me up. "Oi, Rip Van Stinkovic, time to get up," says an Irish accent.

I roll out of my new-found bunk and say, "I'm bringing a mattress next time we're here."

"Bloody hell, you're like a right tramp, you are," says the face of Del that's attached, via a torso and various other parts, to the legs. "Shall I get you a shopping trolley for your gear so you can push it about?"

"I'll be pushing you in the water soon," I reply.

"Don't be doing that now," he replies, genuinely scared.

Right on cue, the unloading starts two hours late at 1100. We fire up the tankers and have a busy few hours filling up a varied collection of vehicles who present to us for fuel. SNP is a hectic place, with wheeled and tracked vehicles coming off the ship at a tremendous rate. It must be a TARDIS, as the quantity of vehicles it's spewing out of the back and down its ramp doesn't seem to match the size of the vessel. There are troops everywhere, and, further down the port, I see the chaos as they try to put everything into some sort of order. The wheeled vehicles will move up country under their own steam, but the tracked ones will be loaded onto the tank transporters of our Regiment. We have a few hoses running out, so we are able to fill up a few vehicles at the same time.

The TC comes to check on us, with Hannibal steering him around, and he suspiciously looks at us for a while before asking, "Is everything going OK?"

"Sir," pipes up Del. "These Jackson suits are ridiculous. I'm piss wet-through under here. Can we not take them off?"

"I'm afraid not. You've got them on for a reason and the reason is to protect you from getting fuel on you," he replies.

"It is a bit over the top, sir," adds Hannibal. "The drivers are fuelling their own vehicles, so I don't really think there's a need for them at the moment."

"Sorry, but rules are rules. Imagine what the CO would say if he turned up later and saw the guys not wearing their Jackson suits," is his reply.

The CO does turn up later and he does his nut when he sees we are wearing rubber suits in the heat of the day. We're immediately ordered to take them off.

"I would have loved to have been in on the awkward conversation between him and the TC," I say to Del.

"Good god, man," says Del is a pompous posh English accent. "Are you trying to kill our own troops? That's my job, Mr Barton."

The relief of getting out of them and feeling the light breeze doing its cooling-by-evaporation effect on us is one of pure release. *[I think it was the last time I wore one, as I can't remember suffering from heat exhaustion as we went into the summer months.]*

The last vehicle rolls down the ramp and we dismantle the hoses and pack up the trucks for the return to Dalma. The TC has either got bored or can't face us after his pep talk with the CO as he has disappeared. Hannibal walks past us, shouting words of encouragement.

"Come on, you lazy fuckers, I've got a date with a cold pivo and you lot are stopping me from meeting the future Mrs Lester."

"Has she got a sister?" shouts Del.

"Oh yes, she's got several sisters and they'll all be coming along if you get this packed up in the next five minutes."

"That's leadership right there in action," I say to Del.

"He's not bad for a Royal Navy security guard," he replies.

Hannibal, who must have been in earshot, clocks this and says, "What was that, Delaney?"

"I said you're not too bad for a Royal Navy security guard."

He laughs and quick as a flash says, "Your date will be with the ugly sister, Hooch, you cheeky bastard."

There is a delay in getting out of SNP. We sit motionless in our vehicles, in convoy, with our engines running and destroying the lungs of anyone within 20 metres. "Good job we did the pre-deployment training," says Del. "My waiting skills were becoming rusty, but this is sharpening them back up to the gold standard."

"What's going on?" I reply, hanging out the window to see what the delay is. Hannibal is having a talk with the Croatian guard. "He's fucking waving everyone in, but looks like he's not letting us out."

"I think he must have read the instructions to being a port security guard the wrong way round," says Del.

After a few more minutes, I see the front tanker pull away and I follow on. I am honestly expecting to see the security guard's legs sticking out of his little hut in the horizontal position. I give him a quick glance as I pass. He's up and about and doesn't look like he's been assaulted.

The Barber of Lake Seville

My name isn't on Troop Orders, so I have the day off along with most of the Regiment. I go for a run with Zero before breakfast around in the tracks behind the warehouse, as we know we have a PFT[63] coming up soon. We could have headed down the long road towards the puddle, but we didn't fancy getting run over or soaked. Zero says she knows a good route and I follow on. The ground is

---

63 Personal Fitness Test.

rough, and as we pass a dwelling which could be a building site, a massive black dog emerges barking violently from the other side of a wall.

"Fucking hell," I say, as I instinctively jump away from the hound.

It's standing on its hind legs as, thankfully, a long thin metal chain stops him from coming any further to rip us to bits.

Zero doesn't flinch. "I forgot about the dog," she exclaims, laughing.

"Of course you did," I say.

We see a few others from Dalma as we trundle along. Nodding to them as we pass, we find most nod back, but a few don't. Some appear like racing snakes and are too focused to acknowledge us, and some look like they're struggling and don't want to expend their spare energy on a greeting.

We spot the SSM from one of the other Squadrons who's running in his professional-looking Nike matching gear. I can't remember his name, but he's a small guy, and he's always out running. He reminds me of a rat wearing glasses from a children's story. He's the type who would bollock soldiers, but only when an Officer was in earshot. The closer the Officer, the more severe the reprimand you'd suffer, and he'll glance sideways, checking to see that the Officer has clocked him.

His career and promotion path are possibly the product of his two favourite things: bollocking soldiers and running. It sometimes feels that what you really need to get promoted in the RLC is only to have an impressive PFT time. I always imagine the promotion boards, when the Officers and SNCOs get together to discuss an individual soldier's performance and suitability for promotion, are mainly focused around what their PFT time is. My philosophy is a 'pass is a pass' regardless of the time you came in at, but I'm lagging well behind the promotion curve. Maybe this is why.

He is pushing one of those distance measuring wheels.

"He must be measuring the PFT route," I say to Zero.

"Why don't they make us run down the straight road and back? It's nice and flat," she replies.

"There's no swimming in the PFT," I say, referencing the puddle. "This will also give him something to do that's not bollocking us when the CO turns up."

"It could be like the steeplechase run with the water jump bit," she says, laughing.

The rest of the day is spent writing a few letters home, reading and generally lazing about. Word gets round that Smeggy Thompson has brought his hair clippers with him and is offering haircuts for 5DM[64] a go. I should really say "haircut" and not "haircuts", as this implies that there's more than one style on offer. There isn't, and, in the spirit of Henry Ford, you may have any haircut you like as long as it's a Grade 2 all over.

It'll do while I'm out here, I think to myself, so I wander off to his pop-up barber shop.

He's put a few chairs in one of the wider corridors for waiting customers and has another for the victim to sit in. He even has a radio tuned into a really annoying BFBS[65] presenter who likes the sound of his own voice.

"Take a seat. I'll be with you in a minute," he says, as I gingerly wander up.

He's getting through everyone at a fair old pace, as his style on offer doesn't take too long to do.

I take my place in the chair as he looms over me.

"Same as everybody else," I say, *"grade zwie, alles uber."*

His first sweep is straight down the middle of my head, which

---

64 Deutschmarks. 1 Deutschmark was worth about 30p back then.

65 British Forces Broadcasting Service.

makes me look like I have a negative Mohican.

As he lines up for the next one, the lights in the corridor go off, Smeggy's clippers fall silent and the annoying DJ on the radio gives us a break.

"You have to be shitting me," I say.

Smeggy, with his hand still in position ready to continue, says, "Err."

I touch my head with my hand and right down the middle I feel a great big trench.

Smeggy bursts into laughter and reaches for his mirror. Holding it in front of me, I see that I look like a total knob.

Power cuts are frequent at Dalma and can last from a few minutes to the best part of the day. They do have back-up generators, but they are only to power the computers in the Operations Room.

"We have to go to the Ops Room, then," I say. "I can't stay like this."

Smeggy, still laughing, says, "You could always wear your helmet." The guys waiting in line are also cracking up in fits of laughter.

Then the lights flicker on, Smeggy's clippers burst into life and the radio resumes the annoying DJ, which is the only time I am glad to hear his voice.

Smeggy finishes the rest of my trim without another power cut. He shows me the back of my head with his mirror, just to look like a proper barber. A Grade 2 is pretty short and there's not a lot you can do with it. I nod in agreement and he then sweeps my neck and shoulders with a brush from a dustpan. "What the fuck," I say, pulling away from it. "What's it been used to brush up recently?"

"It's clean, it's clean, don't worry. It's not the one we use to sweep up the cigarette butts outside with. Fucking hell, I'm not a minging barber you know," says Smeggy, the man who drinks from fire buckets. I pass him a 5DM coin and rub my head with my hand. Feeling the fine sharp bristles is always a rather pleasant sensation. I wander back off to my bunk to get my towel for a shower to remove the itchy bits of hair.

A while later, the power goes off again and I hear laughing coming from the corridor. I know precisely what scene is playing out down there. My curiosity makes me investigate and I am not to be disappointed. There is Geordie Munchester, who had waited a bit too long for a haircut, and Smeggy, clippers in hand, laughing. He was halfway through when the power went. The right side of Geordie's head looks smart and the left side looks like he's been in a tornado. Normally this wouldn't get a laugh, but with the roulette of "How long will the power be off?" it's hilarious.

Smeggy looks like he's having an asthma attack and everyone else is crying with laughter, including Geordie. Cheezy Cheesebourgh is rolling around on the floor, unable to breathe.

"You could play two characters at the local theatre," I say.

Geordie eventually gives up waiting at Smeggy's barbers and heads back to the accommodation to more howls of laughter. From my bunk, it's simple to deduce his location in the large room based on the laughter which reveals his whereabouts as he roams around.

Someone shouts, "You two-faced Geordie bastard," which receives torrents of more laughing.

In the end, the power stays off for another four hours.

Just after 1300, Del turns up asking if I fancy going to the beach for a maybe a swim and deffo a pivo. "I dunno if I can be arsed walking down there," is my reply to his tempting proposition.

"Ish is off to the airport in the coach soon and he says he'll drop us off at the bottom of the road," says Del.

The offer, which is too good to refuse, makes me spring out of my pit like I've realised there's a massive spider somewhere in my bed. I am packed and ready to go in under three seconds.

"He's leaving about 1400," he says and I crash back on to my pit like an exhausted man.

"Yeah, I'll still go, come and get me nearer the time," I tell him.

We bump into Ish as we are making our way over to where two coaches are parked. There must be 30 people milling around them, waiting for a lift.

"Fuck me, Del, how many did you tell I'd give a lift to?" says Ish.

"It's not like you're going in a Lanny now, is it," replies Del? "Just trying to be efficient and all that."

As Ish First Parades the coach, we pile on like excited schoolkids going off on a day trip to Alton Towers.

As we are about to set off, Jimmy Frazer comes walking over and indicates to Ish to open the doors.

"Aff yea git, it's nee a bloody taxi service," he says to us.

"No, it's a bus service," shouts Careless from the back.

"AFF," shouts Jimmy, glaring menacingly at Careless..

We trudge back off the bus, griping at Jimmy's insistence that we can't cadge a lift down the road.

A few of the guys admit defeat and head back to the accommodation, but we are still up for it.

"He's a bloody Judas," says an annoyed Careless.

We laugh and from this day on, Sergeant Jimmy Frazer was thereafter known as Judas Frazer. It was almost a 'where were you when it happened?' moment which went down in the comical history book of the Regiment. It was used so much by everyone that even newly-posted members to the Regiment, including JNCOs, SNCOs and Officers alike, thought Judas was his real name.

We walk down the straight road, and, as we get closer to the First & Last, Del says, "I'm not going in there again. He's stopped giving away free chips, the bloody tight Libyan dictator."

Colonel Gaddafi is smoking a cigarette while chatting to his friend. He sees us, looks up and shouts to us, "Hi guys, I've got cold pivos."

"But no free chips," Del shouts back.

He looks back confused and, being a businessman who's happy to let an opportunity pass him by, he returns to not giving a shit whilst continuing to talk to his mate.

We arrive at the beach and the group splits up. Some carry on to the bar at the harbour, a few wheel off to the bar on the beach and the remainder of us carry on to the beach. Towels out and T-shirts off, we pile into the invigorating, still chilly Adriatic. Within five minutes, we are back out of the water on the beach, shivering and drying ourselves off. I sit with my towel over my shoulders and stare out to sea at the island of Brac in the hazy distance. I have a minute to think to myself and wonder if I could swim over there.

"Bar?" suggests a bored sounding Del.

"I just need a minute. I'm contemplating life, the universe and what it all means."

I pause for a second. "Contemplating done. Let's get us a beer."

Del joins a few others at a table who are already through a round of beers, while I go to the bar.

"Two pivos please, pal," I say to the barman, putting a 10DM note on the bar.

"No problem," is his reply, as he fishes them from the cooler.

"Are you in the picture?" I ask him, pointing to the one with the soldiers posing with the tank.

"Yes, yes, I am," he replies. He points to himself sitting on the back of the tank. I see he's a lot younger-looking in the photo.

"That was my unit until I was injured," he says, now bringing my attention to his leg, which is heavily scarred around his knee and thigh.

"Gunshot?" I simply reply.

"Yes, but no bone damage though, so I don't need a stick like an old man," he remarks, breaking into a laugh.

"Thanks for the pivo," I say to him, laughing nervously, as I return to the table.

Later in the afternoon, we are walking back up the straight road and trying to decide if we will stop at the First & Last for a late afternoon cap. We see the puddle ahead and someone is in it splashing as if they're having a fit.

"Who the fuck is that?" says Del.

"I dunno, but he's gonna regret it," I reply.

As we get closer, we see it's Smeggy laying in the brown water, doing a terrible impression of the front crawl.

"He's pissed as a fart," says Prat. "Must have been celebrating his new haircutting business venture."

"We have to get him out," I say, "we can't leave him in there."

"He might get picked for the Regimental septic tank swimming team," says Del. "Let's see if he does any other strokes and we can enter him in the freestyle race."

"He'll be havin' a stroke if he's swallowed any of dat water," says Prat.

"SMEGGY," shouts Prat. "Your time is up. Yer need to exit der pool."

He looks up, sees us and gets up.

"Whaaay, lads, let's go for a pivo," he says, with brown filthy water streaming down his legs, which makes him appear like he's got a critical case of the shits. His T-shirt was once white, but no more.

"Come on, Smeggy," I say as we try to coax him from the puddle.

He staggers towards us, and immediately we back away as his feet splash through the liquid.

"I want a pivo," he says.

"Yeah, we'll get you a pivo," exclaims Del.

The only time I've ever hoped for the First & Last to be closed is today. Once we are closer, I see the door to the garden is shut and there's no one sitting outside. We breathe a collective sigh of relief at not having the added hassle of trying to keep a stinking, pissed soldier out of a bar.

He stands at the closed gate and wails, "I WANT A PIVO."

"Come on, Smeggy, we'll get you a pivo back at camp once we've cleaned you up," says Del.

Taking turns, we manage to steer him, without touching him, the entire way to the warehouse and smuggle him back in past the Guardroom. It's straight to the shower Corimec, and he's chucked in fully clothed for a good rinse.

Nobody wants to go anywhere near him, so we put a squirt of shampoo on his head and hope he'll sort of clean himself up. We get him to his bunk, he collapses on to his pit, and he falls asleep instantly. The next day he says he had a great night's kip, and apart from a small headache, he's feeling fit as a fiddle.

Any normal person would have been hospitalised after going into the reeking puddle of unknown diseases, but not Smeggy.

Drive me to the Moon, and Back and Back Again

I am on the fuel run-up to Lipa in a 22,500-litre TTF, one of many in convoy for today's trip. Last Friday, they filled up the TTFs at the refinery in Ploče, and now we will be moving our cargo of diesel up to the Lipa BFI.[66] The trucks are lined up, and I am paired with Geordie Munchester, who's now sporting a haircut which is at least equal in length all over his head. We are both still laughing over the amount of time he had to wait for the power to come back on. We've had the brief on the route and the first stop will be at the Kamensko BXP. This is Geordie's initial task up country and he is obviously quite excited. Hannibal appears, walking along the line of tankers, checking if we have our weapons, and saying we'll be departing in a minute. We hold them up so he can see them and he gives us the

66 Bulk Fuel Installation.

thumbs-up back so we know that he's happy. We crawl up Split hill in the fully laden tankers, with buses and trucks also having a go at overtaking us that morning.

Most of the vehicles, including ours, are belching smoke out as the engines work hard to overcome gravity. The smoke from our vehicles is least white while the local trucks and buses is dirty black. The white smoke indicates we possibly have a coolant leak, and it's getting into the cylinders. We're not really surprised, as most of the fleet smokes like this. If we could find an area big enough, we could drive eight abreast and look like a crap Red Arrows. The black smoke from the local traffic shows a lack of cash for maintenance and they'll keep running them until they die. The sun is out, and it's still cool as we drive along Route Gull through the villages. Geordie is quiet, and he is taking in the unfamiliar surroundings. Just outside the village of Dugopolji, as we slow for a sharp bend, a load of armed Croatian soldiers come crashing out of the wood line onto the road. I glance down at them as I pass, and they don't even acknowledge me driving past in this convoy. They are carrying a variety of weapons, including sniper rifles. A few of them are in ghillie suits,[67] which make them appear like green Chewbaccas.

"Did you see them?" I ask Geordie.

"See what?" he replies as he's looking through his window.

"There was a load of Croatian squaddies armed to the teeth back there."

He leans forward to gaze in the wing mirror on his side, "Naaah, I can't see anything."

He sits back in his seat again.

"You been swigging Sleep in the Ditch again," he adds.

"Have I been drinking what?" I ask him.

---

67 It's camouflage clothing made from loose strips of material made to look like twigs and leaves.

"Sleep in the Ditch," he says, looking at me as if I should know. "The local firewater, moonshine, Slivovitz, Sleep in the Ditch."

"Ah, I see," I say. "I've not tried it yet."

"It's awful, tastes like petrol."

"What situation were you in which found you drinking petrol?"

"I've never drunk petrol, but I suspect that if petrol was available as a drink, then it would taste like Sleep in the Ditch."

"Why's it called Sleep in...?" I pause as my brain catches up and answers my own question. "Don't worry, I've worked it out."

At Trilj, we turn right, following the sign for Route Gull that will take us to the border. It's uphill from this point to the BXP into Bosnia. We pass speeding convoys of different NATO nations coming the other way, going down faster than we are moving up. A convoy of our own DROPS vehicles passes us, and we recognise them as they have the small florescent Squadron emblem in the top left-hand of their windscreens. I glimpse my mate Shaun Gilsenan – Gilly or Gilsteamin – driving the front vehicle as he whizzes by. He was the first person I met when I was posted into the Regiment. I've not seen him for days, so I presume he's been up country for a while. He's a proper nutter with a black belt in Karate and a love for beer, and that mix can be a bloody nightmare. He'll get you in a gentle choke hold - his words, not mine - and keep you there until just before the point of unconsciousness. He once gave someone a black eye by sucking their eye socket. I think I'll try to catch up with him this evening, as I now know he's back at Dalma today. I hope it's not over a drink, otherwise a trip to the medical centre might be on the cards.

The tanker is right-hand drive, so, while I give a cursory wave to each passing vehicle, Geordie leans out of his window and screams at them, like he's a madman, "Did you have some Sleep in the Ditch on your cornflakes this morning?"

We pull up to the border crossing and steer off the road. It's out of the cab to stretch the legs and I get Geordie to do the Halt Parade while I go looking for a toilet or bush. I notice the RMP Corimec has a Portaloo behind it. Ignoring the incorrectly spelt sign which says, 'RMP Detachment Personal Only', I dive in and relieve myself.

We continue up Route Gull, past the big lake, and on towards TSG. Geordie sees his first signs of the war as we pass the empty damaged houses and says, "It reminds me of home."

I laugh at this unexpected remark.

As we pass more and more houses that have been damaged, he says, "I feel bad about making the joke now. It's quite sad to see.

"Every house we pass was a home to people who would have enjoyed the same things as us. They'd have gone to work, visited friends, had parties and watched the TV in those houses and seen the news of their world slowly heading for this looming catastrophe coming their way."

He stares silently out of the window for the remainder of the journey.

Upon reaching TSG, I now remember exactly where we turn right on to Route Kite as the way is now becoming familiar. Then it's past the battle bus and the final leg to Lipa Camp. On entering the camp, I follow the convoy through some barbed wire fencing and over to a part I've not been to before. Off to our left is the BFI, which is a network of massive black rubber storage tanks that are more like great, gigantic bags. Each one is dug into the ground with a bank of earth surrounding them. I don't know if this is for protection from incoming fire, or to catch any leaks, or both, if the latter is caused by the former. They're connected to one another by a web of pipes of differing sizes in diameter. There is a collection of big bags of dirt within metal cages down the end of the BFI stacked in neat lines two high. I see these are placed around the Corimecs and I do know these are definitely protection from incoming bits of hostile metal. There are lots of shipping containers next to the Corimecs and they are not protected by anything, so I presume this is what the BFI came in, in its kit form. We pull up and stop, still in convoy, and climb down from our cab. I notice it's becoming quite windy, which is strong enough to pick up the dust and small bits of dirt. I feel a slight sting as they hit my face. Covering my eyes with my hand, I remember the pair of goggles I was issued for such occasions sitting in my locker back at the warehouse. I head to the back of the tanker and get the earthing spike out. At least here I can force it into the soft ground with my foot.

Geordie has attached the other earthing clamp and is now struggling with the thick pipe as he tries to attach it to the outlet valve on the fuel pump compartment. In this wind, he appears like he's having a fight with an enormously long snake in a movie. After we attach it, we wait for one of the BFI operators to come along and check that we are properly connected. Once he's happy, he instructs us to fill him up. I jump into the cab and engage the PTO. I then hear the engine note change as Geordie pulls the outflow knob and we begin pumping our diesel. It takes about 15 minutes to unload our 22,500 litres. There are seven of us tankers, so that's a total of 157,500 litres now in the BFI.

I get my pen and notebook out to do some maths to pass the time and I work out the following. My car has a 55-litre tank, and our total fuel load today would fill up my car 2,863 times. I get about 500 miles from a tankful of fuel, so I'd be able to drive 1,431,500 miles, which is three return trips to the Moon. That sounds quite impressive until you realise this one fuel load would last an armoured battle group one day. The modern military machine is a thirsty one, and without the fuel it's about as much use as my dust goggles right now

.

Polish it Out

A rumour spread around the warehouse last night that there's a PFT this morning in place of the normal PT session. It is part of our MATTs[68] of which we have to do other subjects such as First Aid, NBC,[69] and the APWT.[70] The latter is a day on the ranges ensuring we can shoot at least with some degree of accuracy and we are able to handle a weapon safely. NBC, which is comprised of dressing up in chemical warfare kits, practicing decontamination, how to eat, drink and sometimes how to take a crap. The general consensus during this part of the training is if we ever found ourselves in a deadly NBC environment, we'd hold it in. The SSM has the job to ensure everyone's up to date with their training. A week is normally set aside to get everyone ticked off his list. Since we have deployed on this operational tour, all our training is up to date, but the PFT is required to be done twice a year. Of all the subjects, there is a huge emphasis put on this fitness test. I mentioned earlier that individuals' careers can be judged based on their performance on the test. The same can't be said about the other subjects. If it's a range day, you're a terrible shot, and it's late in the day, the 5.56mm pen will appear. The unquestionable evidence of a few holes in the right place will ensure a couple of things. Your name is now ticked off the list and another day on the ranges doesn't have to be organised just for you. If you can't make the NBC training, don't worry, your name will be on a list somewhere. The amount of emphasis placed on the PFT is such that Mr Burns once declared he'd changed the official time allowed and taken 30 seconds off for everyone. He got around this without having to rewrite the training document by

68 Military Annual Training Test.

69 Nuclear, Biological and Chemical.

70 Annual Personal Weapons Test.

calling it 'Polish Time'. This was in reference to the Regiments' Polish connections. The normal protocol when failing the PFT was to be allowed another attempt. If you failed, you would find yourself on remedial PT until you could show you could pass at least a few in a row. If you came in over your 'Polish Time', you were simply put on 'extra' PT. With the remedial group.

We gather outside the warehouse and almost everyone is there, including Pippen the Chicken, Mr Burns and Buckethands. The only way to get out of this is to either be on guard duty or dead. There is an air of nervousness as Lance Corporal 'Dodgy Daz' Dankworth the PTI[71] walks along the line with his clipboard in hand, taking everyone's name.

Dodgy Daz was a Driver like us, but he'd undertaken the PTI course. Many members of the Regiment did, so we'd always have someone qualified to get us to a point of physical exhaustion. He'd become known as 'Dodgy', as he was always out to make a quick quid. Every time I see him, and I see him most days, he's driving a different car as one of his side hustles is buying and selling cars. He has the gift of the gab and somehow always sells the cars he buys for a profit. *[I heard about him years later, while he was still serving. He had built himself a mini empire of burger vans dotted about on military ranges, feeding hungry soldiers who were on their range days.]*

Some are standing still, not looking particularly bothered, while some jog on the spot, shaking their arms with an anxious appearance about themselves. "Regiment," shouts Dodgy Daz. We stop chattering between ourselves, "Regimeeeeeent, shun."

We spring to attention and there is complete silence.

Dodgy Daz turns to Mr Burns and says, "Sir, do I have your permission to carry on?"

"Please do," replies Mr Burns.

71 Physical Training Instructor.

"Regimeeeeeent, stand at," he pauses, then bellows, "ease."

Dodgy Daz explains what we already know, that the PFT will consist of a 1.5 mile run as a squad around the route. It will then be the same route, but an individual best effort run in under 10 minutes and 30 seconds. Those of us lucky enough to be over 30, or a female, have a little longer. For every five years you are over the age of 30, you get an extra 30 seconds. He explains this is a new route and has been measured out and is exactly the required distance.

"Regimeeeeeent will turn to the right in threes, riiiiiiiight turn," barks Dodgy Daz.

We snap to the right. There is the usual extra movement as someone can't tell their left from their right. They turn the wrong way and then immediately the right way to match the rest of the Regiment.

"Sirs, if you'd like to fall in at the rear," says Dodgy Daz to the SNCOs and Officers, but mainly to Mr Burns.

We head off around the new route, passing the rabid guard dog, which makes everyone jump as we pass it for the first time. Returning to the warehouse as one squad, Dodgy Daz halts us and informs us we are about to start the best effort part of the test. We break from the squad and jostle for a frontline position on the starting line.

Dodgy Daz holds his hand in the air and then shouts, "Three, two, one, gooooo!" As his hand drops, he starts his stopwatch.

There are the customary sprinters straight off the line. It's made up of the ones who are fast and will disappear in the distance, and the ones who are not, but think a sprint off the line is the best option. They burn out in less than a few hundred metres. The rest of us are the plodders, and we follow on, passing the exhausted sprinters. I spot someone ahead who has now cautiously slowed a little on the second pass of Cujo.[72] We continue snaking around the route

---

72 A Stephen King book & film about a huge rabid Saint Bernard dog.

and I am, as always, in the second half, as a pass is a pass. Mr Burns is a quite a fit guy and is a little way ahead of me, but I don't want to expend any more energy to catch him. The last dash to the finish line is always a sprint, hoping to get you in under your allotted time. As I round the last bend, Dodgy Daz comes into sight with his stopwatch and clipboard. If you pass, you are normally directed to one side and if you fail to the other. I see a few already on one side and more on the other. My heart sinks as I already know I've failed. I still make a dash for the line to the shouts of encouragement from the ones who have finished.

I'm directed to the right, into the line of disgrace, and I squat down, trying to catch my breath while my body recovers from the ordeal. My breathing is still heavy as I try to fill my depleted body with oxygen. I stand up to see most of the Regiment, including Mr Burns and quite a few racing snakes, are in the failure gang. They have looks of disbelief on their faces and a few are now asking and are even hassling Dodgy Daz, like a referee who's disallowed a goal, if it's correct.

I bump into a sweaty Del and Prat, who are in the career-ending crowd with me.

"It's fecking hilarious," says Del. "Look at them all, they look like they are gonna cry." He indicates the Roger Bannisters amongst us who'd never failed a PFT in their entire career.

"The distance wasn't right," says Prat. "I'm about a minute slower than normal."

"I agree, even I would have to take a month off PT with remedial eating and boozing to get that time."

"I wonder what they'll do?" replies Prat.

"It'll just be another one next week," says Del.

It turned out that Rat-Face had got the distance wrong, so the PFT was declared null and void. Of all the people we wanted to cock this up, he would have been in the top one. I think the thing which swayed the decision to make it invalid was simply because Mr Burns was on it and the CO cannot be seen to fail. We didn't see Rat-Face much after that debacle. I presume he'd been too embarrassed to show his face and was lying low. Maybe he'd experienced the displeasure of Mr Burns and given some crappy task which didn't involve determining distances.

Del finishes the morning off with some wise words which have us in bouts of laughter. "Mr Burns should have released that fecking massive hound. We'd have passed in Polish, Croatian or any Eastern European time."

Do the Quake and Vac

I have a day without tasks, so it means a morning of trying to hide from Judas and Buckethands. Hannibal is also about and asks me to go to First Parade the remaining fleet of tankers, even though they won't be going anywhere today. It's hard work staying back at camp as there isn't anything to do. We had built a troop rest area outside the MT Offices with a 12x12 tent.[73] We'd only used the roof bit to give us some cover from the sun. Someone had got a few benches and a table and placed them in there too, so we'd have somewhere to sit about when bored. In hindsight, it was a bad idea, as Judas could now find us a lot more easily, so nobody used it.

I am down at the bottom of the vehicle park next to the fruit market. The stink from the fruit which is fermenting away in the big metal bins is rank. It's still better than being told to mop up a leaking Corimec or paint something in the Regimental colours. I take my time going from one tanker to another, trying to drag the

---

73 It's called a 12x12 tent, because when it's erected, it's 12 foot, by 12 foot.

time out. I'm sitting in the cab of a 12,500-litre TTF minding my own business and daydreaming when I feel the tanker bounce slightly. There is a ladder on the back to enable you to climb up to access the filling hatches on the top. I look round and down the back of the fuel tank, expecting to see Del, Prat, or anyone who isn't out that day. I can't see anyone, but I can feel the tanker is now gently bouncing, as if someone is on it, jumping up and down on it. There's still no one visible, so I glance in the wing mirrors to observe who is messing around. There's still nobody on or around the tanker, and I look back out of the front of the cab, trying to work out what's happening. The brown muddy puddle is dancing about and full of ripples. I stare at it, mesmerised, striving to work out what I am looking at when I realise we are having an earthquake. I stay in the tanker as it continues to bounce about for a further ten seconds, and then it stops. The ripples in the puddle now rebound around it and run out of energy, and calm returns to the muddy brown water. I glance at the rear of the tanker and notice it is now motionless. I spot some commotion up by the MT Offices. A few people spill out of the front door whilst looking back at the building, and I ponder if it's about to collapse. I wonder if the warehouse has fallen down into an enormous pile of dust, as that would be an improvement to its current state.

I decide to wander up to the MT Offices out of sheer boredom and listen to everyone's account of where they were at the time and how they survived the earthquake. They have gone back into the building by the time I get to the front door, as they've realised it's not going to fall down on top of their heads. I walk up the fake marble stairs and to the upstairs corridor. A tiny bit of dust lightly sprinkles the hard-wearing dark carpet, resembling a minor accident with talcum powder. I hear the expected commotion emanating from Judas's office, and I slowly put my head around his door.

"Ahh," says Judas, far too quickly as he sees me. "Just the man."

I know a shit job is coming my way now, and I let out a groan.

"The Croatian Cleaners ave done one fee the day. Can ye git the Hoover and give the offices a once-over as they're all covered in basta dust from the tremor."

I knew I should have stayed down by the tankers, but my curiosity has got the better of me. I struggle to get the Hoover out of the cupboard. I then have to fight to detangle its spaghetti-like power cord. Pushing the cheap-looking plug into the sockets, I wonder if I'm about to meet my demise at the hands of a faulty 220 volt ex-Yugoslav Hoover. I flick the on button, and there's no puff of smoke, and the lights in the building stay on, which is a good start. I try to keep my hands away from anything metal on it for fear of electrocution. It makes the most awful high-pitched racket while simultaneously producing an electrical burning smell. It succeeds in sucking up one atom at a time, thus making me go over the same spot several times to make the dust look like I've even attempted to clear it up. It looks more as if I'm moving the dust around on the carpet. I take a simple pleasure from being the creator of noise and gleefully whirl into Pippen the Chicken's office whilst he's on the phone.

"CAN'T YOU COME BACK LATER?" he shouts at me, looking annoyed, with one hand over the receiver.

I carry back out on to the corridor, as the Hoover is still making its God-awful, high-pitched din. I go to enter Buckethands' office.

He just shouts "FUCK OFF!" at me, so I continue on my way, eager to ensure I piss everyone off to the point where I get told to go away. "ALRITE, ALRITE, THAT'S ENOUGH!" shouts Judas at me.

I flick the off button and there's instant relief from the deafening assault on my ears. My hoovering effort has made very little impact on the removal of the dust and a very large impact on the hierarchy's ability to function.

"Jist ge' back tae whut ye were doin' before," says Judas.

Mission accomplished, I think to myself.

"I could just do the corridor," I say to Judas.

"Dinna bother, I'll git the duty POL tae dee it teenite."

I chuck the Hoover back in its cupboard and tie the cable back up in knots for whoever will be unlucky enough to clean up this evening.

Ayrton Mail

I arrive at the MT Offices that morning expecting another day of trying to hide from work, and I am pleasantly surprised by some news from Judas.

"Gee and git yer kit, yir on a post-run up tae Kupres wit DROPS Troop this mornin'."

This is welcome news to me, because I'll have another day off camp and I get to drive a DROPS again. Which is like being in the 21st century. I head down the corridor to their office to get some more details and find out who I will be going with. I am told it'll be Lance Corporal Manbat. Manbat is so called because his name is Wayne Bruce. Simple, effective and funny. He's always laughing, loves a good innuendo, and is a general all-round good egg.

I track him down on their vehicle park and he's already in the process of getting the tools onto the DROPS trucks. "Manbat," I say to get his attention. "I'm with you today up to Kupres."

"Great news," he replies, laughing. "It's just us, two DROPS trucks, no co-drivers, and the post is in the shipping container on the back. Piss easy."

"Super duper," I reply. "I do love a simple job."

"Have you been to Kupres before?"

"Nope, my first time. I've been as far as TSG."

"No probs. Turn right up Split Hill onto Route Gull. Keep going past TSG, and if you get to a tunnel that goes through a mountain, you've gone too far."

"Sounds complicated."

"It's a three-plus-hour drive each way. We'll do the usual stop at Kamensko BXP to say hi to the Monkeys[74] and crack on."

"I'll go and get my gear and be back as quick as I can."

"Cool beans, I'll get your truck tooled up and have the work tickets sorted so we can shoot off as soon as."

I hurry back over to the warehouse to collect my webbing, helmet and body armour. I spend at least ten minutes searching for the duty armourer so I can get my weapon. He's supposed to be in the QM's Department Offices, but he's not. I find him out at the back. He's chatting up one of the stacker[75] girls with a cigarette hanging out of his gob and a cup of tea in his hand.

I walk back towards the vehicle park in a slight hurry, as I don't want to keep Manbat hanging around. But not too fast, as I know he's quite laid back. I still manage to get a sweat on in the morning warmth. He's waiting for me at the front of the two DROPS and says, "We're all booked out and ready to go."

I nod and say, "OK, I'll just need a minute to First Parade the truck."

"Already done," he replies immediately.

I then have a premonition of the truck breaking down because of the engine having insufficient oil. I then have to lie to Pippen the Chicken, telling him I checked the oil because I didn't want to drop Manbat in the shit even if it was of his own doing.

"I'll just check the oil, mate," I say to him.

Dropping my kit by the door, I pop the front hood that the dip-

---

74 British Army slang for the Royal Military Police.

75 British Army Slang for a Storeman.

stick is behind. I pull out the metre-long dipstick to check if the oil is where it should be. It is, so I slide it back in and close the hood. I then go around to the driver's door, open it and put my weapon on the floor of the cab. It's quite a climb up into the cab, but I manage without any of my gear falling off my shoulder. I place it in the spacious back and reach down for my gun. As I look up, I see Manbat is already off and turning out of the camp onto the road.

"Fucking hell," I mutter to myself and start the engine. The door is still open and I haven't even got my seatbelt on as I put the gear selector in Drive. With my left hand, I slam the door shut and then grapple with the seatbelt as I bounce across the vehicle park. I can see Manbat disappearing off down the straight road and out of sight. With my seatbelt now in place, I turn onto the straight road and floor it. I have Manbat back in my sights, but he's got a good distance on me. I see the predictable brown water fountain, as he's not slowing down for anyone. Not wanting to lose him, I keep my foot firmly pressed down on the accelerator as it becomes my turn to navigate the puddle. A white Fiat 126 ventures onto my side of the road to the shallower part. It then stops, as I presume he realises I'm not slowing down. He stops at the water's edge in the middle of the road. The DROPS vehicle is a sizeable piece of kit. I can only imagine that from the driving seat of one of those tiny Fiats it must look gargantuan. Especially with a shipping container poking up from behind the cab. I am close enough now that I can see the expressions of the man with the cigarette in his mouth, desperately trying to find reverse gear. As I enter the puddle, he is now out of the way, but I see his window is open. Just in the right position for a free car wash and a cigarette extinguishing service. *[I reflect on this years later and like to think we were really the forerunner of the Croatian Ministry of Health's anti-smoking campaign.]*

Manbat doesn't stop as he turns onto Route Gannet towards Split Hill. When I get to the junction, there's traffic coming from both directions, which will increase our gap even further. I notice at this point that the wing mirror on the passenger side is too far in. It doesn't give me a view down the right-hand side of the vehicle. The cab is so vast there's no way I can reach across to adjust it. As I hesitate, I'm thinking I might be able to do it while waiting for the traffic. Just as I am about to undo my seatbelt, a car coming from the right turns off the road, presenting me with a gap. I go for it and can sort of slide into the traffic on the opposite side of the road, using my vehicle size as persuasion. I gain applause from the locals, and they use their horns of appreciation. He's now even further down the road and disappears around a bend. I don't see him again until I'm halfway up Split Hill. By now, he's over the other side of the valley as the road follows the contours of the steep terrain.

I continue the rest of the trip, getting the odd glimpse of him in the distance. The DROPS' top speed, limited to 80kph, prevents me from catching him. If he's going flat out, then so am I, and I can't close the distance. I know roughly where I am going up to TSG. I know I'll catch him up at the Kamensko BXP, but I'm more concerned about what will happen if I break down. He'll be clueless to my fate, and I'll have to wait for him to come back. Which will be hours before he realises I'm not behind him anymore.

Arriving at the border, I breathe a sigh of relief to see his DROPS still there, parked up on the side of the road by the Monkey hut.

I pull up behind him, apply the handbrake, and switch off the engine. I feel knackered from having to concentrate on driving a faster truck and trying not to let the gap between us increase anymore. Driving the TTFs up here was more like a relaxed sightseeing trip because of their slow speed crawling up the hills. The DROPS will still do 80kph uphill, even while carrying a modest load and today's load was just the mail so it wasn't struggling.

I grab my weapon and climb down from the cab and hear Manbat say, "Ready to push on?"

"Jesus, give us a break. What's the hurry, Ayrton?" I ask him.

"I'm not in a rush," he replies. "Who the hell is Ayrton?"

"Ayrton Senna, the Formula 1 driver."

Manbat laughs. "I've been driving this route every day since we arrived. I could do it in my sleep. In fact, I dream of it most of the time."

"You'll get a speeding ticket," I say in reference to the Monkeys who often hide round bends to catch the unaware driver just like Manbat.

Manbat stayed on this job for a while longer and, unsurprisingly he did get collared by the Monkeys for speeding. They took his details and passed them back to the Regiment for Pippen the Chicken to begin disciplinary action against him for this offence. He remained cool as a cucumber throughout the entire episode. He was marched in front of Pippen the Chicken and the charge was read out to him that he was doing 75kph in a 40kph zone. When quizzed about it, he claimed he didn't know it was a 40kph zone, as there were no road signs. The Monkeys can sometimes be sneaky but not that sneaky, which obviously would leave them open to the charges being dropped. In light of this additional evidence, Pippen the Chicken assigned Lieutenant Barton to drive to the alleged offence location and determine the presence or absence of road signs. He reported back, after an extensive exploration of the section of road, that he could not find any road signs showing a 40kph zone existed. They dismissed the case. Manbat walked out of Pippen the Chicken's office to threats from Buckethands that he knew he was a guilty bastard and he would catch him one day. The mystery was revealed one drunken evening later in the tour. Manbat knew he would be on the same task for a while yet and came up with a plan so simple, it would be worthy of an MBE. If it weren't a crime. He patiently waited for a Sunday, as there would be less traffic on the road, to put his plan into operation. On his way back to Split, he made sure he was the rear vehicle of the convoy. Purposely driving slower, he let himself fall back from the vehicle in front. By the time he reached the section of road where the speed limit sign was, he was the only person and vehicle there. He stopped in front of the troublesome sign and reversed his DROPS back, right up close to it. He calmly waited, listening out for any traffic. With no one in earshot, he quickly attached a ratchet strap from his tow hook to the pole which the 40kph sign was fastened to. With a little press of the accelerator, the DROPS moved forward. It effortlessly bent the post over and snapped it clean off from its base. He manhandled the post, with its attached 40Kph sign, into the cab and set off again. A few miles down the road, he pulled over once more and launched it out of the window, into a deep ravine, never to be seen again.

I keep Manbat at the border for a few more minutes as I readjust my wing mirror before he's jumping around like an excited child wanting to depart again. As the BXP disappears from both of my wing mirrors, I see a few spots of rain on the windscreen. The sky darkens as we progress on and the few spots become more spots. As it changes from dry to wet, the tarmac road transforms into a darker version of itself. Our big, chunky, off-road tyres won't have much grip on the smooth wet surface of the road. I am relieved to see Manbat has now slowed down. I'm sure he doesn't want to test that the rusty crash barriers can stop a 15-ton DROPS truck from rolling down a steep hill. The familiar war-damaged buildings on the road between the big lake and TSG come into view. My gaze is again drawn to them as we pass. They appear considerably more depressing in the gloom. At TSG we turn right, past the battle bus. Then, not too far past it, we turn left onto the bypass with the word 'Gull' and an arrow unmistakably showing where to go. This is unfamiliar territory for me now as we head along the bypass, which normally would be a wide, bumpy dirt track. With the rain it's now a wide bumpy and muddy track. I bounce up and down in my sprung seat. My foot follows my up-and-down motion, thus bouncing on and off the accelerator, in turn making the DROPS lurch forward. My grip on the steering wheel stops me from being thrown around the cab too vigorously. I have to try either to jam the accelerator fully down or take my foot off it completely to keep the DROPS under some semblance of control. The bypass is, thankfully, only a few miles long, and it's good to get back on to the smoother road. I see the trails of brown mud my wheels leave behind on the tarmac road in my rear view mirrors. They become fainter as the rain and water on the road swills the mud from the tyres. The road ascends and typically follows the best route along the terrain, which produces lots of long sweeping bends. I see a convoy coming the other way and, although they are green, the vehicles don't look familiar. When I see the yellow number plates, I know straight away it's the Dutch Army. Every one of their drivers gives me a friendly wave and I wave back saying, "Well, hello there, scholdier," in a Dutch accent.

We arrive at a junction, without having to look for the words 'Route Gull' spray painted on the nearest flat surface. The faded yellow bullet-riddled road sign indicates it's right to Kupres, which is 25km away. This final stretch of road is now quite straight as it follows a very wide valley. The houses along this section are evenly spread out and are clearly uninhabited due to the severity of the damage. None of them have roofs and they have been peppered with bullets. The randomness of where the bullets struck looks more like vandalism than battle damage, and I guess this was more ethnic cleansing. In the pouring rain up here, it's very bleak. There's high ground to my left which is where the houses are. To my right, it's more like a moorland stretching off into the distance, disappearing into the rain. The houses are facing the same direction and it looks like they were built this way to get the best view. The view opens up on my left and is similar to the view on the other side. I see a huge pyramid or triangle-shaped building a few miles away, and I guess it is, or was, a hotel. It's too far off to see if it's damaged, but I suspect it is. Up ahead, far away, a building stands alone beside the road. As I get closer, I can see what looks like several tanks parked up around it. I can now make out that it's a former petrol station and, like every other structure round here, it's extensively damaged. The tanks turn out to be AS90s[76] from the Royal Artillery. The unhappy looking and wet guard gives me a wave as I pass. I wave back, muttering to myself, "I bet you wished you'd joined the RLC now, eh, mate?"

I see Kupres in the near distance and I am looking forward to a break. It's a rather small town with some drab-looking blocks of flats only a few storeys high in amongst the other buildings. I slow down as I approach the outskirts of town, which is just a pile of rubble which was once homes. The buildings are destroyed, with some still having rusty burnt-out cars in the driveway and wild gardens. Further on in and the destruction reduces. There are a few houses with the damage I have been used to seeing so far, except they have signs of life. Either a light shines dimly through the plastic-sheeting window in the dark of the day, or there's smoke coming from the chimney. There's a hill dominating the town and through the murky rain I can make out the large Croatian chequerboard coat of arms to which I have become accustomed. There's a large white cross on the ground above it, made out of lots of stones. It's hard to tell in this weather. Manbat puts his indicator on, veers right off the main road and onto a gravel track which initially runs parallel to it. I see the asphalt road we were on continuing on to the far side of town. It continues up the hill and disappears into the tunnel

76 They are not tanks but are self-propelled artillery. To the untrained eye they look like a tank but are in fact a huge 155mm gun on a lightly armoured tracked chassis. They are not designed to go up against other tank, but to rain shells down on the enemy from the safety of miles away. The armour only offers scant protection from small calibre rounds and shrapnel splinters.

which he mentioned earlier that morning. About a hundred metres down the gravel track, he again turns right and I see the main gate to Kupres camp.

The barrier is raised and I follow him in giving the guard a cursory nod of appreciation. Kupres camp is an industrial facility. There are no clues as to what it was before the war or before the British Army rented it from God-knows-who. In the middle is a large building – the Troop accommodation – which everything seems to have been built around. The scars of war are very limited here, with only the odd hole, from either a bullet or shrapnel, in the corrugated roof. We finally come to a halt by some Corimecs and I see the sign on the door informing everyone it's the Postal and Courier Detachment.

We both climb down from our cabs and he says, "Follow me."

He goes through the door of the Corimec and is greeted like an old friend even though they only saw him yesterday.

"Did you miss me," says Manbat,

"Whaaaay, Brucey," says one of the guys.

I make a note they are unaware of his nickname and wait for the right time to let them know.

The walls of the adjoining Corimecs have been knocked through, providing a lot of space to, I presume, throw letters and parcels all around the gaff. There is a counter at the front which gives the effect you're in a Post Office of sorts. At one end of it is a varnished wooden box. On it is a piece of A4 paper with the words 'Outgoing Mail' written in Times New Roman. On the walls are posters with pictures of stuff that isn't allowed to be sent in the mail. I notice it doesn't include cigarettes, which are available in abundance and cheaper than the postage back to the UK. Behind the counter are a few desks and lots of mail bags lying about. Some bags are hanging on a frame so they can chuck outgoing letters into them. Right at the back is their rest area. It is made up of a few soldiers sitting about

Dalma Warehouse in Split. The spiritual home of me and the other 500 noisy soldiers living there. I took this picture of it whilst on a holiday in 2018. It had become a cheese distribution warehouse. Oh how the mighty fall . . .

The DROPS truck. At last, a modern vehicle in the British Army's inventory that was easy to drive and in which you could have a decent sleep in the back

The mighty 22500-litre Foden Truck Tanker Fuel. It was a bit of a sod to drive, and it possibly should have consigned to a museum long before Tito passed away in 1980

The first signs of the war as we first crossed the border into Bosnia were possibly of ethnic cleansing

Some towns showed signs of heavy fighting

I can't remember who or what happened to this DROPS truck. Just another statistic showing how dangerous the driving was in Croatia and Bosnia

Every destroyed house I saw was a home to people who would have enjoyed the same things as us. They'd have gone to work, visited friends, had parties, and watched the TV in those houses and seen the news of their world slowly heading for this looming catastrophe

A Second World War M10 Achilles Tank Destroyer, based on the Sherman chassis, possibly knocked out but more likely abandoned due to mechanical failure or getting stuck

160

TITO's legacy was to be seen everywhere, even in the woods

The impressive Dinaric Alps that run through Croatia and Bosnia. They always gave majestic views but were a contributory factor to the dangerous roads

161

The tourist poster view of the Vrbas River that I had seen in my primary school many years before

Route Gull nearing Banja Luka. It was bumpy enough to dislodge the fillings from your teeth

Me getting in some practice for the Banja Luka Best Impression of I'm a Little Teapot competition whilst out on the roads in Bosnia

More pictures of my tour available via this QR code

The view of the outside world when travelling in business class in a Chinook

The old couple we met in the hills overlooking Sarajevo

on a mixture of furniture which looks like it's been salvaged from landfill.

"This is Scouse Lee," he says, introducing me to them.

"Hi, all," I say back to them, giving them a slight nod and a slightly slighter wave.

"He's just up with me for today," he says it as if it's not worth introducing anything to them other than my name.

A female Sergeant Postie[77] puts her jacket on, points at two of the guys lounging at the back of the room, and adds the words, "You two will do."

We pass her the keys to the shipping containers and go back outside into the rain. One of the guys wanders off around behind the Corimec and returns with a set of ladders. The shipping container is at least 1.5 metres off the ground. It overhangs the rear of the truck by a metre. Even Chris Bonington[78] would find it a challenge to climb up to undo the padlock. Ladders are deployed and up scurries one Postie. He calls out the anti-tamper number seal to the Sergeant. She checks it off the paperwork, so she knows we didn't pull over on the way up and steal some of the mail. She passes him up the keys and after inserting each one, with no luck, it's predictably the only one he hadn't tried which pops the heavy duty padlock open. He pulls the handles out and down on the container. Then he moves the ladders out of the way so we can open the doors fully, in jerking movements, as the hinges are probably rusted. The ladders are up, and he goes again into the container. We form a line and the bags of post are passed along and into the Corimec for further sorting.

We do the same with my container, and then we do it again in reverse with the outgoing mail that'll be taken back to Split. Most of the bags are relatively light, but some are somewhat heavy. One of

77 Members of the RLC Postal and Courier trade.

78 The only famous mountain climber I could think of.

them is passed to me and I sink under its weight.

"Are people sending rocks or bricks back home?" I say to no one in particular. The Posties laugh, as if they know the reason, but then carry on in silence, not letting me in on their little secret. I push the stiff door shut on my container. The ladders reappear, the other Postie zips up them and puts the padlock back in place. He refits a new anti-tamper seal and reads the number out for the Sergeant to note it down on the paperwork.

Now that we are done, we go on the scrounge for some food to the cookhouse. It's bang on time for lunch being served, so we join the queue. I go for a very welcoming cat's arse,[79] chips and beans, while Manbat goes for the spaghetti bolognese. We find a table, take a place and tuck in. One Postie clocks us and heads over to us.

"Mind if I join you, he says.

"Feel free," remarks Manbat, gesturing with his arm the choice of the free seats around us.

"Brucey," he exclaims, after sitting down. "Is this the only run you are doing at the moment, as we've seen you every day since we got here?"

"It's Manbat," I say.

The Postie looks at me confused and says, "Man what?"

"It's Manbat," I repeat. "His name is Manbat."

"Oh, for fuck's sake," says Manbat with his head almost in his spaghetti bolognese.

"It's Bruce isn't it?" says the Postie, looking a touch confused.

"That's his surname," I explain. "His first name is Wayne."

The Postie takes a second to compute what's he's just heard from me and then as the computation is complete, he bursts out laughing.

"Cheers, you fucking twat," says Manbat to me, somehow look-

---

79 Readers of my first book will be familiar with this, but, in case you've not read it yet, look at the end of a sausage roll and then look at a cats arse. You'll never unsee it now.

ing somewhat disenchanted while wearing a grin at the Posties reaction to his nickname.

"That's classic," says the Postie, still laughing and trying to eat his lunch at the same time, "wait until I tell the others."

"Dear God," groans Manbat, as he knows this isn't going to pass in a few days.

I heard through the grapevine they never let him forget this nickname for the duration of their tour. They also passed it on to the incoming Posties, who relieved them. They even sometimes dressed up as a 'Manbat' when he arrived. However, I'm still not too sure how you'd dress up as a 'Manbat' to this day.

We head back to our DROPS to ready ourselves for the drive back to Split. Manbat peels off to their Ops Room to call down to our Ops Room at Dlama to let them know we will soon be on our way back. This is just in case we don't turn up, then someone's aware we've gone missing on the road between Kupres and the Monkey hut. "Shall we mix it up on the way back?" says Manbat.

I am thinking his idea of mixing it up might be ramming me off the road as payback for letting the Posties know his nickname.

"Er, we can do," I say, hesitantly.

He climbs up into his cab, grabs the IFOR Route Map, drops back down and, with his finger, shows me his idea.

"Instead of following Route Gull, we can take Pelican to Livno, then Magpie, which will take us back to the Kamensko BXP. It's just a bit of different scenery, that's all."

"Sounds good," I say to his idea.

Then, spotting a potential flaw in his idea, I add, "Does the Ops Room know we're coming back on another route?"

"They didn't ask, and I didn't tell them," he says, shrugging his shoulders.

"There's two of us anyway, so safety in numbers," I say.

→» →» →»

It's still raining as we pull out of the main gate and retrace our journey back down Route Gull, passing the rubble-pile former houses, then the soaking-wet and pissed off-looking Royal Artillery guard at the garage and on to the smattering of empty homes. I recognise the junction where we would turn to stay on Route Gull as we cruise past it. The road now becomes Route Pelican. The road climbs and, with an enormous mountain now in front of us, I see the way heading to the right of it. We pass some Norwegian engineers driving dumper trucks loaded up with earth going the other way. Soon after, I see what must be the brow of the hill, as there's nothing but the grey sky above it. The landscape changes once again as we leave the steep rocky slopes of the mountain behind and it changes to a gently sloping grassed area. We drive past a tented camp whose sole purpose looked like it was to be constructed in the bleakest part of Bosnia. The rain is now coming down sidewards and I recognise the flag flying from the front of the camp as being the one belonging to Malaysia. Maybe they're in shock, as I imagine them huddled up in their tents, wondering what the hell they are doing here and dreaming of the warm weather back home. I'm sure they have a reason that they chose this spot to set up camp. It looks like the picture would be used as an example in the 'where not to pitch a load of tents if you were to find yourself in Bosnia' book. One big storm and the camp will be history. It's on the grass too, which I presume has been cleared of mines, but you never know. We have had it drummed into us again and again not to go onto the earth on the sides of the roads and stay on the hardstanding due to this threat.

Livno is in the distance and it's the usual mixture of houses and low apartment blocks. There's only light damage here, with a few bullet holes in the buildings. Livno, it seems, has avoided whatever had happened up in Kupres. We drive slowly through the town centre, and it has almost a feel of normality to it. There are a few cafés, which add a little bit of colour to the otherwise grey wet day, with their small neon signs above the door or placed in windows. I see inside one of them and get a glimpse of the few people within, sitting at the bar or around the tables talking. The road is lined with a few trees that have shed their leaves and look like they are dead. Small children walk along the pavement on their way home from school and they're carrying the square-styled backpacks that I have seen the kids in Germany use. Some of them wave at me, I wave back, and I try not to splash them as I navigate down the not-too-wide partially submerged high street.

None of the adults seem even to be aware of our presence. I imagine after years of war they are desensitised to military vehicles rolling down their roads. It's not a large town, and soon we are heading out of the other side. I'm looking for a junction with the word 'Magpie' and an arrow spray-painted on to something. I see Manbat put his indicator on. As he turns at the junction, I see the military graffiti on the side of a house telling us to turn left for Route Magpie. We speed up now the town is behind us and the scenery transforms once again. It's now arable countryside, with lots of houses widely spread across the cultivated land. The road winds its way along, rolling over the undulating terrain but with a mainly downward trend to it. The big lake comes into view and I take a moment to realise what I am looking at in the gloom. We are now approaching it from the opposite direction. Over the other side, I can distinguish the road we drove up earlier this morning, meandering its way along the foothills of the mountain to TSG. The road levels off as it gets closer to the big lake and, in time, it's running along the edge of the water. Further on, I see the big lake is held back by an earth embankment, which implies we should be calling it the big reservoir. We pass the junction to TSG, which means we are back on Route Gull and the Croatian border is just around the next few bends.

Manbat dives into the Monkey hut to do the necessary scribbling on bits of paper, and I use the Portaloo. The sign that says 'RMP Detachment Personal Only' is still up and I just happen to have a marker pen on me. So, I cross out the word 'Personal', write 'Personnel' above it, give them a 3-out-of-4 score and add 'must try harder.' The leg back to Split is, thankfully, uneventful and in the distance I can see the blue skies which always bless the Dalmatian coast. The road dries out and Manbat reverts to trying to break the IFOR land speed record.

Even when going downhill, the limiter will ensure the vehicle's speed does not exceed 80kph. If you have a heavy enough load, you can get around this by moving the gear selector from Drive to Neutral, thus letting the vehicle freewheel under its own weight. Top gear is 6th, and this is known as 'silent 7th'. I've heard of speeds of 120kph being reached on some of the steeper autobahn sections back in Germany. I'm not in the mood today to die a horrible death plummeting off into a bottomless chasm, so I let Manbat crack on.

The sunshine creeps closer, the temperature rises, and I am starting to feel too warm in my jacket. I wait until the traffic lights at the bottom of Split hill for the chance to remove it. Managing not to 'dampen' Anglo/Croatian relations, I take it easy through the big puddle. I drive past the turning for the vehicle park, carrying on down the side of the warehouse to the Postie Detachment to offload the mail I've carried down from up country. I see Manbat's speeding efforts have paid off with huge gains of arriving a whole minute before me, as he's still not got his container door open. One of the many things the British Army does exceptionally well is getting the mail delivered reasonably fast. I'm sure I'm not the only one feeling tired this late in the afternoon.

We muck in with the Posties to get the bags out of the container so they can continue on their journey back to families, girlfriends, boyfriends, and HMRC. Now that the load is dumped, it's back over to the vehicle park to fill up from the TTF in readiness for whoever Manbat will be taking back up to Kupres tomorrow. With the vehicles put to bed, I head up to Judas's office to see what the taskings for the morning are on Troop Orders.

Judas is still there and says to me without even a hello.

"I need a guard 2IC taemorra and the other Troop need a Driver fer the mail run again. Which wan de ya wanna dee?"

"I liked Kupres so much today I'd like to go there again, please," I reply faster than Corporal Rory Loughty would if he was being offered a free alcoholic drink. Guard duty is the arsehole of military life and it's made even worse when it's out of the blue like this. I have no intention of doing it willingly if there's an alternative option on offer, even if it was hoovering up the Troop Office all day long.

"Meet Manbat at tae armoury aboot 0730 taemorra morning,"

I move over to the mail tray to see I've had anything from anyone. I go through the few letters and don't see my name on any of them.

"Bloody post," I mutter under my breath, placing the uncollected mail back in the tray.

I move towards to door to leave when Judas says, "Hawd on."

I turn around to see him smiling with a letter in-between his forefinger and middle finger. My spirits are raised at this little surprise.

He flings it in my direction, like one would do with a playing card, and says, "Give that tae Delaney, will yer?"

Shooting down the Beach

I end up doing the Kupres mail run on Saturday too and I'm relieved to find out there isn't any to deliver or pick up on the Sabbath. Judas announces one of the spare coaches will head off down the coast to a beach near Makarska on Sunday. Anyone who wishes to go should be ready by 0900.

"I wouldn't be surprised if he kicks us all off at the bottom on the road and makes us do a PFT in our flip-flops back to Dalma," says Careless.

There isn't much to do around the warehouse on a Sunday, so most of us choose the day out at a different beach. I pack my green daysack with my green towel, a spare green T-shirt and military sun cream. It's not green, but it is in a green tube. I also pack a copy of George Orwell's Nineteen Eighty-Four, for a bit of light reading.

Dodgy Daz is our Driver today and, as I get on the coach, I ask him if he's got a bus licence.

He laughs, as he knows what I am referring to.

A few weeks ago, we had been so bored one afternoon that we decided to take the Volvo 4400 Wheeled Loader for a spin on the roads around the warehouse. They are a big vehicle with huge off-road wheels and four wheel drive so that it can operate in extremely muddy conditions. The axles are fixed and its steering is done by hydraulic rams making the chassis pivot in the middle. They can be fitted with a bucket for digging holes, or as in our logistical role, forks for moving pallets and heavy things off and off trucks. Neither of us were officially trained on it, but we knew how to drive it

Dodgy Daz was at the wheel. I was squeezed into the cab, beside him on a little ledge seat was which was designed just for this purpose. Just as long as you were child-sized. We were going round a corner. I'd like to boast we weren't really racing along as they only do about 30kph flat out, down a steep hill, with the wind behind you. I looked down to my right and I saw the roof of a car below us, up against the wheels. Dodgy Daz didn't feel the presence of the light car versus our 15 tonnes in weight.

"Fucking hell," I shouted.

Dodgy Daz then noticed the car and also shouted, "Fucking hell."

He instinctively turned the steering wheel away from the car. Because of the pivot steering, this only adds to the damage as our wheels now press into the side of the car. In hindsight we would have been best just continuing to drive in a straight line, letting the car steer away from us. We heard the screeching of our rubber tyres on his car's bodywork as the actual damage was taking place. We finally parted and Dodgy Daz brought the Volvo to a halt. The car we had made contact with wasn't a crappy old Fiat 126, but the first brand new vehicle I had seen since arriving in Croatia. The driver, cigarette in his mouth, had to climb out the window in a panic, as the door was so damaged it wouldn't open.

We sat there in shock and both said, "We're fucked."

The Croatian looked at his car, scratched his head, and looked back at his car. He took a drag on his cigarette and looked at us sitting in the cab. We still hadn't moved as we tried to take stock of how much shit we were in. Having an accident is bad enough. Having an accident while fucking around is not great. Having an accident, while fucking around in a vehicle you didn't have the licence for or weren't trained on, is biblically bad.

"How we gonna play this?" I said, with my heart thrashing like a German Techno drumbeat.

"I'm not too sure," said Dodgy Daz. "Let's go and see how angry he is." Opening the one and only small door, I climbed delicately down from the cab and waited for Dodgy Daz to follow me. The damages were around the other side of the Volvo. We looked at each other, took a deep breath, and wandered round to face the music.

The Croatian guy was looking at the damage to his car and rubbing his head with his hands. He took one last drag of his cigarette, flicked it away from him and instantaneously pulled out the pack from his pocket to replace the ones he'd just finished. We gazed awkwardly at him and he looked awkwardly back at us.

"I'm really sorry, guys," he said in perfect English and, knowing nobody speaks Croatian other than the Croatians, and we didn't resemble Croatians. "I didn't see you."

We took a second to realise what he was saying, and it was an admission of guilt. As soldiers, we are conditioned to presume we are always at fault and ready to receive a bollocking.

"Errrrr," is the only thing Dodgy Daz managed to say. We were still in a pile of poo, but this declaration of good news relieved our tension a smidge.

"I was coming round the corner and as I was lighting my cigarette, I took my eyes off where I was going. It's all my fault, guys."

"Accidents happen, my friend," Dodgy Daz announced happily.

His car was quite badly dented. It had black marks on his paintwork from the rubber from our tyres whilst the Volvo got away with just a bit of his white paint on our tyres.

We offered to pass him the details of someone to contact, but he wasn't too bothered. He said he'd claim it off his insurance, of which I suspect he had none. I think he was worried that we'd send him a bill to remove his paint from our tyres and couldn't get away quick enough. A few of the Stackers who worked around the back of the warehouse came over to see what was happening.

"Fuck," said Dodgy Daz. "We can hardly keep this under wraps now, can we?"

"You'll have to report it to Gunny and Squadron Ops," I said, and, grasping the circumstances that I was not behind the wheel, I felt a bit of relief. But my brain swiftly reminded me I was still part of something I shouldn't have been doing.

We jumped back into the Volvo and took it back to the vehicle park, parking it back up where it should have been and where it should remain if you were not qualified to drive it.

Dodgy Daz said, "I have a plan." He explained to Gunny about the incident and put the emphasis on the details that the Croatian admitted blame and there was no damage to the Volvo. Gunny took his word and was fine with it. He even asked Dodgy Daz to drive the Volvo around to the workshops so the Spanner Monkeys[80] could check it for damage. Just as Dodgy Daz was leaving Gunny's office, he said to him, "I didn't know you had a FLRT[81] qualification."

"I got it at my last unit," he said casually, wandering off.

Dodgy Daz was now under pressure to put it on his FMT600 permit before anyone thought to ask. He could just write it on there and put a squiggle for a signature and hey presto, he was in the clear. Nobody asked to see it, or bothered to check the master file in Squadron Ops, so he got away with it and got a qualification out of it. It wasn't like it was rigidly enforced anyway. As mentioned earlier, it was a couple of laps of camp to get the TTF on your permit. My conversion to driving left-hand drive vehicles on the wrong side of the road when I arrived in Germany was simply, "Follow the truck in front and you'll be OK." It was just me in a Bedford 4-Ton truck following another one for hours on end with nobody in the passenger seat to offer guidance or support.

→» →» →»

---

80 Army word for a Mechanic of the REME.

81 Fork Lift Rough Terrain.

The bus follows Route Gannet down the coast towards Makarska with the usual vehicular chaos of the locals trying to overtake on blind bends. We can sit back and sort of relax while Dodgy Daz has to worry about local drivers now. Everyone's heads still snap forward whenever he has to jump on the brakes because another local fancies an early trip to meet his maker. The turning for the beach is off to the right and almost doubles back on us. Dodgy Daz has to continue past it in search of somewhere to turn the coach around. The first appropriate space he finds is miles away down the road and has now added on half an hour to the trip.

"I dunno who found this beach. They were evidently not a coach driver, or a driver of anything bigger than a fucking Mini," he says, while doing a 17-point turn in a small cafe car park.

As we arrive back at the junction, he starts to turn left. Suddenly, a car comes rushing down our left-hand side with its horn blaring. He jumps on the brakes and curses the driver, while we groan at being thrown about.

"Fuck off," shouts Dodgy Daz as the driver hammers off into the distance.

The road to the beach is made from rough concrete, is quite steep in places and, more worryingly for Dodgy Daz, it has rocks, metal posts and tree stumps lining its sides. We are quiet as we know he's now having to earn his wage navigating down this track in an undamaged, almost new coach. At the bottom of the track there's a nice sizeable area. We hear him give out a colossal sigh of relief as he brings the coach to a halt.

"Bet you're glad you volunteered for your coach licence now," shouts Careless from the back. Del, Prat and I find a sweet spot under some trees away from the main crowd of lunatics. The beach is made up of medium-sized pebbles, which make it impossible to walk on bare-footed. Most who attempt this end up looking like they're *The Walking Dead* as they clumsily attempt to get in and out of the Adriatic. They also fall down more than if they had been on the 'Sleep in the Ditch' all morning. I decide to have a swim and stagger down to the water's edge in my flip-flops. Wanting to keep up an appearance of some self-respect, I sit down and put my feet in the water. I brace for the cold shock, but I'm pleasantly surprised to feel it's a more inviting temperature than when I last had a dip. Any dignity I hoped to keep by not falling over into the sea is lost as I slide along the pebbles on my arse into the water.

"You got worms?" shouts Del in my direction.

"It's all this local meat I'm eating. They never cook it properly," I reply as I slide into the water.

I have a swim around, but it's more floating as I have a pair of goggles with me. I am interested in what I can see in the crystal-clear water around and below me. It's teeming with fish from minnow size up to about a foot in length. On the sea floor, I can see lots of sea cucumbers and sea urchins with their sharp-looking spines. Thankfully, the latter are out in the deeper parts, so there is no chance of anyone standing on one and getting to go in front of Buckethands for some self-inflicted injury discipline. I paddle back to the shore and repeat the process of exiting the Adriatic with dignity. Returning to the spot under the trees, I dry myself off. I settle down to read my book and, two pages in, I'm nodding off in the warmth. I try to carry on reading, but I succumb to the sleep monster and I doze off. Slipping in and out of sleep, I hear those who are fooling around in the water shouting and screaming. The noises come and go and my mind starts to dream I'm walking down a street somewhere when I slip off the kerb and jerk awake. I fall back into a state of unconsciousness and this time I dream of nothing. When this happens, I know I'm more fatigued than I realise, and it's like I'm too shattered to dream. I am, of course, woken some time later, not by noise but by dripping water as Del dries himself off right over me.

"Cheers, you bellend," I say to him.

"You're most welcome. Civvies pay good money for this shit," is his stock reply.

"Did you find a bar?" I ask him.

"There's no bar round here that I can see. A few of the lads have wandered along the coast to see if there's anything."

I sit up and declare the obvious. "I think they chose this beach on purpose, so we remain teetotal by the military non-consenting method."

The sober afternoon passes as we talk and eat our sandwiches, which have been sweating in cling film most of the day.

"I've got pink death[82] with a yellow substance that I hope is margarine," I say, as I peel the bread apart.

"Mine's mystery fish," says Del, looking at the brown paste on his. "And it could have been cheese in a former life. I just don't know."

Prat looks at his and declares, "I've no idea what I'm about to eat."

"I wish there was a cafe round here," I add.

I'm now onto my bag of crisps, which aren't a well know brand, when I see Shaun the Yawn coming out the water with what looks like a rifle.

"Has he found a bloody gun?" I remark.

Del and Prat now look to where he is.

"It looks like it," says Del.

"Der sea could be full of guns, yer know," says Prat.

I stand up onto my towel to try to get my toes into my flip-flops. Once fitted, I walk towards Shaun and see it's indeed a rifle. There are now a few of us crowding around him, curious to have a gander at his find. "It's an air rifle," he announces to us, "I found it out there off that outcrop," he says' pointing behind himself.

---

82 Processed ham slices.

"An air rifle," says someone, sounding a bit let down it wasn't something more lethal.

It's not in terrible condition and it doesn't seem like it's been in the sea too long. Shaun says, "I'm gonna take it back with me and see if I can get it working."

"Naah, it's fucking fucked big time," says Prat.

Shaun the Yawn tries to cock the barrel and, surprisingly, it moves.

"I'm gonna get this sorted and then we can shoot things," he says.

"Like what?" says Del.

"Rats, snakes, you know vermin."

"Rats," replies Del, "I've not seen any rats. Apart from up at RHQ, the stray cats keep 'em under check."

"I'll shoot the cats, then."

"But then we will have rats and you can't shoot cats."

"And that's how I'll get to shoot more rats, then."

"You should bloody shoot yerself, bloody loony," says Del under his breath.

"Has he had a knock on the head?" says Prat at the unusual behaviour that Shaun the Yawn is now displaying. Shaun the Yawn was very much the grey man and a bit boring. He'd been posted into the Squadron just before the tour from a real obscure unit that nobody had heard of. Del reckoned he was under witness protection for a crime he did, or did not commit, or was privy to.

It's time to get back on the coach and head back to Dalma for another week of bringing peace to the Balkans. It's silent on board after the day of sun, sea, and no booze as we retrace our journey back along the zigzagging coast road. At the town of Omiš, the coach comes to a brief stop because of a set of traffic lights.

"Fucking hell, check out the melons on that," I shout out of the blue, gesturing to the right-hand side of the bus. All the lads speedily awake from their semi-consciousness to look to where I am pointing, because they can't help themselves. I get a good round of laughs from everyone when they see it's the watermelon seller on the pavement I'm referring to.

Upon our return, we quietly disembark the coach. We wander off in the accommodation's direction, apart from Shaun the Yawn, who heads over to the MT Offices with his suspiciously long-looking towel.

Shaun the Yawn got the air rifle working and over the next few days he stripped it down and cleaned up the insides. He found small tack nails would be adequate for ammo, as they fitted almost perfectly into the barrel. Next, he acquired some baked bean cans from the bins by the cookhouse and then opened up a shooting range in his shipping container store. He made it so if you wanted to sign out tools for the trucks, you had to demonstrate your marksmanship abilities. He said he was doing us a favour and we would thank him if anything happened out on the road which involved a gunfight, as he was keeping our shooting skills sharp.

None of the hierarchy were aware of what we were up to, but then Careless, predictably, let slip to Judas that we were having fun down at the stores. The stores are not normally a place of fun, and that's the reason Shaun the Yawn worked there. This made Judas decide to investigate, and it didn't take PI Judas too long to work out what we were up to. Not wanting the extra work that would come with disciplinary action which involved 'a weapon', he told Shaun the Yawn to make the gun non-existent. With a heavy heart at his predicament and realising he could become the focus for unwanted attention. Shaun the Yawn accepted this advice, snapped the rifle in half and chucked it over the fence into the deep undergrowth.

4

Flirting up Country

I AM called into see the Squadron 2IC, Captain Haywood. As usual, I presume I've done something wrong and I'm about to get an Officer bollocking. These aren't too bad as they are normally just a stern-looking expression with a few big words which I would have to look up in a dictionary later. On the other end of the spectrum, a Buckethands bollocking could leave you severely traumatised and would make your eardrums think they'd been violently assaulted. I presumed incorrectly, as Captain Heywood tells me I have been selected out of a cast of the only one available. I will be heading up to Banja Luka to be the driver for an LRO team.[83] They are tasked with getting contracts in place for local services required by IFOR units. I'm a little excited about it as I'll get to

---

83 Local Resource Officer.

visit more of the country and get away from the stifling Regimental routine at Dalma. The gods are smiling on me once again, as I always seem to land on my feet with jobs like these. I honestly think that I have a Regimental guardian angel looking out for me sometimes.

He tells me I need to pack for a few weeks. I will be flying by helicopter from DJ Barracks tomorrow up to Banja Luka, and I can have the rest of the day off to pack. This day just gets better, I think to myself. Captain Haywood says that I'll be representing the Regiment and should remain professional at all times when I'm with the LRO. Following Captain Haywood's orders, I pack in less than 15 minutes and continue to obey his order of lazing around for the rest of the day.

I bump into Prat and Del and tell them what I am off to do.

"You've sold out," says Del. "Next thing you'll be in the Officers Mess drinking Pimms with Mr Burns and his wife."

"Yer bloody git, dey do say rats always leave der sinking ship," adds Prat. I laugh at their overreaction.

I'm going for a few weeks and know it's only their jealousy because I'm getting away from the Regiment for a while.

Prat went on a similar job a few weeks later, but I wasn't about to give him the same grief in return. He had to drive a Warrant Officer around most of Bosnia looking for shipping containers which the MOD[84] had hired and were still paying for. They found loads of them and most were not being used for their intended purpose of shipping stuff. One particular episode he told me about was that they came across a few at a Norwegian camp which were being used as a windbreak outside their HQ.

The Norwegians were a bit upset when they told them they would be losing their £200-a-day (at no cost to the Norwegian Military)

---

84 Ministry of Defence.

wall. Prat and the Warrant Officer were still offered some hospitality during their stay and Prat recounted how it played out.

"That's too bad that you will remove them," said the Norwegian Captain, unhappy that he'd have to face the winds when he left his office.

"Well, we can't justify having to pay for them to sit about not being used, I'm afraid, sir," said the Warrant Officer.

"Would you like something to eat?" said the now jolly-looking Norwegian Captain.

"That would be great, thanks," said the Warrant Officer.

"After the meal, you must try out our sauna."

"You have a sauna?" exclaimed a surprised Prat.

"No," said the Captain, suddenly returning to being unhappy.

The next morning I am given a lift down to DJ Barracks by Geordie Munchester and stop outside a small empty building near the line of parked Chinook[85] helicopters.

"This is the gaff. I've dropped a few off here before. It's the right place, believe me," says Geordie, as if he knows I have no confidence in his dropping-off skills.

"Look," he says, pointing at a bit of paper stuck to the door of the empty building which gives the game away

'Pax[86] Are Too Report Hear', it says on the piece of A4 paper that's on the door.

"I hope they can fly better than they can spell," I say to Geordie.

"Eh, oh yeah, fucking thick twats. Can't spell passengers."

I don't honestly know if he's joking or not. As I open the door, I slide out of the Lanny and go around the back to grab my gear.

---

85 It's a heavy lift helicopter used for moving personnel and freight. Its tandem rotors make it one of the most easily recognisable helicopters in the world.

86 Abbreviation for passengers.

Geordie doesn't budge from the driver's seat.

"Thanks for the help," I say as I wrestle my kit out the back.

"My pleasure," he replies.

I do not know if he's being honest or sarcastic.

Before I can say 'bye' to him he's started the Lanny up and buggered off.

I report to the empty room as instructed, plonk my arse in a polyprop chair, and wait. I was vaguely told my flight was sometime after 8am, so I am not too alarmed when I'm the only one there. The morning is warming up rapidly and I am already somewhat sweaty from carrying my kit the few metres from the Lanny to the waiting room. A little while later, a couple of girls arrive, and from their green berets I know they are Shinyarses.[87] They are both rather attractive, which gets my attention.

They ask if I'm waiting for the flight to Banja Luka. I reply that I am. They relax as if my being here is confirmation that they are in the right place, even if I'm not too sure myself. A few more people turn up and always ask the same question to give an overwhelming feeling of group confidence. After another period of waiting, a guy arrives wearing a string vest with some very heavy-duty trousers and boots. He must be sweating his arse off, I think to myself, as it has become significantly warmer since Geordie dropped me off. I think he must be one of the fire crew who moonlights as a sort of no-nonsense check-in staff.

"Is everyone here for the heli to Banja Luka this morning?" he announces to a reply of nodding heads and the odd yes.

"Is there anywhere else on offer? I whisper to the Clerk next to me.

"I hear Italy is nice this time of the year," she then laughs with a snort, which gets here the attention of the fire guy.

---

87 British Army slang for Adjutant General's Corps (Clerks).

"You OK," he says to her.

"Hay fever," she says, quick as a flash.

He has a sheet of paper in his hand, looks at it and carefully calls out the names on it. Most, including mine, are on there, but there are a few who aren't here as well as a few who are here but not on his list. He takes their details, including their unit, and writes them down. He doesn't seem too bothered by who has, or not, turned up for the morning's flight.

"OK, we'll get you on in a while and in the meantime, if you could just wait here."

I hear the unmistakable sound of a turbine engine starting up. I get up from my chair to see the big green Chinook that's making the noise. There is someone wearing olive coveralls and ear protection standing in front of it with a large black cylinder on wheels that I presume is there in case of a fire. The fire guy makes another appearance and this time asks, "Are your weapons in the unloaded state?"

We all nod again and a few hold up their guns to show him they don't have a magazine fitted.

"Body armour on, helmets on, and no berets before we go out please."

This is a gentle reminder that if a £5 beret gets sucked into a very expensive turbine engine, it could turn it into a pile of inexpensive scrap.

He then offers us the little yellow ear plugs and says that in a minute we are to follow him out to the Chinook.

I roll the ear plugs between my finger and thumb and insert them into each of my ears and the world becomes a quieter place. He now signals for us to follow him out of the door. I'm now wearing my body armour and webbing with my rucksack hooked over one arm. All baggage is carry-on baggage when flying in the Chinook.

The blades on the Chinook are now up to speed, and I feel the vibrations through the ground. We follow our guy in single file as he

185

leads us out of the waiting room. He stops us behind the helicopter, no more than 10 metres from it. Another person in olive coveralls stood by the rear ramp gives the thumbs-up to our guy, who returns the signal with a matching thumbs-up. He then directs the first one of us in the line towards the Chinook and for the rest of us to follow on. Tailing one of the clerks, I instinctively duck down as I go under the huge spinning blades. I now feel the pressure wave from them cutting through the air. I know they are very high up. Even if I jumped in the air with my arms stretched out, I wouldn't be anywhere near them, but my human reaction for self-preservation is strong. I follow in turn, step onto the back ramp and straight away I get the smell, which you only get on aircraft, in my nostrils.

Go to a plane museum, find one which allows you to go inside and you'll know what I am trying to explain.

I am directed to the left and take my place on a bench seat with my back up against the fuselage. The next person to join me is, to my delight, one of the clerks. I squeeze up against the one who was in before me and she squashes up against me. We search around our sides for the lap belt at the same time and it's chaotic. Once found, we try to work out how to secure them.

The guy in the coveralls is the Loadmaster, and he darts around helping anyone who looks like they are struggling to fasten it.

The back ramp comes up slightly and we remain there for a few minutes. It's a lot warmer on board as the two big fans above us just seem to blow the hot air around whilst adding in more hot air from the engines. The sweat starts to run down my forehead from where the padding inside my helmet is against the skin. I notice I am not the only one as I wipe it away from above my eyes.

The entire Chinook is vibrating, and without the ear plugs you'd probably have permanent hearing damage within a few minutes. It's nothing like in the films, with the characters having a relaxed discussion about how to defeat the bad guys. This is a full-blown onslaught on the senses and quite a buzz as the adrenalin kicks in. The engine's note and vibration change as the blades grip the air, creating lift. The hangar drops out of sight as we lift into the air vertically. It's like being in a noisy elevator. Then the front of the Chinook dips down as it starts moving forward. The sight out the back is now only one of the blue sky. As it picks up speed it levels out, and then I become heavy in my seat as it climbs. The view of DJ Barracks out of the rear of the Chinook now shrinks as we start our journey, flying along the coastline down towards SNP. There are round windows along the side of the fuselage, but they aren't big. I can't really see much from them as our co-passengers are sitting in front of them. The only view is out of the back, and this is where everyone is currently looking. It continues the climb and now turns left and I realise they are basically following the road up Split Hill. It does snake through the high ground which dominates Split, so it becomes apparent this is the best choice of route. The Loadmaster has a door to my left and behind the cockpit. He is looking out as we go and has a mounted machine gun that can be swung out just in case. The flow of cool air through the inside makes it immensely more comfortable and I've finally stopped sweating.

The Chinook levels off and I am able to still see the gap in the mountains which the road traverses through. A few minutes later, the Loadmaster gets our attention and indicates for everyone to look out of the back. I'm not too sure what we are supposed to be looking at. A few of the passengers gaze back at him and again he indicates with a bit more vigour to keep looking out the back. Then we see it. Like someone switching on a bright light in a dark room, there's an eruption of brilliant white and I sense a short burst of heat on my exposed skin. It's the countermeasure flares and they have just tested them. They'd jumped out from both sides and as they spread out, the light intensity reduces and I now see each of the individual flares. They're trailing white smoke as they go and it spirals from the vortex airflow produced by the Chinook in flight. I then notice we're over the big lake as gravity takes over and they start their fall downwards. They extinguish well before they reach the ground, but I suppose starting a massive wildfire is worse for Anglo-Croatian relations than driving through a puddle at speed. It's taken us less than 10 minutes to get to the big lake. It's over an hour by road, even with Manbat behind the wheel.

I sense being lighter in my seat as the Chinook descends rapidly. Spotting the big lake out the back, I guess we are making a stop at TSG. It banks over and circles the town as if they're searching for the landing spot. It then levels out and continues descending, getting slower. The Loadmaster on the back ramp looks over the edge, possibly trying to spot obstacles that the pilots can't see. We are landing on the bypass, and maybe the slow descent is to wait for a gap in the traffic. It goes light again and I sense the familiar heat on my skin. The flares have gone off again and at this height it's obviously not a drill. The engine returns rapidly to full power and we bank over, speeding up as we go. I observe the reaction of the Loadmaster who doesn't appear too bothered by what has just happened, which is sort of relieving. If he'd been screaming and shouting, not that we would have heard him, then I would have panicked more. He's looking out the back and gives the impression he's taking in the view. It's easy to work out something has set the countermeasures off and the crew has reacted accordingly. It's unexpected, and I seem to remain pretty cool, as ignorance is bliss. I'm not too sure what's really going on. After a few minutes, we are now back at our previous altitude. The Loadmaster explains with made-up sign language to us passengers they are going to try that landing again. This time it's with no flares going off, and we bump down on the dusty TSG bypass. A couple of guys come running into view with weapons and rucksacks and step onto the back ramp. The Loadmaster guides them down towards us and they take a seat. As soon as they're in, we lift into the sky again and continue our journey. We seem to fly lower than before. A lot lower. The pilot is now banking the Chinook over a lot steeper and we get to sense the G-force pressing us down in our seats. I get a quick glimpse out of the window opposite me as the person blocking it leans to one side momentarily and I observe rocky cliffs speeding past. Out the rear, I observe we've entered a steep-sided valley and reckon the pilot is either having fun or aware of a threat to us.

Thirty minutes later, we touch down lightly at Banja Luka and are instructed by the Loadmaster to remain seated. The engine continues to run for a while and then I hear it winding down to a stop and the vibrations cease. We now take our ear plugs out and we're able to have a conversation.

"Well, that was exciting," I say to the Clerk.

"Yeah, great fun," she replies, looking very pale. "I thought I was going to barf up."

The temperature has risen again along with the humidity.

"You may have noticed our landing at TSG was a bit different. The countermeasure suite picked up a threat and deployed," says the Loadmaster.

"Like a missile locking onto us?" asks a sweaty-looking Warrant Officer.

"Exactly, but as we are still here, I think it would have been the local Police."

I want to listen to this, I think to myself. "They have the old-style radar guns to catch speeding motorists. Now and again, I suspect they get bored and have worked out it's great fun to point them at helicopters."

"Fucking hilarious," says the Warrant Officer. "I think I'll drive next time."

I make my way off the Chinook with my fellow passengers into the brilliant sunlight and heat of the day. We have landed in a field which is surrounded by barbed wire and next to a huge building that looks like another warehouse. I follow the person in front of me as they are following the person in front of them. I hope whoever's at the front knows where they are going. There is a gap in the fence and a few more people who are evidently waiting to meet others from the flight. I look at my contact and I don't have to search too far as a fair-haired Corporal walks up to me and says, "Are you Lance Corporal Lee?"

"I certainly am, and you must be Corporal Swintex."

"Call me Melba and welcome to Banja Luka Metal Factory. Good flight?"

"Quicker than driving, but more chance of spewing up."

He offers to carry my rucksack as we walk to a Lanny parked nearby and I gladly offer it to him. "I'll take you over to the office so you can meet Captain Triple H and Staff Sergeant Hobbs."

He puts my kit in the back as I climb into the passenger seat. He then jumps in the driver's seat, starts the Lanny and we pull away. He follows the road around a corner, brings the vehicle to a stop and announces, "We're here."

"Eh," I say, slightly confused at the five-second journey. "We could have..." Melba cuts me off mid-sentence, knowing exactly what I was going to say.

"Anyone can make life hard for themselves."

It's Grim up North

Banja Luka is in the north of Bosnia and was the de facto capital of Repbulika Srpska and a Serbian stronghold. BLMF[88] is located to the north of the city on Route Pegasus. The camp is dominated by

88 Banja Luka Metal Factory.

the actual metal factory in the centre. There are a few red bricked office buildings at the entrance. Some other smaller ones, seemingly placed at random around it, are no doubt something to do with its former use. The metal factory building is vast, very rectangular, and made from dull painted corrugated iron. Inside, it's full of the industrial-sized machinery that used to produce steel. There are the usual few Corimecs, which had been added for the troops who are based here. It's soon to become the British-led HQ MND SW,[89] but when I arrive it's still a sleepy hollow.

I only recollect the British Infantry being there and I can't recall which unit they were. However, I do remember there were not a lot of them.

I follow Melba into the office, which is an empty room with a yellow carpet. There are a few desks and chairs, which, judging by their 1970s style, must have come with the property.

"Captain Triple H and Staff Hobbs are out down town putting out potential contracts," says Melba.

"Captain Triple H? I enquire.

"Captain Hanna Huntley-Hays."

"Aha, a two dads surname."

Melba laughs, "I've not heard that one before."

We go on to have a chinwag for a while and he tells me he's a Blanket Stacker by trade. He was sent to BLMF last week along with Staff Sergeant 'Jonny' Hobbs, both from their unit based in Šipovo. Captain Triple H has come out from the UK to be the boss of this particular one. There are a more LROs based around the rest of Bosnia. Their function is to find suitable companies who can offer resources that IFOR will need, such as laundry, bakery, or waste re-

89 Multi-National Division South West.

moval. Once found, they pass the details on the Civ Sec,[90] who will offer a contract. We will need these services, as we are going to be in the country for a few years yet. It'll give a much-needed boost to the local economy, which is still reeling from the war. Our job is a simple one. To be their drivers, look after the Lannys and be a sort of escort, as we will be visiting lots of local businesses in the towns. "Time for some food?" he asks.

"Deffo, I'm so hungry that my stomach thinks my throat has been cut," I reply.

"Come on then," he says. "Leave your gear here. Just bring your gun."

We make our way to the large roller door, which, I think, is the only entrance into the metal factory. The cookhouse is a load of 12x12 canvas tents which have been joined together to make it one large tented mini city. These tents are placed in between the huge dirty-looking machinery wherever there is space. We step inside the well-lit interior and join the queue for food. It's being served by the Cabbage Mechanics from 6ft wooden tables out of Norwegian containers and is apparently Cottage Pie. The mashed potato is served first from its own Norwegian container and then the minced beef in gravy comes next from another onto our white paper plates. We wander through to the seating area with its tables and benches laid out in neat rows, grabbing some plastic cutlery on the way. Sitting opposite one another on a deserted table, I announce an observation.

"Technically, it's Cottage Pie, but I would say it's more mince and potato thrown together by accident," I tell Melba,

"The food's not too bad but it does tend to be gravy-based meat a lot," he replies.

"Maybe they could make it taste better and have called it *Le Pie*

90 Civilian Section, I presume. This was never really explained to me.

Cottarge," I say in a French accent.

I take a mouthful and it tastes better than it looks.

"They get inspected by us three times a day," says Melba.

"Unlike the guys doing the honey sucker job.[91] No bugger inspects them."

Melba laughs but manages to keep his mouthful of Le Pie Cottarge from spraying over the table and me.

We get back to the empty office, and neither Captain Triple H nor Staff Hobbs has returned from town.

"Staff Hobbs will probably be half-pissed when they get back," says Melba.

"Can't beat daytime drinking, but drinking on the job?" I reply, a tad confused at Staff Hobbs's apparent potential state while working.

Melba starts to explain.

"Whenever a service is required for whatever, we need to get three quotes to see which is the best value is for money."

"Cheapest, you mean," I say instantly.

He looks at me and repeats, "Value for money."

"Yeah, the cheapest," I say again.

Laughing, he says, "Word gets around town pretty quickly that we are out looking to award a contract. They can be very hospitable when we turn up to discuss if they are able to supply what we need."

"Like bribes," I say.

"They are a different kettle of fish that comes under gifts which have to go in the gift book. They will normally offer something to drink, such as coffee or tea, but a few will get out the sliv, slivo, slivovi," he struggles to pronounce it.

"Sleep in the Ditch," I help him out.

---

91 The job entails emptying the septic tanks, mostly with a vehicle which has a sucking capability because doing it by hand would just be the worst.

"Sleep in the Ditch. I like that, yeah. Anyway, out it comes in the hope we'll get pissed and possibly offer the contract to them in a half-smashed state."

"Sounds utterly awful, the situation, that is, and the drink."

"Staff Hobbs says it'd be rude not to accept it, plus Captain Triple H doesn't drink, and he's more than happy to take a hit for the team."

I hear a Lanny pull up on the road outside our office, and Melba announces, "Here they are."

Captain Triple H comes into the room first and says, "Aha, Lance Corporal Lee, I presume."

"Yes, ma'am," I say to her, bracing up. I don't salute her because my beret is in my pocket and we don't salute when not wearing it. She offers her hand to me and we shake hands.

"I assume Corporal Swintex has informed you about what we do?"

"He has, ma'am, it sounds rather interesting," I reply.

"This is Staff Hobbs," she says, turning to introduce him to me.

Through his half-cocked eyes he says, "Nice to meet you. I'll catch up with you later."

He reeks like he's had a few.

"If you excuse me, I might go and have a little siesta," he says before he wanders off.

"Hard day at the office, eh, ma'am?" says Melba.

"Oh yes. The buggers are so persistent, it's almost less hassle to accept the offers of booze."

"Was it Sleep in the Ditch?" says Melba with his new-found word for Slivovitz.

"Sleep in the what?" says Captain Triple H, and then she laughs as she gets the joke. "Oh yes, Sleep in the Ditch, very good."

The remainder of the day is spent dossing around. There isn't really much else to do at the BLMF, so I fire Melba some questions his way. "Where's the accommodation?" I ask him.

"You're in it," he replies. "We've been sleeping in here. Well, not the boss. She has a tent in the factory somewhere."

"Showers?"

"The Corimec over the road," he says, pointing at a lone one which has seen better days.

"Laundry?"

"Same Corimec, self-laundering in the sinks, for now anyway."

"NAAFI and/or bar?"

"The resident Infantry unit has a small bar, also in a tent, in the factory. I'll show you later."

"You named after a peach?" I ask him.

He laughs. "Naah, my first name is Colin and I'm from Bury. There's a sort of famous company from up that way who makes traffic cones and road signs... You know that sort of stuff. They're called Melba Swintex and someone had heard of it, so Melba it was."

"Could be worse," I say. "I knew a guy in my last unit who kept pissing himself whenever he'd had a few beers. He was known as Swampy and I've no idea what his real name was."

"Brutal. Life should get better here soon though," he adds. "I've heard that they are going to make this the main British HQ in Bosnia. I reckon we'll have a cocktail bar soon for the senior Officers."

"Can't have them drinking the local pivo, can we now?" I reply.

After some brown, runny, stew-like dinner, served from the Norgies, we head to the bar tent to find they have no beer.

"Might be an early night," says Melba, so we head back to the office.

"I presume Staff Hobbs is still asleep somewhere?"

"He's blagged a room down the corridor and, yeah, he'll be out for the count."

I head outside to enjoy the cool evening air and to read my book, Nineteen Eighty-Four. The only place to sit is on the step of the main door into the office building, so I sit down and observe my surroundings. The grass is overgrown and has more of a wildflower meadow appearance to it. I observe a multitude of insects dancing around the flowers and hear the evening birdsong. The sky is a rich blue and there isn't a cloud in sight anywhere. It's exceedingly serene and I forget where I am for a moment. I am here because of the violence which has happened in this country and it's hard to believe that right now during this late afternoon. The insects soon turn their attention to me and, after trying to swat a few away with my hands, I decide it might be time to go in. I pick a corner of the office and I lay out my foam roll mat which will offer some comfort on the hard floor. I then unpack my dossbag and roll it out too. With the aid of the remaining contents in my rucksack, I endeavour to create a pillow. I take off my combats, unzip my dossbag, and climb into it. I try to get as comfortable as possible and start reading my book. Winston Smith is arrested, taken to the Ministry of Love. Half a dozen pages later, I think it's time to get some sleep, as I feel my eyes struggling to keep open. I put the book down and close them. I hear Melba's shallow breathing, which tells me he's well asleep by now, and then I realise I've left the sodding light on.

"For fuck's sake," I mutter quietly as I get back out from by dossbag, walk over to the light switch, and flick it off. I fumble in the dark as I make my way back to where I know my dossbag was without trying to connect with any of the furniture. Especially my exposed toes. Bending down and feeling around with my hands to where I think it is, I eventually locate it. I climb back in and settle down again.

Sleep comes pretty quickly after the fun-filled day. Yet again, I don't dream and with an almost instantaneous impression, it's the morning.

Kontract Killer

The showers in the Corimec are less 'showers' and more 'slow leaks.'
I try my best to get myself clean under the miserable flow of water
dribbling from the shower head. I soon work out that if I switch
it off for a few seconds, the pressure builds a little. Then, if I turn
the tap back on, I get a short squirt before it resumes back to its
normal pressure, which would struggle to burst a weak expectation.
Half-finished and half given-up, I get dressed and move to the sink
to brush my teeth. I turn the tap, a few drops fall from it and I am
surprised I get this much.

"It's been like this since we got here months ago," says one of the
Infantry guys. "I bet when they make it into a big HQ then there
will be working showers and a cocktail bar, no doubt."

Morning routine is completed, and it's off to the cook tent to
find out if it's a full English stew for breakfast. The Cabbage Mechanics manage to knock up a decent breakfast of sausages, eggs and
bacon. Melba and I wolf it down with a mug of Le Pie Cottarge-fla-
voured cofftea.

> *Dear British Army,*
> *I know you don't offer any commission for recruitment.*
> *However, if you do ever feel like chucking me a few quid for*
> *my ability to sell a life in the Army to the next generation of*
> *soldiers, I will gratefully accept it.*
> *Yours truthfully*
> *James Lee*

Staff Hobbs comes and sits with us and he's looking fresh.

"You feeling all good, Staff?" says Melba to him, evidently expecting a clichéd reply regarding a sore head or having a mouth

that's drier than a nun's crotch. "I'm good. It's amazing what nearly 18 hours of sleep can do for you," he replies.

"Long day," I say to him.

"Oh yeah, the bloody local Super Bleifrei[92] is hard going."

"Same again today?" says Melba.

"I don't know if I can keep this up. I'm going to have to say no to any offers of alcohol today."

Staff Hobbs stands up and says, "Any more brews, you two?"

We both decline and once he's out of earshot, Melba leans over to me, smiling, and says.

"And that's not going to happen."

With our bellies full, we go back to the office and I pack away my dossbag, stuffing it back into my rucksack. Melba tells me Captain Triple H won't show up until at least 0900, so we have some time to First Parade the Lannys. I have to sign for the tools from Melba. We check everything is present and correct, which it is, so I sign my autograph on the 1033 which he produces from nowhere. The office is thoroughly bare of any paperwork whatsoever, apart from a few files that Captain Triple H was carrying, but somehow Melba has found a pad of Issue and Receipt Vouchers.

I laugh at him and say, "You can take the Stacker out of the stores but you can't expect a Stacker not to carry a pad of 1033s wherever they go."

"Sign your life away, sunshine," he says, as I check the tools off against what's written on the 1033 to make sure he's not offloading anything he's lost on to me.

I am driving Captain Triple H this morning and Melba will be driving the duty piss head.

"Have you been to Banja Luka before?" she asks me.

"Nope, ma'am, furthest I've been from Split was Kupres."

92 Unleaded petrol in German.

"OK, I know where we are going, anyway. I have a few companies who I have to check out to find out if they could supply us some buses."

We wander out to the Lanny together, and put our body armour, helmets and my webbing in the front.

"Keep them to hand at all times when we are in town," she warns me.

"Is it that rough down there?" I reply, not too sure what I am now to expect.

She laughs and says, "They'll steal anything left lying about and within easy reach. Make sure the back door is locked too."

We climb aboard and she tells me to drive straight ahead to the front gate. I am not planning on stopping when she says, "Pull over here so we can load up at the loading bay."

The loading bay is a piece of a plastic pipe stuck into a big pile of sandbags. The idea of these is that we put the muzzle of our weapon into it when loading or unloading. If we do then get confused and accidentally pull the trigger, the round would not ricochet all over the place, possibly killing someone. I put the muzzle of my weapon in and she says, "Load."

The muscle memory kicks in. I ensure the safety catch is on, check the change lever is on single shot, and I pull out a magazine. I look to see if the rounds are seated correctly in the top of it and slide it into its place. I feel it click in, and I give it a gentle tug and a wiggle to make sure it's not going to fall out as soon as I remove my hand. I don't bang it in with the palm of my hand like they do in the movies. This will more than likely dislodge the top round and cause it to jam, should I need to start shooting the bad guys. I understand this realistic method doesn't have the effect required for the big screen. I recheck the safety catch is still on before I move away and it's Captain Triple H's turn with her Browning pistol. "We're not flavour of the month around here with some of the population," she says, not having to explain to me that Banja Luka is a Serb area. "So I think it may be for the best to be on the right side of caution and not to be fumbling about trying to load up if a situation arises."

I think what she means in soldier talk is: if it fucking kicks off fucking big time, then we need to be able to deal back some shit faster than a fat kid eating a cup cake.

I decide to keep this thought to myself.

I turn out of the main gate, which has a Warrior IFV[93] parked up by it. It's there to send a message to anyone wishing to gain access for nefarious reasons that they might want to reconsider their life choices. The only flaw in this idea is there's nobody in it, and it looks locked up with the hatches closed. I presume it would take a few minutes to get it ready to go and, by then, the nefarious person in question would be long gone. There's a small service road that takes us to the main road, which is Route Pegasus. Someone has spray-painted an arrow on an abandoned car informing us that Banja Luka is to the left. I carry on, speeding up as the off-road tyres make the noise only Lannys seem to do. Everything looks the same as if I were driving around in Split, except the signs are now mainly in Cyrillic. There is a fair amount of traffic on the roads this morning and the quality of driving is on the same level as everywhere else I've been so far. Utter shite. Captain Triple H doesn't really speak much, apart from when I need to take a turn. She has the habit of telling me this when we are at the junction, so I require the driving reactions of Damon Hill. We turn left and right and right and left, down cobbled streets lined with grey-looking apartment blocks and past piles of rubbish on the pavements. The setting changes from dwellings to more shops and offices until it's nearly only shops or offices, which I presume means we are now in the city centre. She

93 A tracked armoured Infantry Fighting Vehicle that has a crew of three. It can carry seven fully armed infantry soldiers in the back and has a turret armed with a 7.62mm machine gun and a 30mm cannon.

points at a doorway under an unintelligible sign and tells me to pull up by it. I can't work out what the writing says, but it does have a picture of a plane, a train and a ship, so I presume it's maybe a travel agent. I suppose even in times of conflict there's still a market for getting away from it all.

"This is the first company I've got to talk to this morning. If you come in with me, make sure you've still got the Land Rover in view."

"Yes, ma'am," I reply to her.

I get out and reach back in for my webbing. It has my spare ammunition in it and I don't want to have to explain why I need some more. Putting it on, I then sling my gun over my head and let it hang down by my side. Both the doors are locked, but their design means it wouldn't deter the world's worst car thief. At least at my Court Martial I could say that I honestly locked the doors of the Lanny prior to it disappearing for good.

She enters the shop and says, *"Dobro Jutro."*[94]

"Dobro Jutro," says the lady behind the desk with a croak, looking up as if the British Army paying her a visit is a normal occurrence.

"Do you speak English?" says Captain Triple H, now that her indigenous language bank is exhausted.

"Of course," she replies.

Captain Triple H sits down in front of her and introduces herself. She declines the offer of a cigarette, coffee, something to eat and a shot of clear liquid from a glass bottle with no labels on it. She then commences to talk business, describing what she is after and explaining that she would like a quote.

I hang about by the door trying not to look too menacing with my gun and webbing on while keeping an eye on the Lanny as instructed. They talk for at least half an hour and during the entire time, the Bosnian Serb lady chain-smokes her way through half a

94 Good morning, in the local lingo.

pack of cigarettes. The shop bloody reeks of tobacco and I consider going outside to pretend to chase off some imaginary kids from the Lanny. I'm taken back to another time, as I feel like a bored boy again while my mum talks to a friend she's met at the shops. Getting fidgety as time drags on, I look at them talking, then I look back to the to the Lanny and back to them. I almost give out a massive sigh when they both stand up and shake hands. The lady offers me a sweet from a bowl, which I decline. Not because it could be classed as a bribe, but because they look bloody minging. I am then offered a pen, which I again decline as I have plenty of pens. I exit the shop and walk to the Lanny, unlocking the passenger door first and then going round to unlock mine. A small crowd of onlookers has gathered. They're standing silently, some with shopping bags, some with a stoop, but all with cigarettes hanging out the corner of their gobs. Although their demeanour isn't threatening, I do find their muted presence somewhat uncomfortable. I am glad to start the Lanny up and get out of there. Just as I get into second gear, Captain Triple H says, "Turn right here."

I steer the Lanny around the corner and then she says, "There's the next one," pointing to a similar-looking office. We are no more than a 30-second walk from the rent-a-lynching, but we are round a corner and out of their sight. I look in my wing mirror to check if the simple plan has managed to lose them. I repeat the process of locking the Lanny and donning my kit.

As I enter the premises I swear it's the same lady from only a few minutes ago sitting behind the desk. We aren't too far away from the last one, so it is entirely plausible that she's just dashed out the last place and around the back of the buildings. The procedure is repeated. I keep an eye out for the crowd while the usual cordial offers of cigarettes, caffeine, meat and aviation fuel are declined. I now comprehend that Staff Hobbs has the same ability to say no as the Tyrannosaurus Rex had the ability to scratch the top of his head. It soon becomes apparent this lady doesn't speak any English, but she does say, *"Sprechen Sie Deutsch?"* [Do you speak German]

"Nur ein bisschen," [Only a little] I say without thinking and really butting in on the conversation between her and Captain Triple H.

They both look at me. Captain Triple H remains silent while the lady launches into German at a thousand miles an hour.

"Whoa, whoa, mein Deutsch ist serh schlecht," [My German is very bad] I say in an almost apologetic tone.

I can just about hold a conversation in German to give directions to a pub, book a hotel or have an argument as to why Benny Hill isn't funny. The last thing I want is to be speaking in German and agreeing the finer details of a commercial quote. I'd probably end up to agreeing they could have our Lanny, guns and ammunition.

The lady carries on at a breakneck pace and I have to say, *"Langsam bitte, langsam"* [Slowly please, slowly].

I dig deep in my brain and come up with,

"Haben Sie ein Frundin wer kann Englisch sprechen?" [Have you a friend who can speak English?]

I'm hoping I've just said what I wanted to say correctly and if you're a fluent German speakers reading this, you'll notice I used the formal way to address her. *Haben Sie,* and not *Hast Du,* because this is a business meeting. I'm not a total hooligan, you know.

"Ja, er wird in zehn Minuten hier sein." I just pick up the words *ja* and *zehn Minuten,* and sort of guess she's said something along the lines of "Yes, he'll be here in ten minutes."

I breathe a big exhalation of relief and tell an impressed-looking Captain Triple H, "There's someone coming in ten mins who speaks English."

"Aber," [But], says the lady, looking worried.

"Was wollen Sie?" [What do you want?]

"Errrrr," [Errrrr] is all I manage as I try to think what the easiest way to say what we are up to as I don't know the word for quote in

German. *"Sollen wir warten auf dein Frundin?"* [Shall we wait for your friend?] is the route of least resistance, which I decide to go with.

"Ja, naturlich," [Yes, of course] she replies with a smile and lights up a cigarette.

"Are you sure you couldn't translate for me? I mean, it sounds quite impressive," says Captain Triple H.

"Not a chance, ma'am, I really am at the limit of my Deutsch-speaking ability."

"Where did you learn your German, at school or in the Army?"

"No, ma'am, in the pub."[95]

---

95 The Army tried teaching me German but spent most of the time focusing on getting the grammar perfect. It was exceptionally complicated to me and went straight in one ear and out the other. My few German friends, whom I mostly met in the pub, gave me the best bit of advice for speaking Deutsch which was. "We know you're a foreigner, we know your grammar will be shit, so don't get hung up on it. Just say the words you've learnt and we'll probably be able to work out what you're on about. But do note this, never address someone you don't know with the informal Du, it's always Sie." It would have helped more if they'd told me Frundin meant "girlfriend" and not "friend."

Pirate Radio

Word must have got around town that we are out and about, as the next business we approach later this morning seems to be expecting us. The process is repeated, hands shaken, gifts offered and muted crowds driven away from. We go back to BLMF for Captain Triple H to do the paperwork on the quotes and to get some lunch. Melba is with an out-of-character, sober Staff Hobbs in the office when we return.

"Did he drink the town dry yesterday?" I whisper to Melba.

"I think he's turned a corner," replies Melba, also whispering.

"Is that turned into the pub, around the corner?" is my reply.

"Lunchtime," announces Staff Hobbs, standing up from his empty desk. "You two coming or staying?"

Today's gastronomic delight comes in the form of the good old favourite pasta dish, which is Bolognaise Spaghetti. It's the same as what you'd expect, but because of the food being put out in the wrong order, we get the pasta on top of the sauce.

"All goes down the same hole," is Melba's philosophical view on it.

"At least we know what flavour the cofftea will be tomorrow morning," says Staff Hobbs.

"With a hint of bleach from trying to get the Bolognaise sauce-stained Norgies back to their original colour," I add.

"I love the taste of Bolognaise and bleach in the morning," jokes Staff Hobbs impersonating Robert Duvall, in the film *Apocalypse Now*.

"Fancy talking a walk to the CD shop after lunch?" says Melba to me.

"Is that what they are selling?" I reply.

I noticed earlier this morning, as we departed camp, by the main gate, the locals had set up some tables and were selling something.

"Yeah, they have everything, including DVDs, but they are normally very dodgy quality," adds Melba.

"At only two bucks[96] a go, my CD collection is growing nicely," says Staff Hobbs.

"Let me guess which ones you bought?" I ask him.

"UB40, Red Red Wine?"

"Nope."

"Thin Lizzy, Whiskey in the Jar?"

"Er no."

"Dr Feelgood, Milk and Alcohol?"

"Fuck off with the booze-related songs."

Melba laughs and says, "They are quality songs, though, Staff."

The pirate CD industry in Bosnia was massive, and it was bringing much-needed money to the local economy. I have to guess it was being run by people with a background in criminality rather than a PhD in music marketing. There were only a few of them when I arrived at BLMF selling their goods from tables. In time, these developed into tents and then wooded huts or shipping containers that looked like a bona fide music shop with posters and flags. They could be found outside almost every IFOR establishment Bosnia wide and God knows what they were were funding in the long run. I certainly don't think it was the wider music industry. The Chain of Command turned a blind eye as long as the CDs were for personal use. They didn't take kindly to anyone buying in bulk, trying to send them back home to make a quick buck, and the RMPs were always on the lookout for this. Either they were in the pocket of the music industry or they were bored.

A friend of mine, Mugsy Teach, after the tour with the money he saved, took advantage of a perk from serving in Germany. We were allowed to purchase a brand-new tax free car once a year. The dealer would also offer a generous discount on top as a sweetener to get our custom. Mugsy travelled back to the UK to collect his brand-new Mercedes. The salesman showed him around the car, Mugsy signed the paperwork and was given the key as he was going to drive back to Germany in it. He put a CD in the player, ready to listen to Dire Straits' Greatest Hits for the drive down to Dover to catch his pre-booked ferry. The salesman waved him off and, after a few minutes of him sitting in his car and not going anywhere, the salesman realised there was a potential problem.

Mugsy opened the door of the car to the question from the salesman.

"Is there a problem, Sir?"

"The CD player doesn't work," he replied, pressing the Play button again and again.

The salesman joined him in the car and attempted to make it play. After several minutes of pressing buttons, he apologised profusely.

"I'll have to get one of our technicians to look at it," he said, with a repentant tone.

Mugsy was directed to wait in the office with a cup of coffee while the technician tried to figure out why the CD player on this brand-new top marques car wasn't working. He noticed the technician had almost dissembled the entire dashboard to his new Mercedes.

"This is going to take a while longer than anticipated, Sir. Why don't you go and have some lunch? On us, of course," said the salesman.

They booked him a taxi and he was taken to a swanky restaurant half a mile away. He was received like royalty and offered anything from the menu courtesy of the Mercedes dealership. It was during his main course of a roasted rack of English lamb with Provençal vegetables, olive tapenade, and basil pesto that the penny dropped. The CD was the one he bought from outside a camp in Mrkonjić Grad a few months earlier. He nearly choked on his lamb. Not all the CDs we purchased would play on a quality CD player, but they did seem to work on cheaper ones. He also remembered he left the case in the car with its badly printed, slightly out-of-focus and far too much contrast version of the album cover. On his return to the dealership, he was informed by the salesman it was now fixed and his CD should play. With hopefully a not too noticeable red face, Mugsy could not extract himself from the over-remorseful salesman and depart the dealership fast enough.

Melba and I stroll down to the main gate in the afternoon sunshine with our weapons slung over our backs, as if armed shopping is the norm.

"Off to buy some CDs, lads?" says the guard.

"Just going to have a look," says Melba.

"The one on the end with the blonde lass sells the best ones and they do a buy-four-get-one-free deal," he says.

"Good to know," replies Melba.

The CDs are stacked up on hand-made wooden tables, which have been roughly knocked up as I notice bits of bark in places. A piece of brown cardboard states their price of 2DM in black marker pen. Every CD is the same price and I presume this is a gentlemen's agreement by each of the competitors. There are a few others from BLMF browsing their collections, all armed.

On a tour, a couple of years later, inflation had kicked in. This could have been to cover the price of their investment in their sheltered shops. They rose to a whopping 3DM.

We walk along the line of tables, and I expect the sellers to try to hassle us to have a peek at what they are offering. They keep to themselves as we meander, too busy smoking and growing moustaches to bother us. The layout of each stall is almost a carbon-copy of the others. It must be a winning formula.

The one at the end with the blonde lady that the guard told us about was there. She's likewise smoking but not growing a moustache. Her stall stands out as she's the only one offering the buy-four-get-one-free deal.

"Nothing like a bit of competition to get the consumer intersted," I say.

"Two bucks a pop is hardly gonna break the bank, is it?" says Melba.

"It's Day One, Lesson One of the basic retailing course, isn't it? Do something to stand out from the crowd and the Squaddies will come," I say.

"Squaddies love a deal, discount or a freebie," I continue. "If we can blag five quid off a ten-grand car, we'll feel better for it even though it's fuck all."

I glance through the collection of CDs, which are in alphabetical order, and pick a few as I go along. Greatest Hits seems to be a popular theme, and it's not long before I have five CDs. I've gone for the soundtrack to *Pulp Fiction,* and the Greatest Hits of the Cure, Johnny Cash, Bob Marley and David Bowie.

The smoking blonde lady takes them from me and puts them in a tiny plastic striped bag. She then coldly declares, "Eight Deutschmarks."

I pass her a 10DM note.

"I have no change. You pick one more," she tells me in an authoritarian tone.

Her order-like request catches me out. I look around in a panic to see what else they have to offer, as I to try to select something from the swathe of CDs before me.

My eyes dart around as I look, but nothing is grabbing my attention. I sense she's in a hurry to get rid of me now she's got my cash in her nicotine-stained fingers. She looks at her merchandise, pulls out a random one, and thrusts it my way.

"Radiohead, they good band."

"Ok, Radiohead it is," I say, thinking I have little choice.

She whisks the 10DM note away into her money bag faster than it takes Staff Hobbs to say yes to a shot of Sleep in the Ditch.

As we walk away from her stall, I say to Melba.

"You have to admire her entrepreneurial skills."

"Yup, she saw you coming all the way from Split," he remarks.

The Radiohead CD was bloody miserable and ended up as a coaster in Shaun the Yawn's tool store a few weeks later.

Flat Out Tired

Captain Triple H tells me in the afternoon that I need to pack for a few days, as we will be heading out on a road trip. I don't know where she thinks I've been staying in the evenings, other than the office with Melba. I looked at the already-packed rucksack I've been living out of, and said back to her.

"Yes, ma'am."

Officers are sometimes referred to as Lighthouses in the Desert — extremely bright, but not much use. This saying sprung into my head right there, at that moment in time.

Her presence had been requested by a few units around Bosnia. She would discuss what their requirements were with them before getting the quotes to get a contract.

Next morning, after breakfast, with the taste of Italy in my mouth, I bid my farewells to Melba and Staff Hobbs. I have to collect Captain Triple H from her Corimec. I initially think this is the reason she cannot pack light. Then I notice it's because she's bringing a bulky fold-up American cot bed with her to sleep on. They are a whole lot better than the British version as they are sturdier with a box-type aluminium frame. You're higher off the ground and away from the cold. The British one is a wire-frame one. It raises you barely a few millimetres off the deck and, if you roll over too far, it tips over, depositing you on the floor.

The words of my old Staff Sergeant ring around my head at my lack of foresight in not having my own American one.

"Any idiot can be uncomfortable."

I make a note to acquire one at the next available opportunity. That opportunity will no doubt present itself when I find one unattended.

We stop at the gate to load up, and then we are on our way. First halt will be at Gornji Vakuf, about four hours' driving time away. Initially, the route is along Pegasus, but we soon pick up Route Gull, which takes us round Banja Luka and in a southerly direction towards Jajce. The tarmac road finishes not far from the city limits. It becomes a rough dirt road full of suitcase-sized holes and a few football-sized rocks. The gentle rolling landscape soon changes to an increasingly undulating one, then to the more dramatic mountainous setting.

As we progress along the road, it follows the bending Vrbas River as it cuts through the countryside. It's bumpy going even as I try my best to keep out from the holes and away from the rocks. I can't get away from the badly driven, overloaded VW Golfs, which are even more popular here than the badly driven Fiat 126s. Their drivers don't seem to care about any damage they might sustain from the state of the road as they speed past me. Most of them don't spot the holes until the last minute and then their single brake light comes on. I rarely observe a car with both brake lights working. The car bounces in, then out of it, and then carries on to the next hole or around the next rock. With the fillings becoming loose in my teeth, the tarmac appears from around a bend and it feels like heaven as we bounce onto it. The road climbs and the Vrbas on our left widens in places. I get a quick glimpse of the impressive hydroelectric dam which holds back the Bočac Lake before the road curves away and it disappears from view.

The lake comes back into view and the road becomes almost straight as it cuts into the side of the hill. We gradually rise high above the water, and, as we get to the crest, I glance to my left. I then notice something I know I've seen before. The lake has formed a steep-sided valley as it stretches away from me and around a corner in the distance. The sides are lush with abundant vegetation. It's broken up in places as rocks protrude from the steeper parts where no plant life has gained a hold. The water now carries a greenish tint, echoing the color of the undergrowth along the bank. This green, reflected across the glassy surface, mingles with the blue of the sky and the white clouds above, creating a layered scene of intertwined colors and reflections. The view looks so familiar and I try to think where I have seen it before. My grey matter works hard and then I remember it was in my primary school. We had been doing something about European countries and it was on a poster emblazoned with the words 'Visit the Beautiful Yugoslavia'. There is an area just off the road where you can park up to take in the view, but I keep going.[97] The road now drops back down and is level with the lake, which reduces in width until it becomes the Vrbas river once again. Our asphalt path follows the water's edge, continuing to wind along as the sides of the valley become now almost vertical. We cross to the other side of the river via a long, curved brutalist bridge made of concrete. In places, the river is squeezed tightly between the steep sides. The engineers had no other choice but to cut tunnels straight

97 Later in the tour, I stopped here regularly to take in the magnificent view and, of course, take a picture of it. See Page 162.

through the rock. These numerous tunnels are short in length, and like the bridge, have been made with zero architectural flamboyance whatsoever. Some are lined with concrete in a curved style, whilst others are roughly cut through the rock. The frequency of memorials to people who have met their demise in their cars along this route tells me it's an accident black spot. They don't seem to work as a warning to the locals, who still insist on overtaking me on blind bends. After a while, the steep rocky sides of the gorge become a gentler slope and again are covered in the green of bushes and trees. There are a few empty dwellings. These appear abandoned due to something other than the war because of the lack of the familiar bullet pock marks. We pass a three-storey structure made from logs and straw with the word 'Mir' written on a sign on top of the building. The word is in the Latin alphabet, which means we've now departed Republika Srpska and are now in the Federation of Bosnia and Herzegovina. The IEBL[98] is unmarked. It was agreed on at the signing of the Dayton Accords and runs its course roughly based on the territory which was held at that time.

On my return visit in the spring of 2022, I drove down this same road but in the other direction. There was an enormous sign welcoming you to the Republika Srpska, which had been vandalised. Someone had thrown paint over it and there was a 'Z' sprayed on it. This was used by the Russians as a pro-war motif during their invasion of Ukraine.

All this time driving, and Captain Triple H hasn't said a single word. She has the IFOR Route Map on her knee and I think her silence means I'm still going in the right direction. We pass the sign denoting Jajce town boundary and I tell her I'm pulling over for a

98 Inter-Entity Boundary Line

break, to which she nods in approval. I spot a layby ahead and pull in, ensuring I remain on the hard standing surface. Handbrake on, engine off, and I pop the door open, swinging my legs out. I stand up, put my arms in the air, and stretch. I feel the material on the backside of my trousers is extremely damp from the cheap vinyl seat covers. "That was an impressive piece of road, wasn't it?" says Captain Triple H. It's the first time I've heard her talk since leaving Banja Luka hours earlier.

"Yeah, it was pretty cool. Can I have a butcher's[99] at the Route Map please, ma'am?" I reply, knowing Officers are not known for their navigation skills or grasp of Cockney rhyming slang. To be fair, though, it's not particularly hard to find your way around Bosnia because it doesn't have many main roads. We'll continue along Route Gull towards Bugojno where Route Opal starts. From the Route Map, I can't tell if it's a junction at Bugojno or if the road goes straight on. I'm sure some budding NATO graffiti artist has already paid it a visit and it will be well signed. I go to the back of the Lanny to find some bottles of water that I know are in there somewhere. Fishing out a couple out from underneath our kit, I pass one to Captain Triple H. The day is warming up and becoming humid. The warm water going down my throat is needed, but I wish it was a few degrees cooler. As we progressed down the road in the morning, we passed a junction for Route Hornblower. Most of the traffic had turned off this way as it takes them to the other towns within what was known as the Anvil of Republika Srpska. Thereafter, there was no traffic, as our road heads across the IEBL. Parked up in the layby, I study the Route Map on the front wing of the Lanny and I realise how quiet it is. There's no traffic passing us, no sound of life from the nearby town. There's no wind to move the leaves on the trees that are spread around us. The only thing I hear is rushing water

99 Butcher's Hook – Look.

from the Vrbas River, down the hill from us as it navigates some rapids. I look up the hill and notice the few houses which are mere shells, devoid of windows and roofs, with the familiar bullet damage. "Right, time to carry on," says Captain Triple H.

That's the last thing she says to me until we arrive at Gornji Vakuf later in the day. Climbing back into the Lanny, my backside makes contact with the seat. This gives me a brief burst of delight as I realise my arse has finally dried out. I put my hand on my weapon as if I want to be sure it's still there and I wasn't imagining it. Losing a gun is a career-defining moment for all the wrong reasons. It will define it so much that you may as well get out of the military because you'll probably never get promoted ever again.

I ponder for a second over whether Captain Triple H has a sweaty backside like me before rejoining the road.

The Fiat 126 is just inches away as it flashes past us. I've pulled out onto the deserted road without looking in my mirror, just as the only car in a 50-mile radius drove past us. "Fuck," I shout as I jump on the brakes. "Where the fuck did he come from? I think he was waiting for us.

"Where there's blame, there's a claim," I add to the one-way conversation. Captain Triple H remains in complete silence, like her mute button is switched on as soon as we move.

Evidence of the war surrounds us now as every house is damaged. All road signs and the metal crash barriers are sporting many bullet holes. Cars are abandoned at the roadside. Some have turned into an orange rust colour from being completely burnt out. The unburnt ones are peppered with tiny holes from gunfire. The edge of each hole is rusting where the paint has come away, exposing the bare metal to the elements. They're all missing their wheels. The reason why, I can't gauge. We come across a rusty-looking Sherman tank which is off the edge of the road. I'm unsure if it's been on fire or it's rusty from not getting a lick of paint since the Second World

War. There's another similar-looking tank with a turret that is more squared off, which I don't recognise. It looks like it's tried to drive up the embankment onto the road at an angle before being brought to a stop.[100] Further on there's a modern armoured vehicle that's been destroyed by fire and has turned the usual bright rusty orange. Whereas the first ones gave the impression they had broken down, this one has the sense that violence has been inflicted upon it. It has the style of a Soviet personnel carrier with a small sloped turret towards the rear of the vehicle. One of its tracks has been snapped and is now lying flat on the road behind it. It's carried on for a few more feet under its own inertia before coming to a halt and being physically unable to travel any further. One of the two back doors is open. The large metal plate at the front, which is basically the armoured bonnet covering the engine, has been flung back with enough energy to bend it. On the side, there is a metal skirt that's also been bent back with force. Whatever gun was fitted in the turret has been removed and none of the hatches are open. As we roll past, I glance back into the interior through the back door. It's too dark to peer inside and I know it's probably for the best. The entire way along Route Gull to Bugojno, there's damage and destruction. However, daily life appears to be carrying on and growing. I see more IFOR trucks travelling this section of road in an hour than I have seen the whole day. In Bugojno there are IFVs of the Dutch Army parked up on street corners around the town. Some soldiers sit on them, lazing in the sun, and some wander around, keeping an eye on their surroundings. The locals mainly ignore them, with maybe the odd glance their way as they carry on with their daily routine. Children gravitate around them as they look in awe at the huge armoured vehicles. Some of them have overcome their shyness and are laughing

---

100 I did get a picture of it at later on and discovered it was an M10 tank destroyer after seeing one in the Bovington Tank Museum. Again, another Second World War era piece of armour being used in mid 90s Europe.

with the soldiers, while others pass a football to them, trying to initiate a kickabout. Soon enough, the town is behind us, and we are now travelling on Route Opal on the final leg to Gornji Vakuf.

The first thing I notice is the steering of the Lanny has become heavier than usual and it's pulling to one side.

"I believe we have a problem, ma'am," I say to Captain Triple H, who says nothing.

I spot a place off to the side of the road where we can pull off, away from the traffic. The Lanny has a notable dip to the front left now and I realise we have picked up a puncture. I bring us to a halt and jump out to look at what I already know. The tyre is almost flat and I hear the last of the air escaping. I have a gander to where I think the sound is coming from. I spot a flap of rubber, which I peel back easily, revealing a deep cut right into the inner ply of the tyre.

"We must gone over something sharp to do that," I say to her as the hissing air finally stops.

"Bugger, rats and damn," says Captain Triple H.

"I'll put the spare on, ma'am."

I am now having a moment. I know we have the tools, as I only signed for them a few days ago from Melba. But one thing I didn't check was the spare and whether it was inflated. It's on the bonnet of the vehicle and if it was also flat, I would be none the wiser until I take it off. "Why didn't I check the spare?" I think to myself as I go round to the back door of the Lanny to get the tools. I then unfasten the spare and at this point I can't tell if it has pressure or not. It's only when I lift it from the bonnet and let it drop to the ground. It bounces with the noise that can only come from being inflated.

"Fuck, yes," I mutter under my breath.

"You OK?" asks Captain Triple H, thinking I've hurt myself.

"Yes, all good, ma'am, I'll have it sorted in a few minutes."

Thirty minutes later, I lower the jack and give the wheel nuts one last nip with the wheel brace. I'm sweating like I've been for a five-mile run in the afternoon sun. I chuck everything in the back, including the knackered tyre, as I am hoping to get a replacement from someone at Gornji Vakuf.

"Will we be able to get it repaired?" asks Captain Triple H.

"It's beyond repairing, ma'am," I reply to her with sweat in my eyes. "I'll see if I can get it swapped for a new one, as it's not a good idea to be travelling around without a spare."

"My thoughts exactly," she says, nodding in approval, looking dry as a bone.

I put the Lanny into gear knowing it's the last I'll hear her speak until we arrive at our destination. I pull out onto the road, searching with extra vigilance for any speeding Fiat 126s appearing in my wing mirror at a rapid rate of knots.

We go under the rising red and white barrier as we enter the camp at Gornji Vakuf with a friendly, welcome to our base, acknowledgment wave from the gate guard.

"Can you book in, please?" he says as I drive past him.

I give him the 'I heard you' acknowledgment wave back.

I pull up at what must be the Guardroom. As soon as I turn the engine off, Captain Triple H says, "I'll book us in, as I need to find out where I'm going."

"We need to unload too," I add.

Once our magazines are off our weapons at the unloading bay, she scurries off through the door into the Guardroom while I make my way back to the Lanny. I'm still damp from the wheel-changing exertions of earlier.

She comes back and announces, "I think I know where I'm going, but in the meantime, if you head down this road and on the right, you can apparently park up there. I'll come and get you in a few minutes."

"OK, ma'am," I reply.

I drive down the road and I notice it's got the standard layout of a centralised building surrounded by Corimecs and green tents.[101] There certainly is indeed an area which I park up on. I switch the engine off, sit back and relax, watching the comings and goings of the busy camp. Military camps are a funny one. From my experience, I know we always try to appear busy so the shit jobs won't be assigned to us. I wonder if it's the same here and if you got everyone who wasn't doing anything work-related to stand still, and face the same direction, would they resemble the Terracotta Army? There's a pleasant breeze coming through the open windows of the Lanny. I try to slouch back a bit but there's nowhere comfortable to put my head. I then realise Captain Triple H has left her jacket behind, so I grab it, roll it up, and use it as a makeshift pillow. Now in a moderately more comfortable state, my eyes start to close under the weight of tiredness from the long drive and the heat of the day. I dream strange dreams in my not-so-deep sleep as I hear the background noises of what is going on in the camp. Vehicles move around, generators hum, and soldiers shout to each other with more swearwords than normal words. My head nods as I dip into sleep. Then as I dip back out, I raise it again, trying to find the sweet spot as I wedge into the corner on Captain Triple H's jacket.

Her "couple of minutes" seems to be taking a while, but I don't mind as I snooze away the afternoon. Now that my body has caught up on its sleep debt and I'm now balancing the books, I feel a little more awake. I take a swig of tepid water from a plastic bottle I opened earlier in the day and check my watch. I look at the time and notice she's been gone for hours. Sitting up on the seat, I sense the sweaty dampness on my behind and all the way up my back. I remove Captain Triple H's jacket and give it a shake-out so it doesn't look like I've been using it as a pillow. I consider going in search of a cup of cofftea and, as if by telepathic means, Captain Triple H

---

101 I found out later that it was a former school.

comes into view, holding two white Styrofoam cups.

"Apologies for taking so long," she says through the window, and she passes me a cup. I take a sip and it's an untypically very good brew for a change. I was expecting hints of stuff which I couldn't fathom, but I can actually taste the coffee.

"That is an outstanding brew, ma'am," I say to her.

"I used the HQ's coffee filter. It's the best brew I've had for weeks," she replies.

Over our posh coffee, she goes on to tell me the plan and that we'll be stopping the night here. There's transit accommodation, in the shape of tents, on the camp somewhere. In the morning, we will collect a translator. Then we'll drive over to a place nearby to inquire about setting up a contract to obtain some wood for a building project which is going on.

"I'll need to find the REME to see about getting our tyre sorted," I say.

"Sorry, I forgot to ask where they are located," she replies.

"They can't be too difficult to find," I say.

We agree to meet again in the morning after breakfast at the Lanny. She grabs her rucksack from the back but leaves her cot bed behind. I make a mental note that she's left it behind and I may use it to sleep on. I go searching for the place where the Spanner Monkeys hang out and it's easy to find. The gathering of various vehicles in different states of repair, sporting damage or generally not looking too roadworthy is a dead giveaway that I am getting warmer. Locating the office is harder, as it could be in a Corimec, a building or a tent. I have to relent and ask a passing young soldier who bears a resemblance to a Spanner Monkey. He's got no beret, so I have no idea what cap badge, but he's covered in grime and wearing a filthy tee shirt. He may as well have 'I am a Spanner Monkey' written on it.

"Excuse me, pal, are you REME?" I say to him.

"Yeah, I am," he replies.

"Where's your LAD?"[102]

"Over there," he says, pointing to a set of doors on the side of a building.

I thank him, walk over to the doors he pointed out for me, and venture in with a little bit of trepidation due to the unfamiliarity of the surroundings. Inside there's a counter. Behind it are a few 6ft tables strewn with dirty-looking paperwork and piles of vehicle document folders. A Corporal, in a clean T-shirt, is sitting at one of them, writing away. He's so engrossed by what he's doing that he doesn't realise I'm standing there. The young Spanner Monkey, who I spoke to less than a minute ago, comes in behind me, walks around the counter and says, "Can I help you?"

"I hope so," I say. "I picked up a flat tyre on the way here today,"

"Changing wheels is a Driver's responsibility," exclaims the clean Corporal, not even lifting his eyes from his desk.

"I've already put the spare on but the original is pretty fucked," I say, now turning to him.

"How do you know?" he replies, his head remaining down.

"It's got a great big" — I pause for effect — "gash in it."

"Are you based here, and who are you anyway?" he says, looking up. I go on to explain that I am from 7 Regiment in Split but the Lanny belongs to another unit, based in Šipovo.

"Can't help you mate," he says, far too quickly. "You'll need to get back to the unit in Šipovo, or at least contact them so they could order you a new tyre."

"What am I supposed to do if I get another puncture?" I say, recognising the frustration building up in me. "Call a taxi?"

"Sorry, but I can't order spares for other units," he says adamantly. I stand there in silence for a minute, half-expecting him to come up with a solution. He returns to his paperwork and the young

102 Light Aid Detachment.

Spanner Monkey looks at me blankly. I mutter, "For fuck's sake," turn and depart back through the doors.

At the Lanny, I scratch my head trying to think what to do next. I will either have to call Melba for advice or tell Captain Triple H we now have to plan an impromptu visit to Šipovo. Which is at least a two-hour drive away.

Then, like a Michelin Man saviour, I see the young mechanic coming towards me, rolling a fully-inflated Lanny wheel. Notice how I've now called him a mechanic, because the good lad was helping me out? That's how it rolls in the Army, I'm afraid.

"Here you go, mate, you can have this one. Just give me back yours," he says.

"Mate, you're a fucking star," I say, feeling the relief lift from my shoulders.

"We're all on the same fucking side," he says. "I can't stand the 'I can't do that because you're not our unit' bullshit."

"Where did you get this wheel?" I ask him.

"I borrowed it from one of the long-term VOR[103] vehicles."

Undoing the damaged one on the bonnet, I pass it to him and replace it with the new one.

"Nobody will know and it'll get fixed anyway, so who cares?" he says.

"I owe you one," I say to him.

That was the last I ever saw of him. If you're reading this book, pal, there's a pint waiting for you. To Corporal Paperwork, I hope later in the day you had a crap, and it was akin to a massive pineapple.

In the transit accommodation that night is just me, on a British cot bed, in a 12x12 tent, on my own. While I was away dealing

---

103 Vehicle Off Road. The official military term for 'knackered.'

with the REME, Captain Triple H returned to the Lanny and took her cot bed. I curse her 'forward thinking', but I curse my lack of 'forward thinking' more. I try to read my book by torchlight in the evening, but every time I attempt to move, I am tipped out onto the cold, damp floor. It's a long night.

Window Shopping

"Ah, a new tyre," says Captain Triple H, seeing the spare is back on the bonnet. "We're good to go," I say. "I've even tided up the rear of the vehicle for our passenger."

I am introduced to Ivana, who will travel with us today. Like most of the younger generation here, she speaks excellent English.

"Dobro Jutro, Ivana," I say to her, shaking her hand.

"Dobro Jutro," she replies and then jabbers away at me in her language, which sounds like nothing to me.

"Corporal Lee speaks German," announces Captain Triple H.

"Ah, wie geht es dir," [How are you] she asks me.

"Mir geht's gut, danke Ivana," [I am fine, thanks, Ivana] I reply.

"You can call me Iva. It's the shortened version." Iva has a really bizarre accent with certain words and I question her about it.

"Where did you learn your English, Iva?" I ask her.

"At school and from watching the TV, as most things were in English with subtitles," she replies. I've come across this in Southern Germany, in the American Military area. The Germans spoke English with an American accent from also watching telly or speaking to them.

"That's a funny accent you have there. What programmes were you watching?"

She laughs and says, "Most of the British Army units I've been a translator for were Scottish ones."

"Ahhhhh," I say, as the penny drops. It is just the strangest thing to hear her speak English with the odd Scottish twang on certain words.

We stop at the Guardroom to book out and load up while Iva stays in the back of the Lanny. I've tried to make some space for her back there, so at least she will be somewhat comfortable as we bounce around the quality Bosnian roads. There's a little seat she can perch herself on, which at least has a bit of foam padding. As she is the one giving the directions, she'll need to at least be able to see where she is going and, more importantly, tell me where to go. Therefore, I instruct her to climb up on our rucksacks so that she's now in-between and behind us. She can now look out the front a lot better and does not have to scream the directions to us. Our rucksacks are probably comfier than the thinly padded seat, anyway.

We are driving down a street in the town and the damage is the most severe I've witnessed so far. The buildings on either side will not be restorable and look like the only potential use they'll have is hardcore for foundations. The number of bullet holes in the few walls that are still standing are in their thousands. Again, I suspect this is a result of malicious vandalism rather than from fighting. It's hard to imagine the horror which has happened here on this sunny day as we drive along. I almost feel like a tourist experiencing other people's misery from a safe spot and getting a kick out of it.

"It's here somewhere," says Iva in my ear. "Slow down," she adds, as she looks for our destination. I slow and I can't see her, so I've no idea if it's going to be on the right or left.

"Here, it's here," she shouts excitedly. "Turn here."

I still have no idea where I am going. Then I notice her arm appear over my shoulder as she points to the dirty and damaged apartment block to my right.

I turn into a car park that is lacking in cars but filled with people milling around instead. I pull as close as I can to the entrance of the building, which they are queuing to get into.

"Could you not get any closer?" says Captain Triple H as soon as I come to a halt.

I bite my lip to stop myself saying, 'Anyone can be uncomfortable, ma'am'.

We grab any valuable items to take with us into the office, just in case, and I lock the doors.

"Why are you locking the Lanny?" says Iva.

"It's a precaution. You know, in case something goes missing," I reply, now realising where this is going.

"They won't steal anything from you. It'll be fine, don't worry."

I bet she's never had the experience of getting marched into the OC's Office at 100mph for losing stuff, I think to myself.

"I'm sure it will, but I've got this terrible habit of locking things up that will cost me money if they go walkies."

She laughs and starts talking to the people in the car park. I'm anticipating that they will erupt into fits of laughter as Iva points at me.

We squeeze our way into the building. Iva says unintelligible things which make the individuals waiting in line move a little to give us space to pass. We shuffle down the corridor, jumping the queue, with no reactions from anyone, and into the room that's clearly the office. Sat behind a desk is a Captain with a Royal Engineers cap badge. We present ourselves with Captain Triple H in the middle and Iva and me either side.

He sees us, springs up from his desk and offers his hand for a shake to Captain Triple H.

"Hi, Dave Whiterock, Royal Engineers," he says.

"Nice to meet you. I'm Hanna Huntley-Hays, and I believe you've been expecting us," she replies.

"I most certainly have."

"This is Iva, our translator," she says, turning to her.

"Nice to meet you too," he replies, smiling to her, offering his hand again for a shake.

"And this is my driver, Lance Corporal Lee," now turning the other way to introduce me.

"Hi," is all I get and not even a smile. I'm glad I kept my hand on my gun and didn't offer it up before him.

"Marija?" is the next thing he says loudly, calling whoever she may be. A woman, about the same age as Iva, enters the room and, upon seeing Iva, explodes into smiles. They both chatter away in their own language as us unilingual Brits stand in silence, waiting for them to finish.

"This is Marija, my translator," says Captain Rude. "And I presume you two know each other," he adds, smiling at them both.

"Yes, yes," they say in unison.

"We went to school together," says Iva.

"And I also presume you haven't seen each another in a while?" he adds, judging by their reaction to meeting here this morning.

"Yes, yes, no, no," says Marija. "We saw one another last night."

I smile as if it's normal and I ponder to myself, 'Fuck me. If they are like this after one night, what would they be like after a few years'.

"Coffee?" announces Captain Ignore-The-JNCO.

"Yes, please," I say first before anyone else and before he spams me to make it.

Captain Triple H nods to a coffee but the translators decline.

Years later, I learnt why they always turned down coffee from us during a conversation with a friend from Slovenia. Anyone from the Balkans thinks our instant coffee is akin to muddy water.

"Smiiiith," shouts Captain Shiterock. I knew I would come up with a good name for him in time.

"Yes, Sir," says a head that materialises in the doorway, whom I presume to be Smiiiith.

"Put the kettle on, will you please, and Marija, could you please inform the queue we will be a bit delayed this morning?"

"Yes, Sir," says Smiiiith.

"Yes, David," says Marija, smiling at him.

I clock Captain Triple H's momentary frown.

Over the worst coffee of the tour so far, Captain Valentino explains what he does, and what he needs from Captain Triple H.

His job, in a nutshell, is to provide building materials to the local population to help them reconstruct their houses, businesses and lives. Up to now he has been passing over anything he gets his hands on, which was through the military logistic chain. Someone, somewhere in a prominent position, has thought it would be a good idea if we could source these resources locally, thus stimulating the post-war economy. The main things which are in short supply are glass and wood. I have noticed in my travels that most homes are using plastic sheeting for their windows. I guess they want to get them replaced before the winter arrives.

Captain Triple H's mission, should she accept it, is to find a local supplier of the said materials. Iva does say she knows someone who knows someone who might be able to get their hands on the required supplies. This is how it's going to happen, as I'm not too sure the Bosnian Yellow Pages would be too accurate these days.

The rest of the day is spent visiting people whom Iva knows, to find out if they know anyone who could acquire what we need. We end up going round the houses. To save time, I end up waiting by the Lanny while Captain Triple H and Iva do their thing. One address Iva is given is down a dirt track. Before I turn off the asphalt road, I stop the Lanny. We have been told time and time again not to go off-road and stay on hard surfaces due to the undocumented mine threat. The track doesn't look well used, heads off into the

227

woods, and could be concealing anything.

"Are you sure this is the right place?" says Captain Triple H to Iva, sensing my reason for stopping.

"This is how the guy described it to me," she replies.

"We are not driving down there," I say to Captain Triple H. "And the guy who gave you these details looked pretty angry to me. Maybe he's got an axe to grind with us."

"Agreed," says Captain Triple H. "It's not happening."

Maybe there was someone down the track who could have helped us. Maybe there was carnage, pain, and death. It wasn't worth the risk, so we drive away, staying on the hard safe surface.

During the years of conflict here, the worst of humanity was brought out, as that's what war tends to do. The local people I had met so far had been nothing but courteous. I knew they wouldn't boast about anything questionable which they may have done or be wearing a sign around their neck declaring their crimes. I was mindful these awful examples of human beings were still living here, either in hiding or known by the locals. Throughout my total time in the Balkans, which exceeded a year, it's highly likely I encountered or conversed with individuals who had engaged in terrible things.

We carried a wanted list, produced by the ICTY of known war criminals. It had the major players, such as Ratko Mladić, Radovan Karadžić and a host of others whom I'd never heard of. More than half of them had no pictures of them but only their details.

I remember one of them, who was without a photo, just had his alias. Real name, date of birth, address, hometown, all unknown. I could have arrested Colonel Gaddafi from the First & Last on this information alone the next time he didn't give us a free plate of chips.

We finally find someone who would be willing to supply or, more likely, start importing it for us. Details are swapped and these are be passed onto a civilian department somewhere to hammer out the finer points. Normally three quotes are required, but Captain Triple H has to admit defeat today and there will only be the one this time. I'm sure some civil servant administrator out there would say this would be unacceptable in the process of ensuring the best value for money.

Talking Rubbish

After a night of being continually tipped out of bed onto the floor every time I tried to change my sleeping position, it's time to move on. We say bye and thank you to Iva for her help in trying to get us killed and sourcing the much-needed supplies. Captain Triple H has an appointment in Mrkonjić Grad to assist the unit there and set up a contract for the removal of their garbage. We hit Route Opal and Gull as we head back to Jajce for a meeting with someone who might be able to help.

It's another hot sunny day as we continue in complete silence. I can't work out why she doesn't speak whenever the Lanny is in motion. I contemplate getting close to the edge of the road and pretending I'm in a deep slumber to provoke her to react. Would she just sit there if I was asleep in a hushed calm state as we tore through the rusted crash barriers and off into the abyss? I dread a long trip back to Split or to Sarajevo, which would be six hours of enforced quiet. Making a note to myself, I decide I'll have to buy a Boogie Box[104] from the EFI[105] when we next come across one. I can't be doing with hours of only the sound of the knobbly tyres on the tarmac to keep me entertained. I also now have my CD collection to listen

---

104 A portable stereo to you young uns.

105 Expeditionary Force Institute. Basically the NAAFI on a war footing.

to. It'll be growing in size as soon as I get back to BLMF, as I have thought of some other artists to diddle out of royalties.

At Jajce we have to pick up Route Bluebird, which is the road which will take us to the centre of town. Iva suggested we should visit the famous waterfalls of Jajce city and the Museum of the 2nd AVNOJ Session,[106] if it's open yet. I see a sign on the road into town with the letters AVNOJ written on it.

"There's the Museum Iva recommended," I say, knowing I won't get a reply.

I remember the instructions on where we were meeting our contact before we set off. It's the first right after the short tunnel. Across the bridge, right at the roundabout, then go down to the car park and we'll see the Travnik Gate. It's not described to us, but we are told we will know it when we spot it. I'm glad I remembered the directions as I'm not expecting any assistance from Captain Double T. I decided to change her name to Captain Talkative in Transit. I wonder how far we would get if I took a wrong turn and I consider trying it sometime soon.

We drive around the bend and the Travnik Gate comes into view. It's a medieval gatehouse that is the arched entrance into the old town through the city walls. I go around the car park a couple of times before I stop, hopefully annoying Captain Double T a little. Pulling the handbrake on, I switch the engine off and she speaks.

"I believe this is it."

The thought "Thank you, Captain Holmes, for this clarification. I might have carried on driving around looking for an actual gate if you weren't here to guide me" swirls around in my head.

---

106 The 2nd AVNOJ (Anti-Fascist Council for the National Liberation of Yugoslavia) Session was a pivotal meeting held on November 29-30, 1943, in the town of Jajce in Bosnia and Herzegovina, during World War II. It was a defining moment for the Yugoslav resistance movement against Nazi occupation and Axis collaborators and had profound consequences for postwar Yugoslavia.

Jajce is unnervingly lacking of any signs of life. There are no cars parked up and nobody is driving around. I look through the Travnik Gate towards what I think might be the centre and I can't see any people anywhere. Not being able to see them, but hearing their roar, I know the waterfalls are close by. Every building has been damaged but the city walls give it the impression of a tough town. I notice a few window frames have plastic sheeting over them, which tells me someone is living here.

We are to meet our contact at noon. We are early, but Captain Double T doesn't want to go anywhere in case they turn up early. Not that there is anywhere to go.

"I'm going to have a look at the waterfalls," I say to her. "They sound like they are only around the corner."

I stroll over to the side of the road and peer over the low wall towards the river, which is not too far below. It's fast flowing, deep green, and looks cold. I assume it's the last of the melting snow from the surrounding peaks, like most geographical features I've seen out there. *[I learnt later on that it's the River Pliva, and the waterfall is where it feeds into the Vrbas.]* To my left, I notice a set of steps going down to the water and to a park on its bank. To my right, I see a cast iron bridge going over the water to the other side. I walk towards the steps and go down a few before stopping. The deficiency in day-to-day life makes me nervous. I gaze towards it for a minute and I observe the water disappearing over the waterfalls away from me, which is not the best of views. I walk back up the steps, past Captain Double T and to the start of the bridge. Stopping again, I look across it with no intention of going over it. Images flash through my head of bridges blowing up in war films I have seen over the years. I am in the wrong position again, but I am not going to go traipsing round the lifeless tourist attraction to get the best view. I'll wait until 2022, when I return to a city full of life.

At 1pm we hear a car and a VW Golf turns up with no number

plates on it. I clock that there's only one guy in it, and not a load of them. I instantly feel relieved. He pulls up next to our Lanny, opens his door, and says.

"Hi, guys."

Before we can reply, he's out of the car, lights up a cigarette, and has it in his mouth with a big, deep inhale. He holds the packet towards us both in the internationally recognised motion of, 'Would you also like a cigarette?'

We both decline.

We make our introductions and we find out his name is Nemanja. He is in his early twenties, skinny in build but smartly dressed in a suit and wearing a pair of aviator sunglasses. I think he looks somewhat dodgy, not from his attire or the crappy VW Golf he arrived in. It's the aviators which make him look like a criminal to me. Maybe I was stereotyping him, but I'm in a country that's just endured years of civil war, standing in a car park in a lifeless town. I'm armed while my boss talks to a 20-year-old about a garbage contract. We are not in Kansas anymore, and things don't work here the same way as back home during these early days of the formation of a new country. Nemanja lives locally and has an uncle who used to run the local refuse company before the war.

He would now like to get back into business, now normal services are being resumed in these new peaceful times. He grabs a briefcase from his Golf and they both saunter off together to talk details. I remain with the Lanny keeping them both in my sight. They sit down on the low wall. He opens up his briefcase, gets out some paper and jots down some notes while Captain Double T talks non-stop. It's the most I've heard her talk since I first met her a few days ago. They chat for around 20 minutes and when they stand up and shake hands, I guess business negotiations have been concluded. They make their way back towards me.

"Do you like music?" he asks me, opening the back door of his car to reveal boxes of CDs. Pausing for a second, I think I'd like to have a look at what he's got, but then I have a premonition. I'm marched in front of General Mike Jackson,[107] by Buckethands. I am being charged for taking a bribe, which resulted in Nemanja's uncle unfairly winning the garbage contract, which enabled him to make a profit of £10 a week from NATO. "I'm good, thanks," I say to him, gutted that I could have saved a couple of bucks.

Still holding the door open, he looks briefly at Captain Double T, who looks back at him unflinchingly with her poker face before he returns his attention to me. "Hey, man, If you're ever in Mrkonjić Grad. Go to the CD shop outside the bus depot and tell them Nemanja sent you," he says, smiling and putting his cigarette out with his foot.

He shuts the back door, opens the driver's door, gets in and immediately pulls out another cigarette, lighting it. "Adios, comrades," he says, waving his arm out the window before wheel spinning away from us.

"What a lovely chap," I say to Captain Double T, trying to emulate what an Officer would have said in this situation.

"He's an absolute bounder,"[108] she replies, keeping the side up for Officers.

I get out my notebook and jot down this episode, as I think I will have to include it in a book one day.

We get into the Lanny and I consult the Route Map. It's Route Bluebird, then Hornblower, to Mrkonjić Grad and will take less than an hour along the winding road. I am trying to keep one eye on the road and take in the exceptional scenery as we continue on our way. I look onto the side of a hill and I think my eyes are play-

107 The Big Boss. Head of the Multinational Division South-West, which we came under. Not the man who sang Billie Jean.

108 Old word for a dishonourable man.

ing tricks on me as I make out the letter 'T'. It's been cut out in the woods, and new trees are filling the gap, but it's noticeable. I think it's quite a coincidence until I spot the giant letter 'I' next to it. Then I notice another 'T' and another 'O'. My brain then reads out, 'TITO'.

"Can you see that up there?" I say to Captain Double T. "The letters on the hill?"

She looks and nods.

"It's a very impressive bit of gardening," I say to her, trying to get a verbal reaction.

She nods again and we continue the drive in total silence.

The Office Party

After an hour of complete silence, I pass the yellow sign announcing we've arrived at Mrkonjić Grad. It's not hard to find the camp, as the barbed wire and masses of green military vehicles parked up behind it give it away. I spot the CD shops before I spot the main entrance and Nemanja's attractive offer comes back to me. The big board next to the gate tells me it's 8 Armoured Engineer Squadron based here and this place is known as the Bus Depot. The guard stops us and asks for our IDs, which is a first for us. He's happy once he knows we are who we say we are. He then instructs us to unload in the unloading bay and to book in at the Guardroom.

Once unloaded and booked in, Captain Double T says, "I'm off to discuss a few things with the QM.[109] I might be a while, so see if you can sort us both some accommodation for the night?"

Nodding to her, I ask, "Where shall we meet afterwards?"

"I'll find you somehow," she replies.

109 Quartermaster. The one in charge of all the stores and in this case, utilities.

I go straight back into the Guardroom to enquire out about their transit accommodation. "We're full up, mate," says the Corporal Guard Commander, "we're waiting on a load of Corimecs to turn up. They should have been here days ago."

"Ahhh," is only what I manage at the prospect of a night in the Lanny.

"We had the rest of our Regiment arrive last week and no Corimecs to put them in," he continues.

"I heard they have been comman... command... commandeer... I heard the Officers have nicked them for a big HQ somewhere else, so everyone's in the tented transit accommodation for now."

"There's the old Manager's Office in the garage," says a guard from the back room, earwigging in on our conversation.

"Where's that, then?" says the Guard Commander.

The guard comes out of the back room. "In the garage, you know, the big garage? Where they used to repair the buses?" as he tries to explain to the Guard Commander.

"The big garage?" he replies with a slight sign of bewilderment.

"Yeah, in the back of the big garage, there's an abandoned office," he exclaims excitedly.

"There's an abandoned office in the back of the big garage?" exclaims the Guard Commander still looking somewhat puzzled.

"I'll find it," I reply, getting frustrated with the Guard Commanders' lack of geographical knowledge of the camp he is guarding.

"Where's your POL point?" I ask the Guard Commander.

"The POL point?" he replies, with a confused look.

"Don't worry, I'll find that too."

I manage to find the POL point, cookhouse and EFI in record time. If I had asked the Guard Commander for directions, I'd still have been in the Guardroom and thinking of heading to a local bar for some Sleep in the Ditch. I pop into the cookhouse for a lonesome lunch, I clock an empty table in the corner and I claim it like a Billy No-Mates. This is the worst aspect of travelling around on your own on these types of jobs. At least in the bar during the evenings, people will spark up a conversation with you after a few beers. Casting a swift gaze across the tables, I notice a girl staring at me while eating her food. I direct my attention back towards my food, not wanting to catch her eye and make it appear weird. I stare at my white paper plate with its pile of brown on it.

"Don't look up, don't look up," I mutter to myself.

As I raise my eyes, I observe she's still staring at me.

I awkwardly shift my gaze downwards once more, then lift it back up to see she's stood up and is now heading towards me.

I have to look at her now, as it's obvious she's coming to talk to me. She looks familiar and I think I must know her from somewhere.

"James?" she says. "You're James Lee from the Wirral?"

Hearing someone say the name of the area you grew up, and not your unit or former unit, feels just so out of place here, in a military camp, in Bosnia, with my weapon next to me.

"Errrr..." is all I can manage at this weird situation and as I look at her, trying to remember where I know her from.

"It's Dawn. We used to work at Sheldrakes restaurant in lower Heswall together."

The penny drops.

I had a part-time job there washing dishes after I left school. It was a high-end restaurant which was on the shore of the River Dee with views over to Wales. Posh toffs and celebrities frequented it, with the most notable ones being actors from *Coronation Street*. I was eventually promoted to waiter and I often remember bills for their afternoon champagne lunch in excess of a £1,000, which was shit loads, even back then. I was on £1.70 per hour.

"Fucking hell," is my inappropriate reply. "What are you doing here? I didn't take you for joining the military."

She laughs and says, "I didn't. I joined the NAAFI as a manager."

"Aha, that makes total sense."

She was a waitress there and I remember she wanted to go to college to study catering management.

"I've not seen you since, maybe 1988, probably last at Sheldrakes," I say.

"It was. I remember you stopped coming to work, and I heard you joined the Army from Dave Murray. Do you remember him? He worked behind the bar. I think he was friends with your brother?"

"Yes, he was," I reply.

"So what are you doing out here?" she says to me.

"Driving."

"Driving what?"

"A hard bargain at the moment."

"A what?"

"Hey, you don't sell Boogie Boxes with a CD player in them, do you?" I ask, remembering my CD collection and hours of silence on the road.

"Sure we do."

"Ace, can you get me a discount?"

"You cheeky so and so," she laughs and then she says, "Of course you can."

We have a good catch up over my plate of half-eaten brown. I tell her about the job I'm doing at the moment. She tells me how she joined the NAAFI after college and volunteered for this tour with the EFI. "Never volunteer for anything," I reply, offering her my words of wisdom.

She's working in the EFI shop until 2000, so we agree to meet in the bar, after I have picked up my new Boogie Box.

I bump into Captain Double T outside the cookhouse and inform her the Lanny and I are both filled up. She takes a second to get the meaning. "Tonight's transit accommodation is in the Garage Manager's Office," I tell her. "Oh," she says in a guilty-sounding tone, "I've met someone who's putting me up in her Corimec tonight."

"Goodo," I reply.

"It's Samantha Stopford-Sackville. She's a friend of mine and we went to Uni together. She's a Captain with the Royal Engineers."

"You've got to be shitting me with these names," I think to myself.

"Can I borrow your cot bed then, please, ma'am?" I say, now that an opportunity has presented itself to me, hoping she won't need it tonight.

"Errrr, sure," she says, not too sure, but that's good enough for me and I don't do a double check to see if she's *sure* sure.

I inspect the presidential suite for tonight's stop. It is in the garage and it is indeed an abandoned office. It's up the stairs, and where the last few steps should be, there's a space. They've either rotted away or have been stolen, so I climb up through the door, which is minus the door. The glass in the windows at the rear of the office is long gone. No doubt stolen, but more likely smashed. The glass in the ones facing into the garage is still there. A few desks are scattered around, the walls have peeling paint, and bits of brick cover the floor.

I tell myself it beats trying to sleep in the Lanny, and I attempt to set up Captain Double T's cot bed. First, I unfold it and it spreads apart, creating a bed with three cross-shaped supports with one at each end and one in the middle. There are two extra aluminium bars which go at either end. They slide through a looped part in the material and slot into place to create the tension in the fabric that I will lie on.

The first one slots in just fine, without too much effort. Each of the bars has a hole in them which fits into place on the end of the aluminium frame over a small plastic bulge. I notice the other one will require a bit more effort now as the green cloth is going to be under tension. The third one slips on with more effort than the previous two required. When it comes to the fourth one, things get interesting. The effort required has now increased exponentially and is off the scale. I tug and jerk, but I can get the hole nowhere near the bulge. As I try to pull with my hand, the cot bed just moves with me. I reposition myself on the bed, so I can attempt to force it on with my foot whilst using my weight to keep the bed in place. My mass now just puts the material under even more tension and there's no way I'm going to get the last bar on. Experimenting with a different approach, I attempt it while standing up. I jam my foot against the bar and, with my free hand, hold the cot bed in place.

The lack of tension in the material should make this achievable. I press with my foot, increasing my exertion whilst giving a strained groan with the growing pressure I'm adding. Just a few more milli-metres and it'll be on. The cot bed is now off the ground. I'm pull-ing a face now and I feel myself warming up with the energy I'm expending. There's no budging the last bit, no matter how much I am pressing with my foot. Relenting, I let go, and the cot bed falls back to the floor with the fourth bar not in place. I keep this up for another 20 minutes. Eventually, I realise I can't physically complete it alone. It would need the help of a winch from one of the RE's recovery vehicles to get it on.

Admitting defeat, I decide the bar end I cannot get on will be where my feet have to go. The worst case will result in them hanging off the end. The cot bed looks like it's designed for a person of six feet. I am 5ft 7in so I should be OK, theoretically.

I head back to the Lanny to get my rucksack and make sure it's locked up for the evening. Once I am back at the office, I decide to place the cot bed in the middle of the room. I don't want to be near the walls because, apart from looking filthy, they exhibit a significant amount of mould. I have an hour to kill so I give my gun a clean, polish my boots and write a couple of blueys.[110] One to my folks telling them what I have been up to this week as I know they miss me dearly. I still remember the lump I had in my throat the day they waved me off from Liverpool Lime Street train station to start my basic training in the summer of 1989. I'm the youngest of four boys, and I know my Mum must have found it exceptionally difficult to see the last one leave the family nest. I wipe away the tear which has formed in my eye as I think of them.

I write one to Del, trying to disguise my handwriting as I go. The letter begins with me being cordial, by asking him if this correspondence finds him well and I hope he's enjoying his time in the Balkans. Changing the tone, I tell him I know where he resides in Dalma Warehouse. Then adding that he'd better sleep with one eye open and with a LAW[111] under his pillow from now on. With a scribble, I sign it off with: "Not much love and lots of hate, S. Milošević."

With time on my hands, I go in search of somewhere to deposit my mail. I consider asking at the Guardroom, but the world's most useless Guard Commander will still be on duty. A helpful, jolly smiling Warrant Officer, with a strong Welsh accent, directs me to the Post Office. Warrant Officers are normally grumpy bastards, but maybe the Royal Engineers' ones are more fun and approachable.

Next stop is the EFI and time to pick a Boogie Box and see how much discount I can blag from Dawn. I choose a simple one as I know it's going to get battered around in the Lanny and will no doubt be knackered in a few weeks. Dawn gives me a discount and I stock up on a few batteries, just in case. My plan is to wire it into the Lanny's electrical system so I won't need batteries. I bid my farewells and thanks to Dawn and say I'll catch her sometime soon. I unpack

---

110 These were airmail letters that once written would fold in on themselves making an envelope. They were free to send and blue in colour, hence the word 'bluey'. I know those of the older generation reading this would have thought that I was sending something explicit.

111 Light Anti-tank Weapon. A bazooka.

the Boogie Box and leave it in the Lanny for now as I go hunting for the Signals Detachment. There will be one somewhere. I bump into the jolly Warrant Officer again, who happily points out their tent. I head in their direction and, after a bit of charming, I now own a length of D10 telephone cable. I return to the Lanny to implement my plan. The D10 is like speaker cable as it has two wires moulded together. I get out my Leatherman's pocket tool and split the wire. Then I strip each of the wires and pop the battery cover off the Boogie Box, before carefully attaching them to the terminal where the batteries would normally touch, one to the positive and one to the negative.

In the Lanny dashboard is a tiny double-pronged plug socket for the Spanner Monkey to plug in his inspection lamp. I acquired one of these plugs for just this very occasion. I connect the wires into the plug and slide it in slowly. Nothing happens, but then I switch on the Boogie Box and bingo. It lights up and I hear the static of the radio. Not wanting to listen to the drivel of BFBS, I put in the *Pulp Fiction* soundtrack CD and press play. Dick Dale's iconic guitar piece *Misirlou,* the song the film opens with, is now coming from my Lanny in the Mrkonjić Grad Bus Depot. I smile as I now have in-drive entertainment. I spot the jolly Warrant Officer, who gives me the thumbs-up, and says.

"That's fucking class that is, boyo."

I meet up later with Dawn after her shift in the bar, and over a few warm cans of watery Danish lager, we talk about what we got up to at Sheldrakes, people we worked with there, and where they are now. The job was a means to an end at the time to subsidise my YTS[112] pay of £25 a week. It taught me that the hospitality trade is underpaid and demanding, and I realised it wasn't the career path I wanted to pursue. We swap addresses, as these are the days before

112 Youth Training Scheme.

mobile phones are commonplace, and we say our goodbyes, promising to keep in touch and meet up again one day.

I didn't see Dawn on the remainder of the tour or afterwards. We corresponded for a while before the letters became fewer and, in due course, our own worlds moved on.

Walking slowly towards the office in the dark, I tread carefully, as I forgot to take my torch with me. I remember it's packed away securely in my webbing, locked up in the Lanny. Turning to where the Lanny is parked, I mutter a profanity. Thankfully, I have the keys on me and I fish it out of my webbing in the back. Torch found, I lock the Lanny back up and again start my journey. Climbing in through the hole where the door used to be, I wince when I kneel on a piece of brick. I take a spare uniform from my rucksack to use as a pillow. I arrange it at the end of the cot bed with the bar in. For a second, I consider having another go at fitting the bar I couldn't get on earlier. A major workout just before bed probably isn't the wisest of ideas, so I discard this notion. I remove my boots and socks while sitting on the cot bed, as I really don't want to put my feet on the grimy floor. Lying down, I now take off my trousers and place them on my rucksack, sort of folded-up considering the situation. I then wriggle into my dossbag and do the zip up only halfway due to it not being too cold that evening. My compressed spare uniform pillow has the characteristics more of a brick than a traditional soft pillow, but I make it work. I fidget for a while, trying to get the comfortable sweet spot which will enable me to start the transition over the border to Republika Sleepska. I feel my feet hanging off the cot bed, but it's tolerable. Listening to the noises of the still evening in Mrkonjić Grad, I try to differentiate each one. There are the customary ones of generators humming away and soldiers laughing somewhere on the camp. I make out the jolly voice of the Welsh Warrant Officer in-between the laughing and suspect he's the cause of it. Further off in the distance, I hear a car which sounds like it lost its exhaust on a one of the many crappy roads, and a squeak. It's a metallic-sounding one, but I can't work out what it could be. Initially, I assume it must be something being moved by the wind, but there's no wind, or it could be mechanically driven. The picture I get in my head is one of a revolving door and a constant flow of people going through it. It needs a drop of oil on its bearings to loosen them up. That is the last thought which goes through my brain as I drift off. I awake sometime later with my head hanging upside down. The bar at the pillow end of the cot bed has dropped off because of the reduced tension in the material. My *ad hoc* pillow is now on the dirty floor. I try to reattach the bar, but, with no tension to keep it in place, I'm essentially pissing into the wind. To ease my predicament would require getting up and doing a full body workout to get the bar ends fitted. I grab my uniform from the floor and give it a shake-off to get rid of any dirt it's picked up. I decide the best course of action is to slide down the cot bed, putting my now-dirty pillow further along the bed. This is a solution, but not without its consequences. My feet are now hanging further off the bottom with the edge now halfway up my calves. I try to go back to sleep and again my ears tune into the noises of the outside world. The generators calmly hum, the laughing with the Welsh voice has gone to bed, but the squeak is still there. I detect a new sound now and I know exactly what it is. It's a mosquito buzzing around my lughole. I instinctively slap the side of my head. Hoping I've squashed it onto my face, I once again try to sleep. It's back again, making its high-pitched buzz as it looks for a landing spot to have a drink of my blood. I try again with my hand and this time wave it around to scare it off. It returns, so I put my head under the covers of the dossbag for some respite from its onslaught. I manage all of five seconds before I feel the temperature rising and the start of a slow suffocation coming on. My head back out in the cool fresh air is only a tiny relief before the mosquito is back and making a racket down my ear. I wish they would just bite me somewhere else so I don't have to listen to them for the entire night. This goes on for a while longer until I am too tired and I fall asleep.

Coping Cabana

I wake up and I'm on my back with the bottom half of my legs from my knees now hanging down on the floor. I fumble for my watch in the area where I think I laid it last night. Finding it, I feel the cold of its metal casing on my fingers. Holding it up to my face, with one eye half-cocked, I look at what time it is. It's 0615 and I think that's not too bad. I sense an itch on my calf and scratch it, or do I sense a scratch and itch it? Regardless of which way round I do it, I feel the swollen lump of a mosquito bite. I examine my face, expecting to build a picture in my head of the Elephant Man as run my fingers over the lumps and bumps. There's nothing. I go back to my leg and I feel a few warm spots of inflammations. I am glad I still retain my looks, but I can't comprehend how it got to my leg. Was it inside my dossbag all night whilst my fizzog was on show? I unzip the dossbag, letting in the chilly morning air. Sitting up and swinging my legs off the cot bed and slipping my feet straight into my flip-flops, which I had remembered to strategically position the evening before, I rub my eyes and take a swig from my plastic bottle of water. The cool water relieves my dry throat and lips. I am not drinking as much water as I should be, and having had a few beers last night doesn't help, even if it was like cat's piss. I make a mental note to drink more water today. We've a few crates of it in the back of the Lanny so it's not like it's in short supply. The problem is that when it warms up with the day, it's less appealing as it's akin to drinking tepid tea. I pull my trousers on, grab my towel, wash kit, a clean pair of under-crackers[113] and T-shirt and go off hunting in search of somewhere to grab a shower. I notice I am running low on clean kit now and hope we'll find an MBLU[114] on our travels for a chance to do some laundry soon.

With the morning routine accomplished, I take one look back at my accommodation and hope we don't return here anytime soon. After a lonesome breakfast, I keep an eye out for Dawn, but the EFI doesn't open until 1030. I wait at the Lanny for Captain Double T, who turns up with her friend Captain Triple S. I am introduced to her, but she's as uninterested in me as I am in her, as I doubt our paths will ever cross.

Once they've said their goodbyes to one another, I ask Captain Double T. "What's the plan today, ma'am?"

"Back to Banja Luka, I think, as our work here is done," she replies.

"I have a surprise for you, ma'am," I say, pointing at the Boogie Box sitting between us in the Lanny.

We turn out of the Mrkonjić Grad Bus Depot onto Route Horn-blower and I press Play on the Boogie Box. The guitar of *Misirlou* fills the Lanny. I glance sideways and notice Captain Double T has the slightest of smiles on her face. Or it could be wind.

It's just under three plays of the entire soundtrack to *Pulp Fiction* to get from Mrkonjić Grad to BLMF. The CD player doesn't take to the rough section of road. As we near Banja Luka, the music skips as I bounce in and out of the holes.

As we enter through the front gate, I briefly consider that we might have taken a wrong turn and arrived at the wrong BLMF.

113 Underwear.

114 Mobile Bath and Laundry Unit.

It's still the same camp we left, but now it's a hive of activity and Corimecs being moved around by cranes and big Volvo forklifts.

"Looks like the plan to get things rolling has started," says Captain Double T.

We drive around to the front of the office and stop next to a sign which says 'No Parking'. Not knowing where else to park, I decide to dump the Lanny there.

There's no sign of Melba or Staff Hobbs, and the office is empty of everything which was there before we left.

"Oh, this isn't good," says Captain Double T.

"I think we're getting evicted," I add, sensing the ominous signs.

"I'm going to see if I can find someone," she says.

"OK, I'll go and fill up the Lanny and meet you back here, ma'am."

She agrees and I head back out of the office to the Lanny.

As I follow the road around the Metal Factory to the POL point, I spot a Corimec city under construction. They've been placed in symmetrical lines, some with gravel walkways in-between the long rows. Some are even having wooden verandas built in front of them before my very eyes.

With a full tank of diesel, I park back up outside the office.

"You can't park there," says a tall thin Corporal wearing an immaculately-shaped beret and sporting a porn moustache. He points at the 'No Parking' sign.

"OK, where can I park?" I ask him.

What I really want to say to him is, "Do you have a brother who's a Sergeant and works down at DJ Barracks doing the same pointless job?" I swear he must be related or even the same guy, just a rank lower. Maybe he was busted and posted up here for telling General Jackson that he'd better move his car or else. I keep these thoughts to myself in the interest of not getting put in jail and being labelled a gobshite. I was jailed once before back in 1992 whilst dropping some kit off at a stores depot in Dulmen, Germany, for saying what I was thinking. A dull, humourless and bald Lance Corporal told me rudely to put my beret on as I waited by my truck in the baking sunshine. My amusing not very well thought out reply of telling him to 'keep his hair on' cost me an entire afternoon locked up in a cell.

"They've not built the new car park yet," he says.

"So, I can park here for now?" I reply with a sense of confusion, knowing it's going to be a muddled conversation.

"I've just said you can't park there," his tone now becoming aggressive.

The British Army is capable of wonderful things, but sometimes, just sometimes, their logic can just leave you completely numb from the soles of your feet upwards. I dump the Lanny on a stretch of road on which the porn-moustachioed Parking Warden hasn't yet got round to erecting his 'No Parking' signs.

I finally make it back to the office, and Melba is there, waiting for me.

"Aha, there you are. Did you enjoy your trip?" he asks.

"Yeah, it was really interesting."

I look about to make sure Captain Double T isn't hanging around in a doorway nearby.

"I've changed her nickname to Double T," and I go on to explain why.

He laughs at her new name and says he'll let Staff Hobbs know.

"Are we being evicted?" I ask him.

"We sure are. Our office is going to be the new HQ MND SW Cocktail Bar."

"You're fucking kidding me," I reply. "The BLMF Copacabana Bar, with its selection of cocktails for the discerning gentleman and lady."

"On the plus side. We now have modern shower Corimecs, which actually work, and we also have laundry units with the locals doing it for us now," he says excitedly.

"Typical, eh, fuck all here until the Rodneys[115] turn up *en masse.*"

"We might even get some Corimec accommodation, but for tonight, we are in a tent in the Metal Factory."

"Fucking hell, Melba. You build me up and then bring me right back down." Then I remember last night and say, "Can't be any worse than the Bus Depot in Mrkonjić Grad?"

"Come on, I've got us a space in one of the tents. I'll give you a hand to carry your gear over," he says.

"Where did you park?" I ask Melba.

"Ah, the parking issue. Have you met the new Parking Warden?"

"Oh yeah. I managed a brief run-in with him too."

"My Lanny is in a tent," he says.

I wonder if I've just heard him right and repeat, "You've put your Lanny in a tent?"

"I found a couple of empty 12x12 tents at the back of the camp, so I parked in it. What Corporal bastard can't see won't grip his shit."

We drive to the back end of the camp and they are still there. With a bit of coercion and blunt force, we reverse my Lanny into it and tie the doors shut.

"Sorted," says Melba, acting all smug.

The tents in the Metal Factory are full of bunk beds. Every one of them is adorned with a green foam mattress. It's a pleasant reprieve just to sit on it for a while. The floor is concrete, but at least it's sort of clean. Not clean, as in "you could eat your dinner off it," but clean as in "not strewn with bits of brick." A message from Captain Double T gets to us via Staff Hobbs, who has also been kicked out of his room and is now in the tent with us. "You've a few jobs in the

---

115 Nicer than normal term for an Officer, used by the lower ranks.

morning in Banja Luka, and then Captain Double T has booked you on the afternoon flight down to Split for the weekend. You're back up here again on the Monday AM flight."

"That's a result," I exclaim, smiling at the thought of a day off.

"She must be impressed with you. She's never given me a day off."

"Must be your taste in music, Staff," I reply to him.

He laughs and passes me a bottle of clear liquid. I know it must be homemade Slivovitz.

"Have that on me," he says.

"Sorry, I can't accept bribes, Staff, you should know that," I say, inspecting the contents.

"Go easy on it," he warns. "It tastes like petrol mixed with double-strength pure alcohol and paint stripper."

"Am I likely to go blind?" I enquire.

"You might lose your sight, a few days and your career."

"They should use that quote on the logo."

I put it away in my rucksack for another time.

"What's your old room being turned into?" I ask him. "The ballroom, the music room, or perhaps a wine tasting room?"

He laughs. "It's unbelievable they're getting a cocktail bar. Meanwhile, all we can get our hands on is tins of piss weak warm beer from the 12x12 Arms or fucking Satan's bin juice from town. Something in-between would be nice."

I shower and put some clean uniform on and instantly feel a whole lot better for it. With my meshed laundry bag, full of my stinky kit from the last week of travelling, I saunter down to the new washing units. Melba told me they can do it in less than three hours. It seems to be a 24-hour turnaround everywhere else I've been so far. There are several of these Corimecs to choose from and I go for the one that looks least busy. I peer inside and there are a number of large washing machines and dryers. I hand my bag to an old lady who could be my grandmother.

"How long until it's ready?" I ask slowly.

"Yes, yes," is her reply as she takes my bag from me.

I remember the older generation normally speak German better than they speak English.

"*Wie lange bis fertig?*" [How long until it's ready?], I say to her as naturally as I can.

"*Etwa drei stunden,*" [About three hours], she replies with no hesitation.

I thank her and head back to the tent to catch up on some book reading whilst lying on a comfortable mattress.

I return hours later to my still-warm clothes folded up ever so neatly in the laundry bag.

"*Danke, du bist einfach die beste Oma,*" [Thank you, you are simply the best Grandma].

She laughs and goes into replying to me in Serbian.

"Yes, yes," I say.

Don't Even Think of Bringing That Up

After a morning of visiting a few local, lovely-smelling bakeries for a bread contract, we head back to BLMF. We are now allowed to use the new car park, so that's where I dump the Lanny and lock it up for the weekend. I give the keys to Melba, not in case he needs to use it, but more in case I leave them down in Split. After a light lunch of a salami sandwich, I make my way over to the Heliport. It's still only a field with the barbed wire around in. I wait and listen for the unmistakable 'wokka wokka' sound of the Chinook approaching. There are a few of us waiting on the grass with our gear and nobody asks if they are waiting for the flight back to Split. I would have said no and that I was here for a picnic, anyway. Someone turns their head and gazes into the distance, followed by another, and I hear it. The noise of the heavy rotor blades cutting through the thick air comes and goes in the breeze. It increases in volume as it approaches. Someone sees it and points. Everyone scans the blue sky and I notice a spot above the horizon. It looks like it's moving like a snail as it flies towards us. With every passing second, I make out more of its features. I now make out the rotor blades, which appear like they're turning at a leisurely pace. It continues in our direction. Suddenly its massive frame is almost on top of us as it slows to a hover, readying to land. It's as if I have blinked and it's jumped forward at tremendous speed. The noise generated by the immense power of this thing to defy gravity is staggering. I spot a helmeted figure with their head out the side door, looking along the length of the machine. It pauses momentarily before us, magically floating in the air. After that pause, it graciously performs a 180-degree turn. It stops turning when its rear is pointing towards us. I notice another figure wearing a helmet looking over the open back ramp. The Chinook descends and lands ever so gently. It sits in its landing spot with the engines running.

The downwash of the blades now kicks up bits of grass and dirt. I can't see the small specks of dirt that are blowing towards me, but I feel them on my face. The engine note changes and the rotor blades slow as the crew shut the beast down. Its arrival felt almost violent and now calm is returning to this patch of land as it becomes silent again. A member of the crew, now minus his helmet, steps off the back ramp, directing the many disembarking passengers in our direction. They are carrying their kit, wearing helmets, and have their weapons slung across the front of them. They continue past us and out through the gap in the barbed-wire fence. The crew member who showed them where to go now approaches us. He calls out a list of names and destinations. I thought everyone was going down to Split, but it becomes apparent that this flight has a lot of places to visit first. We are called forward in accordance with our jump-off point. The few of us who are heading to Split, the Chinook's base, are boarded first. First on, last off. The Loadmaster reels off all the locations we'll be visiting and therefore it'll be about three hours before we arrive in Split.

One guy with us mutters, "I could crawl quicker."

I am squashed down the front of the Chinook with my way-too-heavy rucksack on my knees. After a few minutes, I don't think I'll be able to have it on them for the next few hours. The Loadmaster notices my discomfort and says I'll soon be able to put my rucksack on the floor once we are ready to go. As the remaining passengers clamber up the back ramp and drop themselves onto the covered benches, the helicopter wobbles on its undercarriage ever so slightly. I fish around in one of my many pockets for the tiny yellow foam ear defenders, which I know are in there somewhere. Finding them, I pull them out of their little oval-shaped box, roll them in between my finger and thumb before inserting them into my ears. As they expand in my lugholes, the world becomes a quieter place and takes on a relaxed atmosphere.

We rise into the air, vibrating. I am able to see the Metal Factory out of the back doors through the sea of people and kit. It's a huge building and could accommodate thousands if it weren't full of machinery. The Chinook dips forward and we start off to our first stop. It's hot and uncomfortable, even though I've now got my cumbersome rucksack off my knees. We land, soldiers get off, soldiers get on, we take off. They pile up the kit along the centre and secure it with straps to keep it in place. It's unstrapped as it's taken off again. It is similar to a busy bus terminal. The Loadmaster is working hard, juggling around the passengers and their kit as they come and go. When we are on the ground, I sweat in the heat, and I pine to be back in the air for the relief of the cooling airflow through the fuselage. When we are in the air, I sense the motion as the Chinook moves, and I'm desperate to get back on the ground. It's a no-win situation. I get a glimpse through the side window opposite me and take a second to comprehend what I am looking at. I observe a flowing river speeding by, but it's on the side of a mountain, defying gravity. Puzzled for a second, I look to the back door and realised we are banking over at 90 degrees. It was the floor of the valley which I was looking at. Suddenly, I get a nauseous sensation from deep within me and it goes away. I try not to think about it in case it comes back again. I make out we are over a built-up area and we are now flying level. The Loadmaster shouts at us to inform us we are landing at Sarajevo next. We touch down. Out the back, with my little tunnel view, I see there's an expanse of concrete with a few green and grey military aircraft parked up. A few more get off the Chinook and a few more get on. Two of the new passengers are in civilian clothes. One has several expensive-looking cameras around his neck while the other carries a large video camera in his hand. They attempt to talk to the Loadmaster over the din of the engines. They take it in turns to hold their ear close to his mouth. When they reply, the Loadmaster must be an expert in lip reading as he's wearing a helmet. After a minute of this conversation, the Loadmaster produces a couple of harnesses which they put on. They sit on the ramp with their legs dangling over the edge. Their harnesses are connected to the fuselage to ensure they won't fall out in flight. The Loadmaster tells us we are going to fly over Sarajevo for these guys to take some pictures. We'll drop them back off at the airport and it shouldn't take too long. I groan to myself at this never-ending flight.

We take off again, picking up speed and altitude as we head for the city centre. I peer out of the rear of the Chinook, but I get very few confined glimpses of rows of high grey apartment blocks splattered with bullet marks. As we bank over, I glance out the side window and spot the UNIS Towers. They are two modern-looking sky-scrapers which were once adorned with windows. The glass is long gone, and I observe the black marks from fire damage. Built in 1986, they were supposed to be a symbol of unity by being named after a couple of characters, Momo and Uzeir. It was from a comedy show and one was a Serb, the other a Bosnian. They managed to remain standing throughout the heavy bombardment inflicted on Sarajevo during the siege and have now become icons of resilience. We continue circling while the cameramen get their shots. The Loadmaster taps them on the shoulder, giving them the thumbs-up, which they return to him. The Chinook now levels out and the nausea returns. I start salivating, and I know I am close to vomiting. I get the Load-master's attention, put my hand on my chest and blow my cheeks up to intimate that I don't feel well. It works as he gets a white paper sick-bag to me in record time. It could have been my excellent acting skills, or more likely I was turning exceedingly green and nobody enjoys cleaning up vomit.

The guy next to me taps my arm and, part shouting, part indicating, he tells me to keep looking out the back. I have the bag open and ready to be filled, but I don't want to suffer the indignity of spewing up in public. I concentrate on my breathing and stare out of the rear as suggested by my fellow passenger, trying not to think of the sickness which is enveloping me. Somehow, through the sheer strength of willpower, I keep the contents of my guts down. I am breathing heavily and sweating profusely so much that I have to remove my helmet. The removal of its weight and the cooling effect of the air across my forehead is just the best sensation. My uniform is soaking wet under my body armour. I wish I could take it off too, but I am stuck on the fabric bench, unable to get up.

We bump back onto the ground at Sarajevo airport and I get a temporary reprieve. I now want to spit out the salvia from my mouth, but I don't think it'd be acceptable inside the Chinook. My passenger friend passes a bottle of water to me. I take a sip which immediately helps with the saliva problem and I start to improve. As the nausea reduces, I continue to try and think of anything other than being sick. He gives me a smile and a pat on the back as he realises I've kept lunch inside me.

We depart Sarajevo and climb up high into the cool air over the mountains surrounding it. It's a nice smooth flight from now, and I suspect the pilots have been informed about the green-looking idiot in the back. Sitting there in my wet uniform, I shiver in the chilly air. I replace my helmet to keep in what little warmth I still have, but it's not a woolly hat. Overall, it's been a miserable trip and not one I care to experience soon. I dread I might have to do it all again on Monday morning. I hope it'll be more like the almost direct flight the week before.

Back at DJ Barracks, the Chinook stops vibrating as it shuts down and the Adriatic air begins to warm me. "Well done for not puking up," says my passenger friend, now that it's quieter and we are able to converse in a normal manner.

"Once one starts, it'll set everyone off, and it becomes utter carnage," he adds.

"It was hard work trying not to, and thanks for the water, by the way," I reply to him.

"I was feeling pretty rough too. The last thing I wanted was a lap full of carrots, and I'm a pilot too."

What a Corker

The RAF let me use their phone to call Judas to sort me a lift. He answers the phone, calls me a skiving twat, and says he'll get someone down to me as soon as possible. This means between sometime in the next hour and before the end of the tour in September. When he asks where I'll be and I say at the EFI, I get a torrent of abuse regarding not eating any NAAFI growlers.[116] I didn't even think of arranging transport on my arrival at DJ Barracks. As I was flying with the RAF, I'd have been late anyway. I think about making my way over to the EFI to see if I can get a brew while waiting for my lift. It's a tadge too hot, I think, to be lugging my gear. One of the RAF bods must have sensed my thoughts as he offers me a lift.

The EFI does a nice range of Bose stereos, Le Creuset pans and Mont Blanc pens, but no coffee, so I end up outside with a Coke. I remove my shirt and the salty sweat marks on the back make it look like a map of Africa.

Using the time wisely, I continue to read my book, where I'm at the cheery part of Winston Smith's ordeal in Room 101, when he finally betrays Julia. Hearing a Lanny approaching along the road, I look up to see Prat's massive grinning face behind the wheel.

"It's the ship-jumpin' rat of Banja Luka," he says through the window of the Lanny, minus his moustache.

"What happened to you?" I ask him, laughing. "Did the slug on your top lip stop paying the rent, so you evicted him?"

"Porn taches are so, er..." He pauses to think of the rest of his sentence, so I finish it for him.

"Last decade, maybe even the one before that?"

I open the back door of the Lanny, still laughing, and chuck my kit in. We catch up on what's been happening while I've been away. A couple of guys in our Troop sustained injuries because of the dreaded brake fade in a fuel tanker. They were driving down the hill on the Croatian side of the Kamensko BXP. With no way of stopping, they were literally stuck between a rock and a hard place. They tried to stick the truck into the rocky outcrop on the edge of the road to slow the vehicle. This achieved very little other than

116 Pies.

damaging the side of the truck as they continued to gain momentum. They caught up with the tanker in front of them, and, with nowhere else to go, they rammed into the back of it. Both vehicles ended up on their sides and it's just by luck that nobody died. The guys in the truck with the brake fade were medically evacuated back to the UK and made a full recovery. The road was closed for a day to complete the recovery process. Both tankers lost their loads, resulting in 40,000 litres of diesel on the road. If they had been carrying petrol, it could have been an even bigger catastrophe with the higher potential of a fire. Knowing the stretch of road, I can only imagine the terror they'd have felt having no brakes and only one terrible option to save themselves.

Back at Dalma, I check if I have any mail first. I feel the snippet of joy which only comes from getting a letter as I notice a few envelopes with my name on them. There's one from my folks, one from my German girlfriend, and a Bluey from the office of Franjo Tudman[117] in Del's handwriting. I visit Judas next to arrange a lift back to DJ Barracks for Monday morning.

"Aye, I'll sort that oot fer yer right noo," he says, turning to Prat.

"PLAT!" he shouts at him, making Prat jump out of his skin.

"Yes, Sarge," he replies.

"Think of a number between one and ten?"

"Errrrr..." he stumbles.

"Come awn, come awn," Judas pressures him.

"Errrrr..." he pauses again before shouting out, "SEVEN!"

"Congratulations, ye win. Make sure yer ready to give this malingering twat a lift to DJ Barracks on Monday morning will ye?"

Monday morning lift arranged, I head back to the warehouse with a moaning Prat in tow. "It's not like you are doing anything else on Monday morning, is it?" I say.

117 The President of Croatia.

"I'm not, but it's der principle of how Judas spammed me."

At the armoury, I drop off my gun. Relieved at the break of not having to carry it everywhere with me for a while. I bump into Gilly outside by the Guardroom. He's been out on the road most of the time since I passed him that day near the Kamensko BXP. "You've been putting the hours in," I say.

"Fuck, yeah, up and down and up and down, like a bastard yo-yo. Do this, do that, yes, Sir, no, Sir, shall I pull your Lanny back onto the road, Sir?" is how he explains his busy few weeks. "Fucking cunts," is how he summarises it.

"Shall I pull your Lanny back onto the road. Sir?" I ask him, fishing for the story behind this sentence.

"Oh, man, don't ask, but it involved our TC and responsibility," he replies.

"I get the picture," I say. Then I add, "I'm off to the harbour for pizza later. You up for it?"

"I can't. I've got to take a convoy up to Banja Luka tonight as they are urgently in need of plastic cutlery," he says, pulling a face.

"Too bad, stay safe, and if you see Marshall Tito, tell him he's dead."

"He fucking will be if I have to pull him back onto the road," he says, laughing.

Months later, I was in the back of a Bedford 14 Tonner, coming back from a night away in a hotel near Makarska. The Troop bus must have been busy elsewhere, so we had the luxury of sitting on the floor in the back of the truck. Thankfully, someone put a canvas canopy on it to keep us 'safe'. We'd been drinking beer most of the afternoon as we waited for the truck to turn up to take us back to Dalma. The rear of the truck is open and the local traffic is building up behind us, desperate to overtake. The winding road didn't afford many passing opportunities for them.

"*Watch this,*" *said Gilly, as he got up and moved to the rear.*

Straight away, I pondered that most disasters in which alcohol was involved start with the immortal words, "Watch this."

He staggered to the back, partly because of the afternoon beer and partly because of the motion of the truck. He waved at the people in the car behind us. They waved back at him, cigarettes in their mouths and with a look which said, 'What is this guy doing?'

Everyone stood up to look over the tailboard to get a better view of what he was about to do. We steadied ourselves by holding onto the metal canopy frame above us. I suspected Gilly was going to have a piss out the back onto the car behind and thought, "Oh, dear God, no, don't do it. It'll spray back onto us." Thankfully, he kept his shorts up and hung out the back to look along the side of the Bedford. With his free hand, the other one grasping the metal frame to stop him from falling out, he signalled to the vehicle behind us to wait. I saw the driver smile and give him the thumbs-up as he worked out Gilly was trying to help him overtake us.

"WAIT FOR IT, WAIT FOR IT," shouted Gilly above the din of the air flow and our truck's engine, still with his hand up, instructing the driver to wait.

We went around a long sweeping bend and then Gilly shouted, "GO ON MATE, GO FOR IT, YOU FUCKING IDIOT, GO GO GO!" whilst waving frantically with his hand. The car pulled out and disappeared from view as it overtook us. Then I heard a car horn blaring from the other direction and the overtaking car came back into view, braking hard to get back in behind our truck. Just as he pulled in, the car sounding the horn flew past us, going the other way. We burst into laughter and when we noticed the driver doing his nut, we laughed even louder. Another nail in the coffin of Anglo-Croatian relations courtesy of a truck full of Her Majesty's drunken finest. We talked of this for years afterwards and sighed, saying, "Those were good times." I imagine somewhere there's a Croatian guy, smoking a cigarette. He's reciting the same story to his friends about a terrifying experience when an idiotic British soldier nearly caused him to crash instead of his own shit driving, for once.

I pass Del in the corridor walking the other way and say to him.

"Congratulations on getting a job as secretary in the Croatian President's Office. But, seriously, they have to use the free Bluey service? Can they not afford a stamp?"

"Times are tight, my friend," he replies to me.

"Where are you going?" I enquire.

"Just to the armoury to sign out a LAW."

We both laugh and I shout over my shoulder, "I'll catch you later."

On our way out to the harbour, I realise a new taxi service has started. Parked up near the warehouse, there are now several British registered trucks, the sides of their covered trailers emblazoned with their company names. I guess they must have been contracted to bring supplies to Split which will be taken up country by us at some point. They've now become a daily sight and in the evenings the drivers hang around looking bored before returning to the UK. Most of them have dumped their trailers and use their cabs to drive to a nearby restaurant for food. A few of our lazier soldiers have talked them into giving them a lift to the bottom of the long road. One passes us that evening, and hanging off the rear of the cab are a dozen soldiers. I notice it's the usual guys from the Regiment, who are in a continual never-ending circle of being in trouble for something. The girls are too sensible to do this, and this is maybe another reason why women live longer than men.

This bus service was short-lived because, as soon as someone in a position of authority saw it, they nipped it in the bud. It was on Regimental Orders, in capitals and bold print, stating that anyone seen riding on the back of these trucks would have the book, and possibly a fist, thrown at them. Prat, Del and I chew the fat, then chew some more fat on our pizzas, with a few beers to wash it down. We make it back well before the curfew for a Pot Noodle before calling it a night and heading off to bed for a quiet evening. It's Saturday night, in a warehouse, with over a hundred soldiers in various states of drunkenness. It's not going to be quiet. Davey Corker, bless him, made the biggest mistake on the tour and he'd never hear the last of it. He's a likeable guy from the West Country and has a thick accent. A few days earlier, someone, I can't remember who, said his name, mocking his accent. Davey broke the unwritten rule that you never ever let another soldier know something that they said annoys you. I'm in bed, reading my book by torchlight, trying to ignore the noises of a hundred blokes scratching and farting when I hear it. Someone shouts in a thick overstressed West Country accent, "DAVEY CORKER!"

It's akin to opening the gates of a dam as everyone shouts it in higher and lower-pitched accents to howls of laughter. Then they start on other people's names in various accents of either their place of origin or just keeping in with the West Country theme. One guy, Si Palmer, who has a stutter, comes in for grief.

"Si, Pa, Pa, Pa, Palmerrrrrr," shouts someone. The room erupts again in waves of laughter.

"Fer-fer-fer-ferk off," shouts Si Palmer back to more cries of uncontrollable laughter as we roll around in our beds. This insulting one another continues for another 15 minutes, gradually quietening but still with the sound of soldiers giggling away. Now and again someone tries to reignite the fire by shouting out, "DAVEY CORKER," to the accompanying giggles.

Poor old Davey Corker has learnt a precious lesson on this tour.

5

Carface

THE NEXT day is spent rubbing a sore head and ribs from the beer and laughing last night. Today's routine is to be a spot of brunch and lazing, mostly in bed. I can't even do any laundry while I'm here as it takes 24 hours and there's none at the weekends, anyway. As the day turns to evening, there's a gigantic thunderstorm. Prat has gone out for a run, so I sit there watching it from the dirty window of my bunk, listening to the rumbling getting closer.

There's a flash of brilliant light at the same time as a sonic boom. I instinctively duck as a lightning bolt cracks its whip directly over the warehouse. The lights flicker and go out to the shout of "Fucking hell," as someone is halfway through a haircut.

The rain is so heavy I can hardly see the building next to ours and in places the water finds its way through our roof. I hear it dripping and the frantic rush as people go on the hunt for the fire buckets. For a short while, when the storm is at its peak, the darkness gives it a feeling of the end of the world.

The rain starts to ease and within a couple of minutes, the sky is becoming brighter, signalling the end of the apocalypse. The sun shines through the dispersing clouds as the storm burns out. I see steam rising from the warm asphalt as the rainwater dries up rapidly. Prat enters the bunk looking like a drowned cat.

"Fucking 'ell, ended up bein' a swim in dat bloody rain," he says dripping water over the floor.

"D'you not take your brolly?" I reply to him.

"It was like running under der sea," he replies, drying his hair with a towel.

"You should have tried flying your kite at the beach with metal wire instead of string so that it wouldn't snap," I say to him.

"I'd 'ave ended up lookin' like der bride of bloody Frankenstein after a day down der coal mines."

"Shocking," is all I can think to say.

→» →» →»

Early the next morning, Prat gives me a lift to DJ Barracks for my ride back to Banja Luka.

"Stay safe, and if yer see dat General Titus, tell him he's dead," he remarks, as I get out the Lanny.

"You what?" I reply to him, recognising something of what he has said. "Where did you get that from?"

"I dunno, I just heard it at der weekend, like," he says.

"It's Tito, Marshal Tito, you tit," I reply as I grapple getting my rucksack from the rear of the Lanny.

"Who's he den?"

"I'll see you when I see you, mate," I say as I wander off to the waiting room.

The flight back to BLMF is on a Puma. The pilot ascends to a high altitude, and I believe he flies directly to Banja Luka, straight over the mountains. I was dreading the trip back up in case it was going to be a repeat of the one the other day. I think if I get the offer of a few days off again, I may just take the hit and stay up at BLMF. At least I'll be able to get my laundry done in a few hours, buy a CD or ten and maybe gatecrash the cocktail bar.

I've no idea where to go on my arrival as we didn't have an office before I flew out on Saturday. I try for the tent first and the bed space, as that was the last known point, but it's now occupied by a snoring lump. They're too big to be Melba or Staff Hobbs. I head back outside to take a moment to think about where to go next when I see Melba walking along the road.

"Oi, Melba," I shout to him. He looks in my direction, smiles, waves and changes direction towards me. "Aye up," he says cheerily. "Did your weekend go well?"

"Where are we living now?" I ask him.

"We got moved into another tent yesterday. I'll show you where," he says, lifting my rucksack. We go back into the Metal Factory, and we find it next to another piece of huge industrial machinery as big as a house. "I hope it's not the thing that makes asbestos?" I say, looking up at it before going through the flap into the tent.

He puts my rucksack on an empty bed and says, "You're off out soon with the Boss on an interesting one."

"Go on," I say, becoming interested.

"They, the MND bods 'ere, need a car for an impending very important person visit."

"Keep going," my interest level continues to rise.

"They want a decent car, a good car, a posh car, and not a shitty VW Golf."

"We're going back to Germany to collect a Mercedes?" I say, wildly guessing but hoping it could be true.

"Not quite, but I suspect Germany may be involved in it."

Melbe tells me they want a Mercedes or BMW for this visitor. They looked into the feasibility of sourcing something from Zagreb, which is not too far away, but they want to purchase it from a local business in Banja Luka. Mercedes and BMW are a few years away from opening a dealership anywhere in Bosnia. The only people who can get their hands on what we need are the local mobsters. The Boss and I are off round to visit them this afternoon.

"Are we taking a section of infantry and a Warrior with us?" I ask.

"They want to keep it low-key, so no," he replies.

"Yes, this will be interesting," I say.

"I've got you a mafia DVD film so you can get up to speed on what to do if it goes pear-shaped."

I pause, I think, then we both burst out laughing.

Captain Double T tells me the same thing Melba said regarding our visit today, apart from the DVD bit. She gets the paperwork together and we both head off to the Lanny. "We have to pick up the interpreter from the Guardroom," says Captain Double T.

"Shit," I say, realising Melba still has the keys.

"What's up?" says Captain Double T, not realising that I don't have them.

"Corporal Swintex has the keys to the Lanny, ma'am," I say to her. "I'll go and get them from him."

"Oh, OK, I'll go and meet the interpreter at the Guardroom and I'll see you there," she says.

I head back to the tent, hoping he's not already buggered off into town with them.

"Please still be there, please still be there," I repeat to myself, walking towards the tent.

I pull the flap back and see his big smiling face holding his hand out with the keys in them. "You after these?"

I drive around to the Guardroom and see Captain Double T waiting by the loading bay with the interpreter.

I am introduced to Danica. She is small and predictably of the younger generation.

Captain Double T and I load up our weapons together and pack Danica into the back of the Lanny. There's less crap in the back today and I fit the tiny seat onto the side for her.

There's the usual chit-chat about where she learnt her English, which was from university and on the telly. We find out she's fluent in Russian, Polish and German, which doesn't come as a surprise to me anymore. This local younger generation is making us Brits look bad. I managed a few years of French at school before they realised the entire class was useless and binned it for us.

There just isn't the necessity to speak a foreign language for us English speakers. When ze Germans speak to Italians or the Spanish speak to the Polish, they will resort to English. Europeans are exposed to lots of English often, whether it's through music on the radio or films on the TV. Whilst the only German I remember being exposed to on TV was *'Vorsprung Durch Technik'* from the Audi advert. Even Nena's *99 Luftballons* was sung in English for the non-German speaking world. What is the second language of Europe? Perhaps it's English for most, if not all of them. With those thoughts going round my head, while I should be listening to Captain Double T's directions, I don't feel guilty for not speaking four languages. "You've passed the turning," says Captain Double T to me.

"Shit, sorry," I reply to her as I am back at the wheel of the Lanny, "I was daydreaming."

I look for somewhere to turn the Lanny around.

The house is huge and has an Alpine look to it. There's a tall fence and a just as tall sturdy-looking gate in front of it. This increased security, marking the boundary of their land could mean a couple of things. The crime rate here is high or they are protecting themselves from the competition. There are a few vehicles parked up behind the fence on the rough concrete driveway. There's not a VW Golf or a Fiat 126 in sight. I see a mixture of ominous-looking Mercedes and BMWs. All are dark in colour and have blacked-out windows. A few have no number plates, whilst some are fitted with German ones. I see plates denoting they are from Munich and Frankfurt.

"I think there's an intercom on the gate," says Danica, "I'll go and speak to them."

"I'll come with you," says Captain Double T.

I wait in the Lanny as they both approach the entrance. A couple of great big Alsatians bound up to the gate, barking at them. Captain Double T hesitates, while Danica doesn't even flinch. She presses the button on the intercom and speaks into it. I can't hear her voice over the din of the Lanny's engine and the dogs. I'm keeping the engine running just in case we need a quick getaway.

A bearded man appears and shouts incomprehensible things at the dogs, making them quiet. He grabs their collars and holds them while he talks to Danica through the gate. She talks, he nods, she introduces him to Captain Double T. He nods at her, she points my way, and he nods at me. I don't know why, but I nod back. The bearded man shouts something back towards the house and a younger guy comes out. He hands him a set of keys and takes the dogs from him.

The gate is opened, Captain Double T and Danica are beckoned in by him. Danica gestures for me to move forward through the gates. I put it into gear and drive towards them, whereupon the bearded man points to a space next to one of his BMWs. I switch the engine off and get out of the Lanny, grabbing my webbing with my remaining 90 rounds in the pouches. If I get into a gunfight, it better not be longer than a minute, otherwise, I'll be getting the white flag out. Life doesn't always imitate art, unlike in Hollywood films, where I would never run out of rounds in my magazine. The bearded man smiles at me, points at our Lanny and says in-between laughing menacingly, "Rolls Royce." I laugh back and say, *"Super Dobro Rolls Royce,"* giving him the thumbs-up.

This makes him laugh even more and, out of nowhere, I wonder how many people he's strangled while laughing.

We are ushered into the house while Danica is talking and looking quite relaxed. We'd unload our weapons when entering a building, such as the barrack block, but I keep my magazine on when entering this family home. I get a flashback of Melba saying the words "mafia" and "pear-shaped". Once inside, we are greeted by a well-dressed lady, who I presume is his wife, and his children. Danica is struggling to keep up with the translating and we shake hands with everyone. There are a few guys who hang around, eyeing us up. They look far too intimidating to be grumpy relatives, such as uncles, and I guess they are his henchmen. He guides us to a table and invites us to take a seat. I remove my webbing and when I do, the potential wife offers to take it like a coat.

"It's OK," I say, and she looks momentarily confused. The bearded man understands as he says something to her and she concedes her claim to take my ammunition-filled webbing. She moves away, and I place it by my feet. I take my seat in a very expensive-looking chair and place my weapon on my lap. The bearded man says something to Danica and I make out, slivovitz and coffee. "He wants to know if you'd like to try a plum brandy or maybe a coffee?" says Danica.

"Coffee will be fine," says Captain Double T before she looks at me. I'm so tempted to say, "Slivovitz please, and make it a fucking massive one." I expect, if I go for the massive shot of 'Sleep in the Ditch', I'll end up in the back garden with the bearded guy, firing his AK47. I'd give him a go of mine and we'd blast my 120 rounds off on full auto. He'd then bring out weapons of increasingly larger calibres for me to try, finishing with a Howitzer or a dirty great big tank. It'd be up to Captain Double T to drive us back to BLMF with me, unconscious in the passenger seat, dribbling from my mouth. I'd be charged, jailed, tried at a court martial and summarily discharged from the Army. It'd be a career-ending decision, but what a way to end it. It'd have entered the unofficial history books of the British Army. On Mess functions for years to come, it'd be used as an anecdote and my place in military folklore would be assured.

In the end I go with, "Coffee will be good, thanks."

His kids, most of whom are young, jump on my webbing and reach out to touch the gun. I laugh, but my laugh is forced, originating mostly from nerves. The coffee arrives and the bearded man says something, and, just like that, the kids disappear. It's Turkish coffee, which is served up in the tiniest of cups but contains a month's worth of caffeine. I take the sugar and milk as if I am having a normal mug of coffee and try to stir it into the thimble-sized cup.

Negotiations go well during the afternoon and in the end a deal is reached on what car will be supplied. It's very peculiar sitting in the bearded man's house drinking Turkish coffee with a loaded gun on my lap. I wonder if it will it be stolen from Germany to order, or if they are legitimate and we'll get it from a dealership in Belgrade?

Standing up, I try not to scratch the lavish furniture with my gun. I pick up my webbing, hoping that it still has its ammunition in it and that his kids didn't steal it from me earlier. Everyone shakes hands and Danica feels she has to translate for us, even though it's obvious everyone is saying their goodbyes. I shake hands with the bearded man and he grips my hand firmly and says something mostly incomprehensible. I pick up the word 'Slivovitz', as he taps my gun whilst grinning. Danica translates and says, "He wishes you all the best and next time you come round we should drink Slivovitz and fire our guns together."

"Please tell him I'd bloody love that," I say whilst thinking "He's a mind reader." He no doubt got to where he is today, at the top end of the gangster ratings, by always being one step ahead of his rivals.

Danica pauses, as I'm sure she wasn't expecting this reply, then translates away. The bearded man gives out a cry of delight and pats me on the back.

The rest of the tour is going to feel rather dull after this bizarre episode today. I could stay up here doing this job for the rest of my time here, I think to myself. It's away from the Regiment. I am getting to visit interesting places, meet interesting people, and listen to my entire CD collection in silence.

Unfortunately, as if my thoughts of the job cursed me, this slipper city job was to come to an end. On our return to BLMF, Captain Double T breaks the bad news to me.

She'd been waiting to start a course back in the UK and the details had come through to her a few days ago. It'll be starting soon, and she'll be departing in a couple of weeks. It's been decided to downsize the LRT team to only one crew, based at BLMF, and that crew was to be Staff Hobbs and Melba. I'm gutted I've got to return to the Regiment. I do enjoy driving the trucks, but I know it'll be driving in circles on the same few routes. She senses my disappointment and tries to cheer me up with the news of the next job, that will be in Sarajevo.

Leave a Light On For Me

A few days later, we head off on the road again. I pack a fresh uniform and chuck a few packs of water in the back of the Lanny. More importantly, I choose a selection of new pirate CDs to listen to during the drive. Our destination today will be a place called Kiseijak, which is home to the elements of the ARRC.[118] It feels like anyone and everyone in the military is trying to get a piece of the action out here this year. Our journey will be along Route Gull to Bugojno, turning onto Route Emerald. Then a left turn onto Route Diamond, straight through Vitez and pick up Route Swan.

Most of the roads are familiar now, but parts of it are new to me. I expect it will be the same outstanding scenery with many reminders of the war. The ARRC are using a hotel known as the 'Kiseijak Hotel'. As they arrived before the bulk of the IFOR units, they picked the better accommodation. The drive is a long and a sweaty one, but one at least we have music to pass the time. I stop every hour to stretch my legs and back, but more importantly, to keep myself alert. I peel my top from my back, which is now as wet as a well-used dishcloth. The rise in temperature and humidity is energy-sapping. More than a few times, my eyelids become heavy as the heat tries to put me to sleep. The temptation to shut them for a second is overwhelming, and I take this as my cue to pull over for a few minutes. Captain Double T falls asleep as soon as we get moving, only to wake when I pull over again to stop the onset of sleep.

We arrive late in the evening at the hotel, but at least we are expected. Even in the dim light, I make out the shape of its brutalist outline, which uses concrete as the main material. The strange design makes it stick out amongst the older buildings surrounding it. It was built as a winter sports hotel and, like every other building in Bosnia, it has seen better days. The Corporal, who was expecting us, tells me where I can park the Lanny for the evening and waits for me as I do so. He gives us a quick tour, showing us where the cookhouse, Corimec toilets, and showers are before taking us to our digs. I notice outside the rooms are pairs of boots and I approach the Corporal. "Are we not allowed to wear our boots in the rooms?" I

118 Allied Rapid Reaction Corps.

say, thinking they must have really posh carpets.

Without even cracking a smile, he replies with a straight face, "You leave them out. They will be cleaned and polished for you during the night."

I wait for him to burst into laughter, but he carries on walking. He says it in a tone, which I think he does on purpose, to make me appear thick for not knowing the hotel's etiquette. Maybe he is an actual butler.

"This will be your room, ma'am," he says to Captain Double T.

"Meet you tomorrow at the vehicle, about 0830ish," she says to me as she disappears behind the door.

"Yes, ma'am, see you then," I reply.

I am shown to my room, which is a concrete shell with a few cot beds in it. It's still better than the Mrkonjić Grad Bus Depot Manager's Office. The fixtures and fittings have been removed, leaving bare walls and the floor. I think they were removed, not by a tradesman, but more likely by an opportunist thief. A lamp has been put in the room so at least I can see the bareness of my surroundings. It's plugged into the wall as the thief must have been OK for sockets.

An attempt has been made to make getting around without your boots on easier by putting cardboard on the floor. At least it gives a little bit of comfort and insulation from the chilly surface. I get my kit out and unpack my dossbag onto one of the cot beds. Once done, I head off back in the direction of the showers to get cleaned up before bed. As soon as I'm showered and in clean kit, I go looking for the bar. After searching most of the hotel for it with no success, I admit defeat and return to the room for the night. I strip off and get into my dossbag to settle down. Exhaling heavily, I stand up once more, recalling that I've failed to leave my boots outside the door for Jeeves to clean. Hastily getting back into my dossbag, I make an effort to turn off the lamp off, only to find the switch is missing. Because I'm lazy, I tug the cable to pull the plug from the wall but the plug comes away, still attached to the socket. The bare wires from behind the socket are now on show and I decide against trying to poke it back in with my fingers. I now have a night light to keep me company and am awake all bastard night.

Dog on a Log

Morning arrives, but I wouldn't know it as it's been light all night long. I retrieve my now-clean boots from outside the front door. After the morning routine and an agreeable breakfast of food not served from a Norgie container, I wait at the Lanny for Captain Double T. I look at the hotel in the day's light and I see it's a dirty white with plenty of battle damage, but the holes are bigger this time. I soon work out the hotel is covered in plaster and, where the bullets struck, they knocked a sizeable chunk of this plaster out. The sun is already high in the sky and burning hot. I try to keep in the shade. The temperature and humidity are rising, signalling another uncomfortable day. Captain Double T arrives with another interpreter in tow. Her name is Mirza, and I don't even want to know how many languages she speaks just to highlight my lingual inadequacies. Joining us today is Corporal Cyril Norman from the AGC.[119] When he's not in Bosnia with the TA,[120] he's an accountant in the real world. He has a shopping list of office equipment he requires and companies who could supply it. He'd done his homework, making things easier for Captain Double T.

They both squeeze in the rear of the Lanny and off we go to the first business of the day. Soon it's lunchtime and Mirza says she knows a wonderful restaurant where we can stop at for lunch. We pull up in front of a place with seating outside under cover from the

119 Adjutant General's Corps. The clerks or shiny arses as more commonly known.

120 Territorial Army. Part-time reserve Soldiers.

burning sun and exit the Lanny.

"Oh, my God," exclaims Corporal Norman. "They're bloody cooking greyhounds."

I turn to see what he is staring at and I notice a couple of carcasses skewered on a spit slowly turning over an open fire. They still have their heads, and to be honest, they do look similar to greyhounds. During the rest of my time in Bosnia, I notice more and more of these on the sides of the road being sold. They end up being imaginatively named by everyone as, 'Dog on a Log.'

Mirza laughs, and he replies, "This is no laughing matter, Mirza, it's bloody well disgusting."

She is now in hysterics and is attempting to explain it to him through her laughter.

"Cyril, it's lamb, not a greyhound. It's a Bosnian delicacy," she says, trying to calm him down. We take our seats at a table, where the waitress approaches us and speaks to Mirza. They talk for five minutes before she goes back inside before reappearing with the menus in her hand. Now, I don't speak the local lingo, but that was a long conversation to get a couple of menus and I suspect it went something like this:

> **Waitress:** Hi, what do you want?
> **Mirza:** Hi, we'd like to order some food please.
> **Waitress:** You want food?
> **Mirza:** Yes please. You are a restaurant, are you not?
> **Waitress:** I thought you were going to ask for something else.
> **Mirza:** Why would you think that?
> **Waitress:** Because people stop here all the time and ask us questions.
> **Mirza:** Really, what questions do they ask?
> **Waitress:** Normally things like, how do you grow seedless

grapes, or is that really a greyhound?

Mirza: That's interesting. We are rather hungry, though.

Waitress: I suppose you'll want to see the menu?

Mirza: That is how a restaurant works, I believe.

Waitress: But they're inside.

Mirza: We'll you'd better get them.

Waitress: It's far away.

Mirza: It'll do you good.

Waitress: Are you sure you want to eat?

Mirza: Yes please.

The menu is in Bosnian, using the Latin alphabet. Underneath it's also in English, German, French and Italian. The owner must be a budding entrepreneur and has spotted an opening in the market by enticing in well-paid NATO forces to come and eat at his establishment. Today's choices are meat, meat, or meat.

"What is the main type of meat the Bosnians eat?" I ask Mirza.

"Goooood meat," she replies, laughing.

I decide to go for the chicken and chips with a Coke to drink. Everyone follows suit, apart from Mirza. She opts for a cigarette as a starter, followed by a Turkish coffee and a cigarette, and finishes with another cigarette for dessert. I notice Corporal Norman and Captain Double T both look at the Dog on a Log and pull a face, before making their choice. The Cokes turn up and they are in cans with the style of ring-pull I've not seen for years. The type which comes off from the can and would litter parks in the UK until someone invented the one where you push the tab into the can, keeping it attached.

"Didn't Blue Peter ask us to collect these to make kidney dialysis machines?" I say, holding up the ring-pull, inspecting it closely.

"Yeah, I remember," says Corporal Norman. "They had an appeal and a totaliser which would light up in sections, getting closer to the target amount."

"I remember collecting tin foil for the blind," says Captain Double T, shrugging her shoulders to emphasise she didn't know why.

"Remember this," I say, as I break the ring-pull in two and use the flat bit as a spring to flick the ring part, spinning it across the car park.

Captain Double T and Corporal Normal both laugh while Mirza looks on, bemused, with the cigarette hanging from the corner of her mouth. I imagine the conversation that evening with her husband about her day at work must have confused the hell out of him.

The food arrives, and it looks decent. We tuck in as Mirza looks on, sipping on her coffee and topping up her monthly caffeine level in one cup.

The chicken looks like it's been cooked on small skewers and then cut into smaller pieces. Putting a piece in my mouth, I notice it has the texture of chicken, but it doesn't taste quite right. I continue eating and take another piece and think, this chicken is the oddest I've ever eaten.

"Has anyone seen any chickens since they've been here? I know I haven't," I say, asking them. They both shake their heads and Mirza continues to watch us eat. Suddenly, I don't want to eat any more chicken. The others carry on, unaware of my hint. I turn to the chips, as I'm still hungry. Not wanting to disrespect the restaurant owner, I do take a few more mouthfuls of the meat. I scoff enough to make it appear like I've made the effort. Needing to wash down whatever the hell I scoffed, I order another Coke. Glancing at everyone else, I see they have eaten a token amount of the meat.

We get the bill, pay up in Deutschmarks and move onto the next business visit of the day. I don't feel right for the rest of the afternoon and I swear what I've eaten wasn't chicken.

I get Corporal Norman on his own for the first time later on that day. "The chicken taste funny to you?" I ask him.

"Yeah, it wasn't quite right," he replies.

"You eaten there before, by any chance?" I enquire.

"It's the first time I've been out the hotel since I got here months ago."

"I'm sure we've just eaten someone's pet."

"You reckon it was dog or cat?"

"I don't know. They say most things taste similar to chicken."

"You feel OK?"

"To be honest, I'm feeling... a bit woof."

Corporal Norman lets out a massive groan.

I continue through the day casting pet puns at him, to his utter dismay.

We pull up at another business, and Captain Double T and Mirza both get out of the Lanny. I pretend my door won't open and call to Corporal Norman in the back.

"My door is stuck. I can't open it. Can you come round and let meow?"

He puts his head in his hands.

I wait with the Lanny to make sure it's not stolen and when he comes back I ask, "Was that a paws-itive meeting?"

"Lord, give me strength," he mutters.

While he is away I remember I have Hound Dog by Elvis Presley on a CD. I play it on the drive to the hotel.

I imagine him behind me, wishing he'd never volunteered for this tour now and stayed at home doing his boring accounting job.

→» →» →»

Back at the hotel, Captain Double T and Corporal Norman go off to do whatever they have to do. Mirza disappears off for a cigarette, I presume, while I'm left with the rest of the day to myself. We aren't departing back to BLMF until tomorrow morning, so I have time to kill. First job is to fill up the Lanny, which takes me all of 10 minutes. I give the windows and lights a clean, sort out the back, and check the spare tyre still has air in it. That only kills another 10 minutes, so I wander off to find a coffee in their cookhouse. Even though it looks closed, I spot a water boiler with coffee kit laid out next to it. My decent coffee made, I make my way to one of the many empty tables to sit at, and decide to pen another letter to Del. I mull over which character I could pretend to be this time as I take a Bluey from my jacket pocket. I write his name and address on the front and I reflect on the day so far. The only reason by which I'll remember Kiseljak is being the place I ate a pet. It'll will always now be etched in my memory for this one reason alone.

"May I join you?" says a voice from behind me.

I turn round to see a Padre standing looking at me.

"Yes, sir, you can certainly join me."

"How's it going?" he asks me, and before I answer he adds, "I'm the Padre."

"All good, thanks, and I think I already worked that one out," I say, smiling.

"You're not based at Kiseljak, are you?" he enquires.

"Nah, I'm passing through. I'm the driver for the Local Resource Team. They go round setting up contracts and buying things from the locals."

"It must be a very interesting job."

"It has its moments, believe me. Last week we bought a top end BMW from a..."

I pause, thinking I'm going to incriminate myself and the entire team. "...We bought it from a garage in Banja Luka."

"I suspect the only people who are able to get their hands on a top end BMW over here are the criminals, and they no doubt steal them from Germany to order," he says.

That's uncanny, I think to myself.

"What have you been up to today?" he enquires.

"I've just got back from a trip out with someone from here."

"Did you enjoy it?" he asks me.

"Yeah, I'm only the driver, but we stopped for lunch somewhere."

"Was it the place next to the timber yard?"

"I think it was."

"Did you have the chicken?"

"Yes I did, in fact we all did," I reply hesitantly, with an idea of where this conversation could be going.

"Did it taste weird and was the texture a bit odd?"

"Yes it was."

"You know why that is, don't you?"

"Because it's cat, or maybe dog?"

He erupts with laughter.

"It's rabbit. Stand your guts down."

I experience a rapid burst of relief and my stomach instantly feels better.

"They can't get hold of any chickens, so they use wild rabbits instead."

"Thank fuck for that. Sorry, apologies for the cursing," I say to him.

"That's brilliant, cat or dog, I'm going to tell my wife," he says, struggling to get his words out in-between his bouts of laughter. I see Corporal Norman later on, before we depart. Because of the kind and caring compassionate person I am, I opt to keep this nugget of information to myself. Do I feel guilty about it? Not at all. So, Cyril Norman, the accountant from Leamington Spa, if you're reading this, you now know you didn't eat a pet. My conscience is eternally clear and I will sleep soundly forever on.

You Just Can't Keep Away

We stop one more night in Kiseljak before heading back to BLMF. The journey is uneventful, and driving through 'damaged and destroyed' villages has now become normal to me. There are still strange things to see from time to time. On one such trip, I remember there being a pair of shoes in the middle of the road. I gave them a wide berth just in case, but as I passed them, it was clear there was nothing dangerous about them. It was awfully sinister to come across a pair of shoes laying in the middle of nowhere on Route Parrot near to the IEBL between Kupres and Sipovo, with no houses in sight. It made us think an old score had been settled. If we had gone looking off the road, would we have found a body? We didn't go looking as the 'stay on the hard road surface' rule prevailed. Another time, we came across a horse with its front legs crudely bound together with wire. We intervened on this one, cutting the wire which had been digging into its flesh. Not too sure what to do, we secured it to a crash barrier as we didn't want it wandering off and blowing itself up on a mine. We made a note of the grid reference so we could report its location. The first IFOR base we came to on the route was a unit of Czech Infantry. They had set up a camp in the remains of a ruined farm building and they thanked us for informing them and sent a patrol to rescue the poor animal.

Soon it's time for Captain Double T to think about departing back to the UK for her course. We wish each other the best and she thanks me for my help, especially the German translating. I thank her for all the talking she did when we were driving and am called a cheeky so-and-so. I never found out what was going on there. The vehicle toolkit is signed back to Melba, and he says he'll drop the Lanny back at Sipovo if Staff Hobbs manages to stay sober for a day.

"Keep safe, buddy," I say to Melba. "Thanks for everything."

"You too, pal, it was good to meet you. We may bump into each other one day, and don't get too depressed being back with your Regiment."

I turn to Staff Hobbs.

"Thanks for the 'Sleep in the Ditch', Staff, I've not drunk it yet. I'll keep it for a special occasion."

"You'll need it in the winter. You can use it as cold-start to get your Lanny going?" he says laughing. "But seriously, be careful of it."

I think that I should book a seat on the afternoon Sickhook back to Split. Then, as if by magic, I spot Careless wandering around BLMF, looking lost.

"Oi," I shout at him, and a dozen other people turn to look at me, including a snarling Warrant Officer.

"What are you doing here?" I ask him.

"I brought the TC up for a meeting."

"Are you going back today?"

"Yeah, we will be."

"Great, can I cadge a lift?"

"I dunno if the TC will like that?"

"Fuck him, I need a lift back to Split as my job has finished here."

"I'll ask him when I see him."

"Don't ask him, just tell him, for fuck's sake."

The journey back to Dalma in the rear of the Lanny with Careless at the wheel is worse than the previous trip on the Chinook. It's a long drive from BLMF back to Split. I try to make a bed from the kit in the back, intending to sleep most of the way. Apart from being thrown sideways and up in the air, it's akin to a mobile sauna. They have the front windows open but there isn't one in the rear. Unless the rear door is open, there's no air flow. We are on the unmade stretch of road out of Banja Luka when I relent and have to open the back door. The back of the Lanny fills up with the dust from the

281

dirt road faster than soldiers filling the First & Last when he's giving away free pivo. I am blinded and coughing my guts up. I hear Careless and the TC swearing as the dust makes its way to the front of the Lanny. I have two choices of comfort. Breathe easily and boil or be cool and suffocate. I wish I'd booked my seat on the Chinook now, even if it meant barfing up. We get onto the smoother asphalted sections of the road and the motions are now only sidewards. I can now pop the back door open without dying from a dust induced lung disease. I sit right at the back, holding the door open and enjoying the fresh breeze which it affords. After a while, my eyelids begin to droop and I am worried about falling out the back. I have this vision of Careless and the TC looking in the back of an empty Lanny at Split. They're both scratching their heads, trying to figure out where along the 150-mile route I could be. I do eventually manage a kip, but I wake several times covered in sweat.

We arrive back at Dlama in time for dinner, which is needed, as I'm now starving. Before I hand in my weapon, I bump into Judas and he tells me the great news. I have to drive a DROPS up to BLMF tonight as part of a convoy. They are running low on paper plates and plastic cutlery and they need it urgently. I try to protest, saying I've only just got back from Banja Luka, but it falls on deaf ears. He explains we have most available soldiers away on taskings, the R&R[121] has started and there are a few on courses back in the UK. Also, the Regimental football team has a game with a local club in the morning. I love it when Army sports come before operations. He says to be ready to go at midnight and meet Manbat over at the MT Offices. He'll make sure someone gets the truck ready and I am to get my head down until then. I am now glad of the extra sleep I managed on the way back to Split, even if it was hot and sticky. After scoff, I head back to bunk and find out Prat and Del are on

121 Rest and Recuperation.

the same tasking. Prat and I try to force ourselves to sleep, but it doesn't come as the accommodation is way too noisy early in the evening. At 11pm, I give up and decide to get ready. With our gear in hand, we head over to the MT Offices to find out what's happening. I meet Manbat, who is watching the loading the last of the pallets onto one of the DROPS trucks by a Volvo.

"Aye up, mate," I say to him.

"Aha, you're with us tonight. We're nearly done with loading," he says to me.

I notice the cutlery and plates are placed in cardboard boxes which are sat on pallets for ease of moving.

"What happens if it rains?" I ask him, thinking the boxes will fall apart once soaked.

"Fuck knows," says Manbat. "They're a royal pain in the arse to strap down too. We should have shipping containers to put them in."

He points to where my truck is already loaded, I walk over to it, chuck my gear in the cab, and plug in my Boogie Box. It's going to be a long night, and I want it to be my companion to keep me awake on the drive. I climb on the back of the DROPS to check the straps holding the flimsy boxes in place. I feel for movement and there still is some, so I tighten the ratchet strap which collapses the cardboard box further with every click.

Midnight arrives, and Manbat shouts for everyone to gather round him at the front of the lined-up convoy of trucks. He goes through the route, which is familiar to most of us. He says he'll stop for a quick break now and again so we can check the straps on the boxes, as they are bound to come loose. If there are no more questions, then we will sod off in five minutes. We stare at him for a few seconds before he declares,

"Right, let's make like a baby and head out."

To the tune of Johnny Cash's *I've Been Everywhere,* I don't splash nobody at the puddle nor hold anyone up on Split Hill. The roads are empty, apart from the odd Policija vehicle parked up on the side of the road, hoping to stop an unsuspecting local for a bribe. Blinded by our headlights, they were probably trying to pull the first truck over as they came towards them. The moment they identify that we're IFOR, they give up, waving us on frantically, as if they've realised it was their boss they were about to pull. I've had them jump out on me a few times, but I'd just keep going as we had been told they had no jurisdiction over us. Soon we are at the Kamensko BXP, and straightaway everyone is tightening their ratchet straps. I give mine a few more clicks to get the balance between being tight enough that I don't lose any of them and loose enough that they don't squash the box too much.

Soon we are on our way again. The only other traffic we pass on the roads belong to IFOR of varying nationalities. The next stop is outside the base at Kupres and, again, the loads are rechecked and re-tightened. I change the CD to David Bowie and we set off to the tune of Heroes. My truck is number three of the six in the convoy. I'm following Prat, keeping close to him, and checking if Del is still visible in my mirrors. We wind our way along Route Parrot with the odd glimmering light from a dwelling far off in the distance. I have my window open to experience the cool and still night. There's no moon and I am able to make out the Milky Way in the sky above me. I'm feeling tired, but David Bowie and the winding road keep me alert. I remember doing night drives in Germany years previously on exercise down the autobahns. Trying to stay awake was a real problem on those long, straight and boring German roads. At least if you fell asleep, then the new and rust-free crash barrier was likely to keep you on the road. Out here, if you go off the edge, you're more than likely ending up in the bottom of an abyss. Maybe it would even be littered with a few mines to make it even more exciting. If there even was a crash barrier, it'd be about as much use as a sunroof in a submarine, and over you'd go. Soon enough, we pass the battered sign for Sipovo. I hope Manbat will schedule another stop so I can tighten my straps, and, more importantly, un-tighten my bladder. As we enter a built-up area, the brake lights of the trucks ahead illuminate the darkened street. Six DROPS vehicles take up a lot of real estate and, not wanting to go searching for somewhere suitable, we stop in the road. I climb down from the cab and choose a wheel to relieve myself on. The truck behind me puts its main beam on, lighting me up for the Bosnian population to see, and I hear Del cheering whilst beeping his horn.

"Could you not wait until the morning, you dirty sod?" he shouts at me.

Our engines are still running, and there's the usual commotion from others further along the convoy as they check their loads. A few lights of the houses nearby come on as our noise has woken them from their slumber. I become aware that our sudden arrival and commotion at this ungodly hour might be frightening to the people in the surrounding dwellings. We are only having a quick break, but to the locals we are a load of soldiers turning up in the dead of night with vehicles and making a racket. I am conscious of the ethnic cleansing which went on here in the previous years and how we may present to them right now. We don't hang around, and, within a few minutes, we are disappearing down the road, and peace returns to the darkened street. As we pass the picturesque Bočac Lake, the first hints of dawn turn the sky behind the mountains beyond the lake a light blue. I have an enormous yawn and try to stretch as best I can while at the controls of a truck. I rub my eyes, grab a bottle of water, and hold the steering wheel sort-of straight with my knees as I open it with both hands. A convoy of American Humvees passes us going the other way. Each one of them has a soldier poking out the top manning a huge black machine gun, looking ready for a spot of early morning war. They are very wide vehicles, and we kick up a load of dust as we are forced right over to the edge of the road to get past them. We're close to BLMF now and I know the section of the unmade road is around here somewhere. I see the cloud of dust up ahead as Manbat arrives at it first. I reduce my speed to a walking pace, and even then I bounce up and down in my sprung seat. My seatbelt stops my head from contacting the ceiling of the cab. More than once, as I go up, my foot comes off the accelerator pedal, making me lurch forwards as the truck slows. I then come back down and put my foot back on the accelerator pedal and I'm pushed backwards as the truck speeds up. More than a few times, I have to remove my foot away from the pedal, as this is getting out of control because of the rutted surface of the road. I am glad I used a bungee cord to secure my Boogie Box, as I hear the tools crash around in the toolbox. Once we're back on the tarmac road, we speed up again. I feel like I've had a full-body workout, with a few punches to the head from Mike Tyson.

→» →» →»

When we arrive in a cutlery-free BLMF, no one hails us as heroes. We're instead told by the stroppy Corporal with a porn moustache where we can't park. Manbat works it out and finds out where we should be for the unloading. We congregate at the front truck and have a natter between us. Some light up a cigarette, some lie on the grass. I sit on the kerb and give my eyes a rub. Manbat comes back from wherever he'd been and says, "They can't unload us for another hour yet."

We make a collective tired-sounding groan.

"However, breakfast is on."

The groan changes to a tired-sounding cheer.

Del climbs up onto the back of his truck and begins ripping open a few of the boxes.

"What are you doing?" says Manbat.

"I'm thinking inside the box," he replies as he removes a handful of plastic cutlery. "We may need these diggers."

"Good shout," says Manbat.

"Squadron Ops informed me of something last night and it sounded mission critical. If we can't get the KFS[122] to Banja Luka this morning, we are going to have to start retreating," he says, passing a load of white plastic knives to me. We claim a whole bench to ourselves inside the tented cookhouse. The Norgie containers have gone, to be replaced by brand-new hotplates, which have quite a selection, consisting of bacon, eggs, and sausages. Even the coffee now tastes decent and not with the added flavours of the prior evening's main course.

I spot Melba on another table. He stares at me, blinks a few times, and then smiles. He walks over to where I am sitting and says, "What are you still doing here? I thought you left yesterday."

"I've left and come back again," I reply to him.

"Did you fly back up again or what?" he says.

"I brought you up a resupply of diggers by road this very morning. We heard you were about to run dry of eating implements."

"Fuck me, they're working you hard back there."

"Well, the Regimental football team is through to the final in the 'skiving bastard's championship' and there was no one else available to drive them up to you. Otherwise, you'd have been scoffing with your fingers."

"I've got my own metal ones," he says, showing them to me in case I don't believe him.

"How's things been with you since I last saw you?" I ask him.

Melba laughs, and then I laugh too.

"Take care, pal, I'm sure I'll bump into you up here again soon,"

---

122 Knives, forks, spoons.

he says as he wanders back to his table.

The trucks are unloaded in quick time once the stackers get going with their forklift. The boxes are not heavy, and we could have unloaded them even quicker if we threw them off ourselves. Soon enough, it's time to set off back to Split. I'm not as fresh as I could be before a six-hour drive across a country with the most dangerous roads in Europe. Manbat does the customary brief, and in his rush to get back, it's quicker than usual. He says where we will be stopping for breaks, and to keep an eye out for the vehicles behind and in front of us. Weapons physically checked, so he knows we have them on us, we make our way to our trucks and he shouts out to us, "Departing in two minutes."

I make sure the Boogie Box is plugged in and primed with a Bob Marley CD. I climb over to the passenger side to open the window, as I'll need the maximum amount of breeze to keep me alert on this one. Further along the convoy, the truck in front pulls away and I mutter, "Two minutes, my arse."

I rush across the cab and back to the driver's seat. I fire up the DROPS, flick the gear knob into Drive, and follow the disappearing truck in front of me. In my hurry to get moving and not split up the convoy, I forget to put on my seatbelt. In my mirrors, I notice the truck behind me is not moving and Del is, no doubt, muttering the same words as me a few seconds earlier. Once on the road, we squeeze up to look like a real convoy and not individual trucks in the morning traffic. Banja Luka is now behind us, and the unmade section of road is getting nearer. In the distance, the dust cloud signals to me that Manbat is now on it. I reduce my speed as I transition from the smooth asphalt to the uneven and bone-jarring part. The dust from the DROPS in front fills my cab as I bounce in my sprung seat. I hit a hole, which causes me to realise I've forgotten to put my seatbelt on, as am launched upwards, causing my head to make contact with the ceiling of the cab.

"Ow, fucking hell," I curse, as I now drop back down into my seat. I keep one hand on the steering wheel and with the other, I fumble for the seatbelt, which is hanging uselessly somewhere to my left. It's a genuine struggle to find the buckle whilst getting thrown around and keeping the truck on my half of the excuse of a road. I take both hands off the steering wheel as I attempt to click it in. The truck is now veering around as I battle with the bumps and the buckle. I feel the reassuring click through my fingers as it locks in place, and I'm now strapped securely in my seat. My bonce is safe from any more trauma. I rub the top of my head and can't notice any swelling, but I notice the dust in my hair. Head injury averted, I now concentrate on keeping my truck on the road as we speed along the route which we had taken earlier in the morning. The day is warming up, and it begins to be dreamlike. The battle to keep my eyes open commences. Bob Marley struggles to keep me focused on keeping this great big truck on the road. I put my head out the window in the hope the blast of cooler air will revive me a little. It does momentarily, but the tiredness and the warmth soon set off the drooping eyelids process once again. I sing to myself, I talk out loud, I rub my face, and I drink warm water from a plastic bottle. It works, but it's a short-term fix because as soon as I stop, I sense myself going. I should pull over, but I don't want to be the one who breaks up the convoy. We are approaching TSG and I am hoping Manbat will let us have a break there.

There is a tremendous bang and the steering wheel jolts in my hands. My eyes open and, for a split-second, I don't know where I am. Then, as the adrenalin kicks in, my body goes into fight-or-flight mode. I am now aware I'm in the driving seat of a DROPS and I've fallen asleep. The vehicle has veered too far over to the right and a rusty yellow crash barrier has saved me from heading over a very steep rocky embankment.

"Fuck this," I shout to myself, scared that I have nearly gone off the road, likely to my demise. My heart rate is through the roof and now in time with Bob Marley's *Iron Lion Zion*. I am wide awake during the final part of the journey to TSG. I breathe a sigh of relief as the front vehicles slow and pull off to the edge of the road. The first thing I do as soon as we come to a halt is to inspect the truck. I'm dreading what the damage is and how much shit I'll be in. It's the military mentality which we all have. Even though I have been exceptionally busy for quite a few days now, and awake for a long period, I presume the worst. I am immediately full of the guilt that it's my fault and I, and only I, have fucked up. The area doesn't appear too badly damaged and, after having a good look, I believe I've got off lightly with only the bottom foot-step showing any noticeable signs of an impact. It has been bent inwards but has still held its shape. There are scuff marks on it too and I see bits of shiny metal where it's taken the paint off. There are marks on the front wheel's metal hub in faint yellow.

Del comes wandering up the side of our parked trucks and asks, "What happened there?"

"Nodding dog," I say to him.

"Oh yeah," he replies.

"This is serious business on these dodgy roads," I say back to him.

"I'm struggling too in this heat and have had a few near misses. I must have been asleep when you hit the barrier, as I didn't notice."

Manbat now appears to inspect the damage and says, "You'll be able to sort that out, no worries."

We stay there for over half an hour and, instead of taking a power nap, I keep walking around in circles. As I chat to Prat and the others, I'm sort of relieved it's not only me struggling to keep awake.

Then we are on our way again. The final part isn't too bad, as Manbat stops a couple of extra times. Back at Dalma, Del and Prat give me a hand to hide the damage. We attach a ratchet strap to the foot-step and then to the tow hook on the back of Del's truck. Ratcheting it up, I manage to unbend it almost back into its original position. Prat gets hold of a tin of green paint and slaps it on anywhere which shows the shiny bits of metal or yellow marks.

"No one will ever know," says Prat, eyeing up his handiwork as as the thick olive-coloured liquid drips on the ground and over most of the tyre.

We trudge up to Judas's office to check the mail and find out what tasking or torture they have thought up next for us.

"Ah, just the man, I've git a great the job for yee," says Judas to me. I want to say, "You have to be kidding me," but I don't as I'm too tired.

"Fancy a trip to Sarajevo?"

My ears prick up in interest. "I am, but as long as it's not in a helicopter or in the next hour."

"It'll be in a few days an' it's wuth Lieutenant Fairfax. She's git tae gee an' visit a few of the Detachments."

"Perfect, that'll give me time to catch up with my social calendar," I say mockingly back to him.

"Captain Haywood recommended that y'dee it as he received good feedback from the last job ye did," he replies, either ignoring or not listening to my sarcasm.

"Sounds perfect," I say, adding, "Who's Lieutenant Fairfax when she's not at home?"

"She's the new TC of the stacker section who are attached to us. That's who she is." The thought of a few days checking trucks and doing menial tasks sounds almost appealing as I pick up my kit in readiness to head back to the accommodation.

"But in the meantime, you're on the gas run in the morning," says Judas, putting a massive spanner in the works. My shoulders droop as I walk off, dragging my gear behind me with a dejected look about me.

Dry Me a River

The next day of the gas run turns into a few more days of gas runs and another stint as the duty POL. The trip to visit the Detachments is delayed and I even fear it will not now go ahead until I get word that Lieutenant Fairfax wants to meet me. I head over to the stacker section to find her and finally track her down in a Corimec, behind a desk covered in paperwork.

I salute her and I introduce myself.

"Lance Corporal Lee, ma'am."

She salutes me back and stands up from her chair.

"Ah, Lance Corporal Lee," she says, offering me her hand for a shake.

"It's nice to finally meet you. I believe you've been up country a few times now?"

"I have, ma'am," I say, shaking her hand back, feeling a bit out-of-place shaking an Officer's hand. She'll soon stop doing that once she's a Captain.

"Well, we'll leave tomorrow around 8am, so where should I find you in the morning?"

"We could meet over by the MT Offices if you're OK with that?"

"That'd be great," she replies, smiling.

She then runs through the plan which is to visit the MBLU's up country as she is responsible for them. We are to check in any of our Radio Detachments, or Rad Dets, as we call them, which are on our way, so they don't feel forgotten by the Regiment.

"Do you have any tips on what I should take with me?" she asks me.

"CDs, ma'am."

"CDs?" she replies, confused.

"It's an abbreviation for the term Compact Disc, ma'am."

"I know what a CD is," she says. "I meant military kit."

"Just the normal gear you know, dossbag, cot bed, and your gun. But if you have any CDs, it's worth bringing them along as the Lannys don't have radios in them and it's a long drive to those places you've just listed."

"Oh, OK, I didn't bring any CDs with me," she says.

"Don't worry, I know a few places who sell them on our route."

→» →» →»

The next morning, we are navigating up a busy Split Hill in our Lanny. I am in second gear and the engine is screaming its head off, but when I shift it into third it labours. Who designed the gearbox, I wonder? They must have got their gear ratios mixed up. I put it back into second and the engine reverts to screaming again. U2 are playing on the CD but I can't hear them above the noise. I notice an impatient bus in my mirrors, having a look to get past as we traverse the bending road. He's so close and I make out the wrinkles in the driver's face from too many years in the sun. I see he's smoking a cigarette, probably along with every one of his passengers.

"The buses are faster than our Lanny. Have you got the handbrake on?" shouts Lieutenant Fairfax.

"I'm flat out, ma'am," I shout the reply to her.

"Is there something wrong with the engine, then?" she shouts back.

"You need to be aware, ma'am, this vehicle has been made by the lowest bidder, and is therefore a pile of shite."

A Mercedes driver behind the bus snaps and starts to overtake it. I think he was planning on getting in front of the bus but doesn't realise we are there until he's halfway along. There's traffic now coming around the bend, in the form of a truck, and the Mercedes is on the wrong side of the road. The gap he left as he started his manoeuvre has no doubt been replaced with the next cigarette-smok-ing Croatian with a death wish. His only option once past the bus is to force us off the road. This is what he goes for and I pull over to give him room, but I am up against the edge of the road. The truck coming the other way, horn blaring, pulls over as far as he can go. I notice Lieutenant Fairfax in my peripheral vision, tensing up and bracing against the dashboard.

Normally, I'd say something like, "This guy's driving is just dreadful," but with the closing speed of the truck coming down the hill, it's over in an instant. I lose the power of speech as my brain devotes all of its run time to survival. The Mercedes squeezes past us and accelerates to the next vehicle in front of us, less than a hundred feet away. On this day I've learnt that you can fit a Lanny, a Mercedes E190 and a truck side-by-side on Split Hill. If the distance that sep-arated us from a catastrophic accident could be measured, it would be in millimetres.

"Is this normal?" shouts a stressed-looking Lieutenant Fairfax above the racket.

"Rush hour is worse," I shout back.

Once we are at the top of Split Hill, the Lanny is able to at least achieve a mediocre speed, which means the irritated locals calm down. We continue our journey up country, crossing the Kamensko BXP, heading up to Kupres, before taking Route Parrot to Sipovo for our first night's stop. Lieutenant Fairfax is quiet as we pass the first of the war damage on Route Gull. She gazes out the window as we pass the empty houses, and, now and again, she comments on how sad it is. On Route Parrot, which crosses the old front line, I see a few graves off the edge of the road. The soil looks like it was dug up recently and they just have sticks at the head of them. This makes them look more of a marker, and maybe someone's planning on retrieving them one day. We arrive in Sipovo later in the after-noon and track down the MBLU gang on the camp, which isn't too hard. We spot a soldier carrying a white laundry bag over his shoulder and follow him. The guys and girls of the MBLUs are busy in their never-ending quest to keep everyone's uniforms clean. They are the unsung heroes of the Army, along with many other trades which keep the military functioning.

All you normally get to see is the stuff at the sharp end, but this could only be achieved by everyone pulling together. The chefs do a marvellous job, as we know an Army marches on its stomach. The Posties get the post to and from the troops, thus keeping up the morale. The MBLU bods make sure we have clean undercrackers. This often gets overlooked, but, believe me, a clean set of undercrackers is up there with good food and a letter from home. They're genuinely pleased to see us, and I get the impression they feel forgotten about with just their small team up here. Giving us a personalised tour of a facility, they proudly explain the process and how they run the gaff. They tell us they used to run showers too, but now they have Corimec ones on site, so there isn't much of a call for their showering services anymore.

The industrial-sized washing machines and dryers are self-contained in a frame which is the size of a shipping container and can be carried by a DROPS. They are manned by RLC TA and, for reasons that I never get to find out, they are all from Liverpool.

They introduce themselves as Corporal Scouse 'Moses' Rush, who is in charge, and his Lance Corporals, Scouse 'Windy' Gale and Scouse 'Merky' Murgatroyd.

Lieutenant Fairfax says, "Lance Corporal Lee is from Liverpool."

"Whereabouts, lad?" says Moses to me.

"I'm from the Wirral," I reply to him.

"Ha, eez a bloody woollyback,"[123] says Scouse Gale.

"I know, I know," I say, now thinking I'll have to explain to Lieu-

123 A term for anyone who lives in the North West of England outside of Liverpool.

tenant Fairfax about the Geography of the North West.

Scouse Moses tells us of a problem they've had a few times. It's like watching a play with the three of them standing in front of us. I take it in and make a few notes later that evening . . .

Der Laundry Lads
Written by IFOR

EXT. IN FRONT OF THE MBLU, LATE AFTERNOON.

SCOUSE MOSES
De 'eavens opened, like, and it pissed it down, yer know, it was like dee end of der werld, ma'am.

SCOUSE MERKY
We've a bone to pick wid Mother Nature. Whenever it rains, heavy like, dee MBLU terns into a bastard water park.

SCOUSE WINDY
Dat evenin', der water was so high dat der laundry bags decided to go white water raftin' down de hill and we had to rescue dem all.

SCOUSE MERKY
I'm a soldier, not a bloody lifeguard, ma'am.

SCOUSE MOSES
I had to channel me inner Duncan Goodhew just to rescue a dozen runaway laundry bags.

SCOUSE WINDY

Maybe we should start offerin' white water raftin' trips as a new service?

SCOUSE MOSES

We had to do all der laundry again. It was a right pain in der arse. I missed der footy dat evenin'. Liverpool were playin' Everton. I've talked to der powers dat be about tryin' to get the Royal Engineers to build some flood defences, or just relocate us to another part of der camp.

LIEUTENANT FAIRFAX

What was the outcome?

SCOUSE MOSES

It was a draw.

LIEUTENANT FAIRFAX

Not the football.

SCOUSE MOSES

Dey said dat dey would see what dey could do, but we are still here and still gettin' flooded.

SCOUSE MERKY

If dee higher-ups won't listen, den maybe it's time we take matters into our own hands.

SCOUSE WINDY

If day won't listen to reason, den maybe day'll listen to the sound of soggy socks squelching in der Corimecs?

The scene fades out with the sound of distant thunder, hinting at more rainy misadventures to come for der Laundry Lads of the MBLU.

I leave Lieutenant Fairfax with the troops and go to find somewhere to sit and boil in the afternoon sun.

The rest of the week is a repeat of the above, driving to wherever there is an MBLU. They're always Scousers, happy to see us, and always wanting to give us a tour. We get to meet up with the Rad Dets, who are equally glad to see us.

There was an episode during this trip, but the details have faded from my memory in time, and so I cannot remember how it came to be. We were invited to a barbecue in a village with a load of Croatians. We must have been invited by maybe a Liaison Officer who we met whilst on our travels. I didn't dream it, as I have the pictures to prove both that it happened and that I was there. It was somewhere near Glamoc. I seem to recall it had been occupied by the Serbs. They had been forced out by the Croatian military offensive the previous summer, and the Croatians were very proud to tell us this. After the barbecue, we were shown around an abandoned children's hospital and told all the equipment was taken by the Serbs when they left. Anything which was left behind, of which there was little, had been smashed with the intent of not allowing anyone else to use it again. They had destroyed the main fuse boxes and adorned most of the rooms with graffiti. This consisted of the Serb coat of arms with the white cross and a 'C' in each corner. I found pencil drawings on the wall in another room that looked like they were drawn by a child. They were of planes bombing a castle and a battle going on with lots of tiny soldiers. One picture was called "The Final Countdown," and there were dates underneath it leading up to something which meant nothing to me. Outside the back door and down the bottom of the steps was a load of kit. I saw a gas mask on top of it and straightaway thought it had to be booby trapped. I then remember thinking that I really shouldn't have been in there as we couldn't have trusted the locals to ensure the building was safe. Making my way out, I hinted to Lieutenant Fairfax as I passed her that we should get out.

Sarajevo

We make our way to Sarajevo for the last visit and the highlight of our mini road trip, as we'll be dropping in on the Rad Det at Zetra Stadium. Everyone knows Zetra Stadium, if not by name then because of the British figure skaters Torvill and Dean and their perfect score at the Winter Olympics of 1984. We enter the city on Route Snake from Kiseljak, passing the airport which is at the end of the valley that the city sits in. Mountains dominate the city all around it, and it's where the Serb Army was positioned during their siege. They would have fired shells and heavy weaponry from these vantage points. I can see further on that the high ground is closer to the built-up areas, and in places the city has spread up into the foothills of the surrounding mountains. The main road in runs almost straight with high-rise blocks on the right and factories on the left. The tram tracks run in-between the carriageway. Everything has signs of damage, but the rebuilding is happening. The tram has new electric overhead cables, the streetlamps have been replaced, and there are recently planted saplings on the roadsides. I read that they used them for firewood during the siege.

As we approach the city centre, I notice the damaged yellow Holiday Inn where the journalists stayed. Behind it are the UNIS towers with their upper floors damaged and looking burnt out. On the right is one of the largest and most modern-looking buildings in

Sarajevo, the Parliament Assembly of Bosnia and Herzegovina. It is heavily damaged, and again the upper floors have taken the brunt of the violence inflicted on it.

I find out later this area was known as Sniper Alley as the front lines came close to the edge of the city. At a set of brand new-looking traffic lights, if we had turned right, any buildings in front of us would have been occupied by those deadly snipers.

At a junction, the roads diverge. We take the one following the Miljacka river and we skirt around the city centre. Every building has bullet marks in it and more than a few have bigger holes from heavier weapons. There are many bridges crossing the river and I recall that Archduke Franz Ferdinand was murdered somewhere around here by Gavrilo Princip, a young Bosnian Serb whose actions started the First World War. Or as Prat put it: "Der guy with der turkey for an 'at who was shot by a principal and den it all kicked off big-time in the mud in France or Belgium wif der Germans."

"You can't teach that," I thought when I heard him say it.

The traffic is light and driving standards seem to be relatively calm compared to what I have experienced in the last six weeks. It's a mixture of Fiat 126s, VW Golfs, Ladas and strange looking Jeeps sporting IFOR logos. There is high ground all around us now and the main road bends round to the left and almost back on itself.

"I think we may have missed a turning, ma'am," I say, as I sense it's not feeling right.

"I think you might be right," she replies, trying to look at the Sarajevo part of our IFOR Route Map.

As I continue to drive along the road and she says, "It can't be hard as it's on the only road heading north out of town."

There are traffic lights on what appears a main road. I guess that turning right will get us heading in approximately the correct direction. "Shall we take a right here, ma'am?" I say.

"Go for it," she replies.

After I turn, the road starts ascending and in the distance I spot the TV tower on the top of a large hill. On our left, on the side of some high ground, are modern-looking apartments. Like every building which is still standing, they give the impression they've taken a right battering.[124] An immense graveyard comes into view on our right. Most of the headstones appear improvised and the mounds of freshly dug soil give away the truth that they've been recently buried. This is one of those moments that will stick with me. I've been here less than two months, but yet I have already become accustomed to being surrounded by the evidence of the suffering, death and destruction. The troops deployed on the earlier tours, from 1992 to 1995, had to sustain it happening right in front of them. They do paint a thoroughly different picture of what I was experiencing. I was aware of the high numbers of those killed during the war, but it's hard to picture thousands of people in your mind. When I see the sea of individual graves, it puts it into something I could visualise. However, this wasn't all the people who'd been killed, which made it even more disturbing.

We carry on up the road and, as it levels out, a large black building, damaged as usual, comes into view. It's the Zetra Stadium. To be honest, at first I think it's just another warehouse as it has a dull appearance about it. It's dark and square, and the graveyard runs right up next to it. The corrugated outer shell looks like it has collapsed in places, revealing the tubular framework. Around the outside, there's a collection of military vehicles parked up. I identify them as British and know this must be the place. At the front gate, the guard asks us to book in and unload before progressing any further. Lieutenant

---

124 During my return trip many years later, I was told by my ex-Bosnian Police Officer guide that this was the expensive part of Sarajevo, where the better-off residents live.

Fairfax books us in and gets the directions to our Rad Det, who we have come to visit. They are to be found in a couple of Corimecs at the top of the vehicle park.

Lance Corporal Alex 'Two Wrongs' Wright is there to meet us and he was expecting us. I know him from the HQ Squadron back in Bielefeld and we shake hands, asking one another how it is going.

"So so, you know, can't complain" is the consensus from us both.

"So, how's it going?" Lieutenant Fairfax asks Two Wrongs. He is up here with another two guys from the Rad Det: Lance Corporal Kenny 'Kit-Kat' Fulmer and Sergeant 'J9' Jones.

Kit-Kat's name comes from the missing finger he lost in a motorcycle accident years before. He now has three remaining fingers and a thumb on his left hand, but that's good enough to qualify as the four fingers you'd get in a Kit-Kat. Sergeant Jones is only called 'J9' when he is out of earshot. He is an older member of the Regiment who looks like he's spent far too many hours in the sun. He has thinning hair on top, so he shaves off the rest. J9 is short for Junction 9 on the M25, the turn off for Leatherhead. I don't know who thought of that one, but it's a classic.

Two Wrongs blabbers on about stuff which doesn't interest me. I decide to bask in sunlight on the bench behind the Corimec. Sergeant J9 is sitting and doing the same, but with his eyes closed, working on trying to get more wrinkles.

"Good afternoon, Sergeant Jones," I say to him. "It's been a while since I last saw you."

He opens one eye, looks at me, and closes it again.

"Ah, it is you who's driving Lieutenant Fairfax Machine. I was informed she was coming, and I was wondering which idiot would be driving her."

"Only the one and only, *moi,*" I reply to him, pointing at myself with my thumbs.

"Well, I suppose as the head of this outfit, I'd better go and speak to her," he says, opening both his eyes and sitting up.

"You having a quiet time up here away from the Regiment?" I ask him.

"Fuck, yeah, I don't want to be in Bullshit City with you lot. It's a lot more relaxing up here. Mind you, though, when we were told you were coming, we swept out the Corimec."

"I've managed more time away from Split too," I say.

"Have you been to Sarajevo before?" he adds.

"Nope, first time for me. Got as far as Kiseljak a week ago though and ate a rabbit."

"A what?" he says, bursting out laughing.

"A rabbit, you know, the long-eared fuckers? Fond of carrots?"

"A rabbit, fuck me. Had you run out of food and had to catch one?" he says, still laughing.

"I thought it was chicken, then dog, but found out later it was rabbit. Thank fuck."

"Do you want a tour of Sarajevo later this afternoon?" he asks me.

"Hell, yeah, that would be ace," I excitedly reply.

"We have an interpreter here. Can't pronounce her name, so we call her Susan. I'll get her to take you both on a tour later."

He gets up, stretches, and mooches around the corner to talk to Lieutenant Fax Machine. I overhear their muffled talking in the Corimec behind me as Lieutenant Fax Machine asks questions and Sergeant J9 and Two Wrongs reply to her. They continue to talk inside the Corimec for half an hour. When they come outside, I make out the end of their conversation.

"It went off in his hand and then he was covered in the stuff," says Sergeant J9.

"That'll teach him for mucking around with things he's not trained on," replies Lieutenant Fax Machine.

I try to think who or what they are on about, but I have no idea.

"Susan says she'll be here in 10 minutes or so and she'll take you on the city tour," says Sergeant J9.

"That's very kind of you to arrange for us, Sergeant Jones," replies Lieutenant Fax Machine.

We meet Susan, who doesn't have the appearance of a Susan but, when she tells us her real name, we agree Susan is better. She is older than any other of the interpreters I've met so far. She is dressed as if she's visiting a friend for afternoon tea, which makes her look out-of-place standing next to our dirty Lanny. Lieutenant Fax Machine offers her the front seat, and she accepts, as I doubt it would have been at all ladylike for her to clamber in the back over our kit. The back door shuts and Lieutenant Fax Machine's head appears between me and Susan, so I fire up the Lanny and we head off. Susan shows us around the city first and takes us close to where the front lines used to be. The destruction here is total. I don't make out any houses with roofs or any which look occupied. They're only masonry shells and full of rubble. We pass large lines of people queuing up for water with armed IFOR Soldiers, of an unknown nationality, either keeping an eye on them or keeping one out for them. Lots of people wave happily to us as we drive past them. Susan tells me where to turn next and the road takes us up into the foothills. She asks me to pull over here and says we should get out to explore. Not too far away, I spot the UNIS towers and the Parliament Assembly building. We are looking at it from a different angle from when we drove past it earlier in the day. On the side that we couldn't see before, there are several large holes in it, big enough for someone to climb through. Everything from the edge of the road to the towers is trashed. A little way along the road are a few Ford Transit vans laying on their sides, minus their wheels. Bullets have peppered them, leaving them with more holes than a colander has. Susan is quiet as she looks with us across the devastation, and I can't imagine what is going through her mind. A bunch of kids walk up to us and say,

"Hello." They point at my gun and want to touch it. I let them, but I put the sling over my head first, as I don't want have to explain how I lost it to a 10-year-old. They ask for sweets and I give them my remaining Polo mints. Lieutenant Fax Machine goes around the back of the Lanny and gets them a couple of bottles of water, which they are grateful to receive. Susan talks to them, laughs, and pulls a face. Even though I don't know what they are saying, I know they are being cheeky to her and us.

We get back into the Lanny, waving bye to the kids, and she directs me again along the roads.

"We will now go to visit the bobsled track up on Trebevic Mountain," says Susan.

Soon we have left the urban destruction behind and we're now in the woods driving up a steep road. The Lanny excels itself with the choice of screaming engine gear or labouring engine gear. I have to choose the former at the expense of everyone's hearing.

"Is the jeep broken?" shouts Susan to me.

"It's a very cheap jeep," I shout back to her.

We continue going up and up and I get a glimpse of something concrete in the woods, which is long and thin. It is running parallel to the road we are on and as we come around a bend, the curved track goes over the road.

"OK, stop here please," says Susan. "This was built for the 1984 Winter Olympics."

On the high-sided turn, there are gaping holes along it at regular intervals. A large calibre weapon has been fired at it, which has punched a hole straight through the foot-thick concrete. Because of the regularity of the holes, it looks more like malicious vandalism than something from the chaos of a battle.

I express that thought to Susan and she replies, "Yes, yes, I think so."

We continue along and, as the road flattens out, there is a clearing in the trees, and I glimpse a house. It's a two-storey dwelling with a damaged roof and no windows or doors. There is rubble around the outside. There are signs of the wooden doors and window frames having been on fire as the black soot marks carry up the side of the house. The lower half is covered in a flaking, faded, white plaster which makes where the bullet struck stand out. Despite having just as many bullet holes, the upper floor, constructed of red brick, hides them better. In front of the house is an old couple. The woman is brushing up, and the man has a small axe in his hand as he uses it to whittle a piece of wood. They stop what they are doing. As we approach them, they smile at us.

"Stop here now, please," says Susan.

I pull up and switch the engine off.

"There is a good view of the city from here. Go and see. Don't go on the grass. Mines and booby traps go bang bang," she says, smiling at me.

"I'll be sure to stay on the road, Susan," I reply reassuringly to her.

I get out of the Lanny and Susan goes over to talk to the old couple. As I pass them to take in the view, I say, "Hiya, *Dobar Dan,*" and nod at them.

They reply, *"Dobar Dan IFOR,"* in a strong accent, smiling.

We must now be at least 2,000 feet above the city. I see the now tiny-looking UNIS towers, the Parliament Assembly building, and the graveyard that appears colossal even from this distance. I can make out almost everywhere we have been, even the road which brought us into Sarajevo. It disappears off down the long valley into the distance in the late afternoon heat haze.

"Was this their home?" Lieutenant Fax Machine asks Susan.

"It still is their home," replies Susan. "They are returning now the war is over, but their house will need a lot of work."

The old woman talks to Susan. She listens while the old woman chats away. "They say this is where a few of the big guns fired into the city. They were told to leave many years ago,"

The woman says something else, takes Susan's hand, looks at me and smiles. "She wants to thank you for bringing peace so they can now return home and live their lives like they used to," says Susan, not taking her eyes off the old woman.

"Tell her we are glad they are able to return and may they have many happy peaceful years ahead of them in their home," says Lieutenant Fax Machine.

We give them the rest of our bottled water and I climb in the rear of the Lanny, looking for our emergency ration packs.

"We aren't going to really need these, are we?" I say looking at Lieutenant Fax Machine.

She nods in agreement, and I hand them over to the couple. They express their gratitude, through Susan, with lots of talking with which I am sure she cannot keep up, but she says, "They are extremely grateful."

Torvill and Bean Soup

It's back to Zetra we go, with a drive by the Latin Bridge, to see the exact spot where the Archduke Franz Ferdinand was assassinated. We pass it in the blink of an eye. It looks just like any other corner street next to a bridge except there's a gathering of IFOR Soldiers taking pictures of one another. I suppose we are the first of the tourists who will return to the country now that peace has broken out.

Back at Zetra, we thank Susan for her time and she nods appreciatively, smiling before mooching off.

Kit-Kat has now appeared in the Corimec and says to Lieutenant Fax Machine, "Did you enjoy the tour, ma'am?"

"It was fascinating," she replies.

"Scoff's on, if you're hungry," he then announces.

The cookhouse is inside the stadium and on the part where the ice rink used to be. I look up and I see the blank scoreboard that displayed Torvill and Dean's perfect score. On the left of it are the Olympic rings and the official logo that was a snowflake, along with the word 'Sarajevo 84' underneath it. The other end houses the workshops with numerous vehicles lined up. Lannys have their bonnets open and trucks are missing wheels or have their cabs tilted forward so that the Spanner Monkeys can work their magic on the engines. I sit at the 6ft wooden table with the others. Tucking into my funny-tasting chicken supreme with rice, I find my mind constantly plays the Bolero as I eat. I wonder if everyone's thinking the same thing as my jaw chews my dinner in time to the beat of the music.

Out of the blue, Two Wrongs says.

"Wouldn't it be funny if we could get the scoreboard up and running again, and we could give the chefs our score of their food?"

I knew they were thinking about it, I just knew it.

"Make it so," says Sergeant J9 to him.

"My chicken supreme would be a 4.9," I say.

"A 3.2 for my... Errrr, I think it's a pork chop," says Sergeant J9.

"And 6.0 for the chicken curry," says Two Wrongs.

"I've also got the chicken curry but I'll have to drop it to a 5.8 due to the lack of a naan bread," says Lieutenant Fairfax Machine.

"This red bean soup is a bit thick, I'd give it 2.0," says Kit-Kat.

"That's because it's chilli con carne, you thick twat," replies Sergeant J9, bursting out laughing.

Desserts are a rice pudding or bananas and neither make it into the Bolero grading. The rice in the pudding is still hard and the bananas are nearly as green as the Lanny.

Sleep in the Ditch

Two Wrongs shows me to the transit accommodation for the evening and it's a very agreeable Corimec with a bunk bed. There is even a green plastic covered mattress on it. Green, because nothing says 'Army' more than the colour green, and plastic, because at least they could be used again if someone pisses themselves while asleep. I chuck my gear on the floor and roll out my dossbag. I have the Corimec to myself, which should make for a good night's sleep.

"We've got some beers in the office fridge. You fancy one?" asks Two Wrongs.

"Does the Pope shit in the woods?" I reply, my spirits lifted a little.

We make our way back to the Rad Det Corimec Office and J9 and Lieutenant Fairfax Machine are sitting in there, with a can of beer each.

"Is the bar open, Sarge?" says Two Wrongs.

"The Officer's and Sergeant's Mess are both open. I don't know about the Junior NCO's bar though," he replies.

"I've asked the duty bar manager, and he said it was OK," says Two Wrongs, standing next to the fridge.

"Who's the duty bar manager?" enquires Sergeant J9.

"It's Kit-Kat today, Sarge."

"Well, I am not going to argue with the duty bar manager, so crack on."

I take a second to grasp this act is just that, an act. Thinking he was being serious there, and it was going to be a dry evening, I'd had a mild panic attack.

I donate a few Deutschmarks to the beer kitty in anticipation of drinking more than a few. We carry on into the night and eventually we run out of booze. This is the cue for Lieutenant Fairfax Machine and Sergeant J9 to knock it on the head and retire to their accommodation.

"Is there anywhere we can get any more booze from?" I ask Two Wrongs.

"I don't think so. The Yanks here are dry and always come scrounging and the REME bar will be closed, I reckon."

Then I remember the bottle of Slivovitz which Staff Hobbs gave me a while back. It's still in my rucksack. "Hang on a minute, mate, you'll like this," I say as I pop over to the transit accommodation. I feel around in the bottom of my rucksack, through my spare clothes, and then I touch the cold of the glass bottle.

"Ta dah," I say, coming back into the office Corimec, proudly showing Two Wrongs my bottle of Slivovitz homebrew.

"Is that Slip in the Ditch?"

"It's better than that. It's Sleep in the Ditch," I announce, "and it's fucking homemade."

"Oh, dear God."

"Hang on to your career, Two Wrongs, as we are about to go cuckoo."

I twist the cap off, and cautiously take a whiff. It burns the back of my nose and I immediately pull it away from my face, screwing up my eyes.

"Jesus Christ on a bike," comes out of my mouth like a natural body reflex.

"You might want to put that cigarette out, mate," I say to him.

I hold the bottle up to the light and I notice it's got a blue tint to it. I swill it around, examining it.

"Are you going try it or are you looking for bits in it before putting it in your car?" says Two Wrongs. I bring the bottle to my lips, hesitate, whilst holding my breath and take a sip. Just the one sip.

→» →» →»

I open my eyes and I cannot remember where I am. Not as in where I am in the local vicinity, but where I am in the world. I don't initially recognise the surroundings, but I recognise the inside of a Corimec.

My brain starts talking to me and it's like a computer rebooting.

Corimec, I know this word, but where do I know this word from?

They had them in Bosnia, yes, I did a tour of Bosnia once.

Why was I in Bosnia?

Ah yes, I remember, it was because I was in the British Army.

When did I get out of the British Army?

I didn't. I am still in the British Army and I am still in Bosnia.

Why does the inside of my mouth feel like a leather flip-flop?

I drank something foul last night.

The memories, no matter how fuzzy, suddenly reload back into my brain.

The first sip is disgusting and I nearly spit it out on the floor. It burns my mouth and that burning sensation goes down my throat and into my stomach. I'd like to say it was like drinking petrol, but I have never had that pleasure. However, if I had to imagine what it would be like, what I was experiencing now would be my best guess. Two Wrongs has the same reaction and manages to keep it down. We take a few more mouthfuls, each one becoming easier as we became accustomed to the firewater.

"Fancy going over to the gym for a kick about?" says Two Wrongs.

"Yeah, why not?" I reply. We grab a ball and head over to the main building. The gym hall is in the basement and is still in a half decent condition. We start off kicking the ball to one another and then I go in goal, still with the bottle in my hand. I take a sip now and again, and when Two Wrongs scores he comes up to take a celebratory sip too.

We are trying to be quiet, but, no doubt in our ever-increasing drunken state, we are getting louder.

"Hello," I hear someone say as it echoes around the empty gym. I hold on to the ball which Two Wrongs has kicked to me.

"Psssst," I say in his direction. "There's someone here."

I spot an American soldier in full kit come through the door. He's got his helmet on, with his webbing and body armour, and is holding an M16 rifle. "Dave," says Two Wrongs. "You on guard duty again."

"Hey Alex, yeah, man, whatcha doin' in here?" says the American soldier called Dave.

"We're having a game of footy, I mean soccer. Wanna join in?"

"Nah, I'm good, man," says Dave.

"This is James from Slipper City, Split," says Two Wrongs as he introduces me to Dave, "and James, this is Dave from Boston, Massachusetts."

"Nice to meet you, Dave," I say to him.

"Nice to meet you too, man."

"Fancy a swig of this," Says Two Wrongs pointing at the bottle of clear liquid.

Dave's eyes light up. He can tell by our state that whatever is in the bottle is alcoholic. The Americans are on a dry tour and, soldiers being soldiers, they all like a drink.

We take a seat on a bench at the side if the hall. Dave takes his helmet off and sits down with us.

"When you next on guard duty?" Two Wrongs asks Dave.

"I've just finished, and I was on my way back to my bunk, but then I heard you two," he replies.

I pass the bottle to Dave.

"Get your laughing gear around this Bosnian Moonshine, good buddy," I say in an American accent, which undeniably confuses him.

He takes his first mouthful and utters the immortal line.

"Jesus H Christ on a bicycle."

"How's your tour going?" I ask Dave.

"Not too bad man, we've had a few incidents, but it all seems quiet now."

"What incidents did you have?"

"There are a few diehards around the city, hiding in the rubble, still trying to shoot people when they get the opportunity."

"The POL point was under fire last week," adds Two Wrongs.

"Was under fire or was on fire?" I ask him.

"Under fire. One of the REME guys was filling up a truck when he sees sparks and puffs of dust. He didn't quite realise what was happening and just stood in place trying to work out what was going on."

"One of our Bradleys[125] spotted where the shooter was and gave him some career advice with their 25mm cannon. That shut the fucker up," says Dave.

I remember the soldiers from earlier today, standing watch over the long line of people waiting for water.

"That happen much?" I ask them both.

"About once a week," says Two Wrongs, looking at Dave, who nods in agreement.

As we continued talking and drinking, my recollections of the rest of the evening from that point became muddled. I have snippets, which involve more talking, jumping around on a crash mat, climbing up wall bars, and taking mouthfuls of Satan's bin juice.

I sit up, and I feel like my head is still on the bed. Once it's caught up, I attempt to stand up. I find my trousers, pull them on, slide on my flip-flops and head for the door with the idea that a shower might reinvigorate me. It's a bright day outside but still early, so the camp

---

125 The American version of the Warrior IFV.

has a sense of calm to it. I look around to see who may be up and about. I see Dave's helmet on top of our Lanny. Not too far away, I see the unmistakable shape of a body in a shallow storm drain.

"Shit," I say to myself, and I make my way slowly over to it. I see it's an American uniform and then I recognise it's Dave from the night before. I have no idea if he is dead or sleeping and I am now quite alert as the onset of a bit of panic is happening. Dave is on his side, still with his webbing on, and his rifle attached to him by his sling.

"Dave, can you hear me?" I say to him, tapping his face lightly, thinking I'll make it increasingly harder if he doesn't respond.

He gives out a cough, followed by a groan.

"Thank fuck you're alive, you OK, mate?" I ask him.

"Yeah, man, who are you?" he asks me without opening his eyes.

"It's James from last night in the gym, remember?"

"Oh shit, yeah. What the fuck happened, man?"

"We were drinking Bosnian Moonshine in the gym."

"Were we?"

"Dave?"

"Yeah, man."

"You're a fucking legend, mate."

"Why's that?"

"You're sleeping in a ditch."

Epilogue

THE TRIP back to Split was hard because of the heat and the 'Sleep in the Ditch'-induced hangover. The icing on the cake was us forgetting to replace the water that we'd given away the previous day. We stopped off in Mostar to have a look at where the famous bridge, Stari Most, had once straddled the river Neretva before the Bosnian Croats had destroyed it in 1993. The remainder of the tour was just as busy as the first couple of months. There were still the gas and fuel runs to keep going with, and further trips to many locations to deliver more and more plastic cutlery. I spent a week up in Kupres learning how to operate some brand-new fuel tankers and bumped into an old school friend. We even managed to fit in a few days' stay at a hotel down on the Makarska Riviera, watching Gilly skim metal serving trays across the pool, to the dismay of the waiters.

I spent a week in August in the UK attending a course. I was required to learn how to use some new equipment that we could carry on a DROPS. It could offload shipping containers from a rail flat. On my return to Split, they subjected the entire plane to a drugs test, and we had to hang around for hours in DJ Barracks while everyone provided a urine sample. I returned to Germany at the end of September, not by RAF aircraft, but by bicycle. Captain Haywood had organised a cycle ride from Split back to Bielefeld in aid of the charity BLESMA.[126] It took us 10 days to complete on mountain bikes with knobbly tyres that a tax-free car dealership had donated. As hard as it sounds, the actual issue was navigating, as this was in the days before Sat Navs, so we had to rely on paper maps. Cycling up the Croatian coast and over the Alps was a doddle, as there are not too many routes that you can choose from. From the southern

126 British Limbless Ex-Service Men's Association.

German Border to Bielefeld was considerably harder as we stuck to the back roads. We arrived back at camp on time to a tremendous welcome from the Regiment, getting our only puncture less than 20km from the finish.

After our post-tour leave, we returned to the Regiment for the customary re-organisation of people and posts. I ended up working in the SQMs with Del and found the job rather dull. I continued in there for a year before being chosen to become the CO's Driver and deploying back on another Op Resolute tour, but this time under the guise of SFOR, Stabilisation Force. It was a totally different experience from the tour I have written about in this book. The Regiment HQ was based at DJ Barracks with 17 Squadron, up at Kupres. I was accommodated with the CO, at a private residence in the nearby town of Trogir. I spent most of my tour taking him to a weekly meeting at BLMF and to visit the troops around the theatre. It was an interesting tour, but not as interesting as this one. I would remain in the Army until 2013, eventually retiring as a Staff Sergeant. I had further postings in the UK, Cyprus and back to Germany and deployments on tours to Iraq and Afghanistan.

I returned to Croatia many times on holidays from 2000 onwards, either driving down from Germany or flying in from the UK. When either arriving or departing at Split airport, I would look at my fellow passengers, and wonder if any of them had served here. I still found it all somewhat bizarre that I was back, but in my flipflops and on holiday.

I finally returned to Bosnia in 2022, on my own personal pilgrimage. I flew from Luton to Sarajevo and my intention was to visit all the places that I could remember. I wanted to see how the country had progressed and modernised. It was nice to appreciate the brand-new glass-fronted buildings, and the super-smooth motorway out of Sarajevo was a revelation. There were still plenty of marks from munitions on the city's buildings. There was obviously a plan to repair all the damage, but there was so much of it that it was going to take more than the 28 years that had passed since the guns fell silent. The remaining damage seemed to be more evident in the poorer parts of the city, which were dominated by a jungle of grey high-rise tower blocks. As we drove out into the countryside, we passed plenty of still-damaged abandoned houses, but the armoured vehicles had long since been removed. I visited the bridge in Gornji Vakuf, where Lance Corporal Wayne Edwards, the first British soldier killed in Bosnia in 1993, had died. The town's municipal council named the bridge after Wayne, in tribute to him and all the other peacekeepers who subsequently lost their lives during the conflict. The ceremony was attended by Wayne's sister, retired Colonel Bob Stewart and British Ambassador Nigel Casey.

I saw plenty of murals and one in TSG caught my attention. It was of a figure named Slobodan Praljak. His face was painted in black and white in front of the unmistakable red-and-white Croatian checkerboard coat of arms. There was also some text and I asked my Slovenian friend to translate it.

"Every Croat will know for their entire life that General Praljak wasn't guilty."

I was aware of him as he'd been in the news a few years earlier for committing suicide by drinking cyanide during his appeal trial in The Hague by the ICTY. He addressed the Judges and said, "Judges, Slobodan Praljak is not a war criminal. With disdain, I reject your verdict!" He then drank from a small bottle, collapsed, and was pronounced dead later that day.

Mr Casey said at Wayne's ceremony, "The citizens enjoy a normality that they value all the more because of the horrors they endured during the conflict." These words stuck with me, giving me hope that the horrors wouldn't happen again. When I saw the mural of a convicted war criminal, I thought that a quarter of a century might be enough time to heal the wounds, but it's also enough time to forget the mistakes.

Did we bring peace to the Balkans? Yes, we did, but one can argue that it'll just be until the next conflict. Once peace was guaranteed in Bosnia for the time being, Mr Milosevic turned his attention to Kosovo until that was also quelled. With the invasion of Ukraine, tensions are again rising. I was told by my Bosnian Guide on my 2022 visit that the Balkans are known as being the land of blood and honey. They will have periods of conflict followed by years of peace as the cycle repeats itself. From 1992 until 2007, the British Military served in the Balkans under the UN, then NATO under IFOR, SFOR, and eventually EUFOR. British troops have been back there in 2019 under EUFOR. The ultimate figure for causalities during the deployments all over the Balkans between 1992 and 2019 was 72 killed, and many more injured, the majority being from vehicle accidents attributed to the poor roads. Estimates suggest that the number of civilian casualties from just the Bosnian part of all the war was around 100,000, with 80% of them being Bosniaks.

For now, peace is assured in Bosnia, but trouble was brewing elsewhere and, given that, the world is an ever-changing place. But that's another story.

Acknowledgments

I would like to extend my deepest gratitude to my editor, Gary Bainbridge. His expertise has been invaluable in transforming the memories in my head into the books of which I've always dreamed.

I'd also like to show appreciation to my proof-readers. Your attention to detail and thoughtful feedback have brought clarity and polish to these pages. Any remaining quirks are entirely my own.

My heartfelt thanks go to Julia Lemon for her outstanding artwork, which brought so much character to the map. I still remember the look she gave me when I showed her the IFOR Route Map and explained my vision. Her creativity and talent truly brought the idea to life, and I am grateful for her exceptional work.

I'd like to say a big *"Hvala"* to Blaz Gindiciosi, my invaluable Balkan advisor. Without his help, I wouldn't have remembered, or been able to pronounce, half the names of things I encountered. A proud Slovenian, Blaz humorously claims to be either Southern Austrian or Northern Croatian, depending on who's asking. His knowledge and good humour have been a constant source of support.

Thank you to Neill Williams for the time he gave me re-educating me with the details of the fuel trucks that I forgot about the minute I got home from the tour.

I am deeply grateful to the people of the Balkans, who have endured tremendous hardships yet have consistently shown me kindness throughout my time there on all my tours and visits.

Lastly, I cannot express enough appreciation to all members of the British Armed Forces who served in the Balkans, especially to the unforgettable characters of 7 Transport Regiment, who fill these pages. Their antics, bravery, and occasional questionable decision-making have become a vital part of this story. You couldn't make some of this stuff up, though I might have tried!

Also from JAMES LEE

'The alarm sounds again. We hit the floor. Another salvo of impacts interrupts the rocket attack announcement. Rocket number one is close, number two is closer. "Here we.." is all I manage to say just as number three detonates. It's the closest one yet. We hear the building flex around us as the shockwave passes through. Somehow it remains standing as it strains with the passing wave. I'm hoping this might have fixed some of the squeaking doors...'

Licking The Taliban's Flip-Flop is the blackly comic story of a British Army 'Mover', and his final Operational Tour in Afghanistan. Find out how Staff Sgt Lee narrowly avoided death by drone, what on earth Black Nasty is, how our hero managed to bounce Prime Minister David Cameron into taking a special package back to the UK... and exactly how much money it would cost for a British soldier to lick a Taliban prisoner's dusty flip-flop...

... Not all forces memoirs are Bravo Two Zero, you know.

Available in Kindle and paperback here

BA Press

Printed in Great Britain
by Amazon

61537255R00181